Buddhist and Christian Responses to the Kowtow Problem in China

Also available from Bloomsbury

Buddhism and Iconoclasm in East Asia, Fabio Fambelli and Eric Reinders
Silver Screen Buddha, Sharon A. Suh
Adaptation and Developments in Western Buddhism, Phil Henry

Buddhist and Christian Responses to the Kowtow Problem in China

Eric Reinders

Bloomsbury Academic
An imprint of Bloomsbury Publishing Plc

B L O O M S B U R Y
LONDON · NEW DELHI · NEW YORK · SYDNEY

Bloomsbury Academic
An imprint of Bloomsbury Publishing Plc

50 Bedford Square
London
WC1B 3DP
UK

1385 Broadway
New York
NY 10018
USA

www.bloomsbury.com

BLOOMSBURY and the Diana logo are trademarks of Bloomsbury Publishing Plc

First published 2015

© Eric Reinders, 2015

Eric Reinders has asserted his right under the Copyright,
Designs and Patents Act, 1988, to be identified as Author of this work.

All rights reserved. No part of this publication may be reproduced or transmitted in any form or by any means, electronic or mechanical, including photocopying, recording, or any information storage or retrieval system, without prior permission in writing from the publishers.

No responsibility for loss caused to any individual or organization acting on or refraining from action as a result of the material in this publication can be accepted by Bloomsbury or the author.

British Library Cataloguing-in-Publication Data
A catalogue record for this book is available from the British Library.

ISBN: HB: 978-1-4742-2728-5
ePDF: 978-1-4742-2729-2
ePub: 978-1-4742-2730-8

Library of Congress Cataloging-in-Publication Data
A catalog record for this book is available from the Library of Congress.

Typeset by Integra Software Services Pvt. Ltd.
Printed and bound in Great Britain

For Vivian

Contents

List of Illustrations — viii
Acknowledgments — ix

1 Ritual Topography — 1
2 Buddhist Obeisance — 27
3 The 662 Debate — 51
4 The Editor's Conclusion — 77
5 Christian Objections — 95
6 Theories of Obeisance — 123
7 Disobeisance Today — 139

Appendix: Further Information on the Debate Participants — 146
Notes — 152
Bibliography — 176
Index — 183

List of Illustrations

Figure 1.1	Doorsill or bridge of traditional Chinese doorway. Jingye Temple, near Xi'an. Photo by the author	5
Figure 1.2	Longshan Temple, Taipei. Main courtyard. Photo by the author	14
Figure 1.3	Longshan Temple, Taipei. Twelve zones of obeisance. Diagram by the author and Diana Fouts	15
Figure 1.4	*Baidian* in zone 5 of Longshan Temple. Photo by the author	17
Figure 1.5	Longshan Temple. Pattern of traffic flow. Diagram by the author and Diana Fouts	20
Figure 1.6	Simplified ritual topography of Longshan Temple. Diagram by the author and Diana Fouts	22
Figure 2.1	The vertical topography of monastic obeisance, according to the four Buddhist rules	31
Figure 5.1	"Parents training their Children to worship Idols." *A Quarterly Token for Juvenile Subscribers* No. 21 (April 1861), p. 4	110
Figure 5.2	"Persecution in China." *A Quarterly Token for Juvenile Subscribers* No. 49 (April 1868), p. 8	111

Acknowledgments

Since I started on this topic, I've talked with almost everyone I know about bowing. But I should single out my dissertation committee: Bill Powell, Alan Grapard, and Richard Hecht. Also, the Philosopher Tribe, D. K. Reinders, Bob Reinders, Bill Gilders, Barry Schwartz, Fabio Rambelli, the Iconoclasms Network, Mayfair Yang, Dave Valadez, Heng Sure, and the various contributors to an epic Buddha-L thread in 1996–1997, especially Joy Vriens.

1

Ritual Topography

A door is a hole in a wall. You go to all the trouble of building a wall, a structure that can't be walked through, but without a door it's useless. As through all holes, things leak in and leak out. Anxieties about boundaries and transgression converge there. So in China, as elsewhere, there are many taboos and subtle injunctions associated with walking through holes in walls. For example, if the front façade of a temple has three large doors, we are supposed to enter through one of those on the sides, not through the central door. According to a Ming text,[1] to go through the central gate would be acting proudly. If you enter by the left of the three gates, you put your left foot in first; if through the right gate, the right foot first. In other words, even the first foot in the temple is furthest from the center of the three gates. That's one modest footstep.

A door takes you to a different kind of space. You step through a door, and you have to change your behavior. You have to put out your cigarette, stop chewing gum, be quiet. And you even change what's in your mind—think pure thoughts, perhaps. A whole different self descends upon you at the door. At least, that's how it feels, if through years of habit you have become cultured. Still, the most oblivious foreigner, the least self-conscious child, nonetheless has to walk through the door. If you're a novice, you might need some help.

Daoxuan and doors

The monk Daoxuan (596–667), famous as the founder of the Chinese vinaya (monastic discipline) school, wanted very much to maintain clear boundaries between monastic and non-monastic space. One might summarize Daoxuan's entire corpus as a lifelong effort to keep the Sangha *other*. In Buddhist rhetoric, the monk was a "guest from outside the boundaries" (*fangwai zhi bin*). This expression suggests both foreignness and, at the same time, a rejection of the ultimate validity of any boundaries. On the one hand, Buddhism was not from China; on the other, Buddhism was not from anywhere.

Daoxuan had visions of certain ideal architectures: of the original ordination platform as constructed by Sakyamuni Buddha himself and of the Jetavana monastery of the Buddha. He wrote on the physical construction of monasteries but more extensively on the bodily discipline of monks and nuns and on their legal status. Most of his work concerned the boundaries of the body: robes, rituals, postures, gestures, paraphernalia, and ordination. His writings on bowing, to be considered in the next chapter, and his role in the bowing debate of 662 to be considered in Chapter 3, make him a particularly good focus for thinking about bowing.

How did Daoxuan want monks to walk through doors? Let us look at his basic training manual, the *Jiaojie xinxue biqiu xinghu lüyi* (Admonitions for New Student-Monks to Maintain Discipline, abbreviated as *Jiaojie lüyi*).[2] It consists of a short preface, followed by 466 rules of conduct, in twenty-three sections. Most of the rules in this long list are very bluntly stated commands and prohibitions, dos and don'ts of the monastery. The rules are grouped by topic, with a clear inner-outer organization. The first section deals with "How to enter the compound." Once inside the gate, of course, the new monk must know how to behave in front of his superiors, so sections two and three concern correct etiquette in dealings with the Master. Then follow some pointers on behavior within successively smaller spatial designations: compound (*si*), cloister (*yuan*), and room (*shi*). Then, the new monk was introduced to a series of "internal" topics: dealing with the Teacher, behavior at the two mealtimes, leaving the mess hall after eating, washing and protecting one's bowl, entering the assembly, entering the Buddha Hall to recite the monastic vows, the bathroom and wash-house, dealing with monks of higher status, sweeping the ground, and handling the water jug. Whereas the first section was on entering the compound, the last section is called "How to enter villages" (i.e. exit the compound). The first and last sections form an in-and-out frame for the text. Here is a tour of a Buddhist temple, with a scribe following Daoxuan around, recording all the instructions of this famously nit-picking monk.

Along the way there are many doors to go through. So what does Daoxuan say about the act of passing through a gate or door? Be careful: "All who exit their room or yard must not collide with old venerable monks."[3] "If, when returning from the outside, [you find that] someone has closed the temple doors, you must knock softly; you must not alarm people."[4] "All who close the gate should be careful. You must not do it carelessly to the point of damaging it."[5] Just as you avoid the center gate when entering a temple, so too, "All who enter the Master's room, should go through the door to one side."[6] The cardinal virtue here is dignity (*weiyi*), a kind of self-possession of the body and its robes. "When outside of the monastery gates, maintain dignity."[7]

Some of the instructions seem comical for their tendency to make explicit behavior we might think would never need to be named. "When you reach the front of the toilet, if you know there is a venerable resident [of the monastery inside], you should avoid it."[8] "When you reach the front of the toilet, snap your fingers three times or make a coughing sound. If thereby you know there is no one inside, then go in."[9] "If there are people waiting urgently outside, to allow those who haven't gone yet, you should come right out of the toilet."[10] Even the toilet door requires ritual behavior.

In fact, the whole text begins with a doorway:

1/1. When outside of the monastery gates, maintain dignity (*weiyi*).
1/2. When entering the monastery gate, bow (*libai*), and then, kneel (*gui*), and recite the customary praises to the Buddha.
1/3. Gather up your sitting-cloth, join palms and bend the body. Then, with a serious expression, walk slowly on one side of the walkway, looking ahead.

In the *Admonitions*, he is describing the ideal behavior of monks. But in a section called "Method for pure believers to enter the monastery" (*qingxinshi rusi fa*) of his *Xingshichao* (Guide to Practice), he specifies how a lay person should enter.[11]

Chinese people who come to the outside of a monastery gate, put their clothes in order and bow once, enter the gate, and again bow once. Calmly and carefully go straight ahead, not looking around to the left or right. First go to where the Buddha is, and bow three times, circumambulate three times, and chant a verse of praise three times.... After you have bowed to the Buddha, then go to the outside of the monks' quarters. Bow once, and then go in to see the abbot, and in sequence bow to those under him, bowing once to each.

Then follows a section on purifying one's attitudes before entering. We should certainly not consider this merely a pious formality. Ideally, going through a temple door is an occasion for self-reflection and moral change: a new subjectivity.

In the same text are instructions on the method for female pure believers to enter the monastery.[12] The conduct in general is as above, says Daoxuan, but he adds a series of additional rules against such behavior as laughing and making yourself up. Did he think women were more giggly? The repression of laughter is itself a remarkable transformation of the subjective self. We are never told when the right time to laugh is, whereas a section of *Jiaojie lüyi* specifies "Six times when one must not talk or laugh." 1. When bowing to Buddha. 2. When listening to the Dharma. 3. When the assembly is gathered. 4. During the large meal. 5. During the small meal. 6. When going to the toilet. Laughter is in the same category as other bodily reactions that are hard to control: sexual arousal, hunger, the need to go to the toilet, bumping into people, scratching, belching, yawning, loud speech; and thoughtless movements like sitting in the wrong place, slouching, or not paying attention. Daoxuan lays down the law on all sorts of involuntary or semi-voluntary behavior: "Facing people, you must not scratch yourself." "When facing people, you must not unceremoniously blow your nose or spit." "You must not make a noise belching" or rinsing your mouth. Still, laughter is, perhaps, unique in being a behavior often stimulated by attempts to repress it.

The *Xingshichao* also describes the correct method for laity to exit the monastery.[13]

> When your business is completed, notify [the monastic personnel] that you are exiting the monastery gate, and perform obeisance according to the correct method. [Note, in smaller font:] Three bows before the Buddha, one bow as you reach the gate, one more bow outside the gate. When there are a few monks, bow once to each in order. When there are many monks, generally bow three times.

Bowing to the Buddhas is not only done in the halls; one begins to enter their presence just outside the front gate. But what exactly are you bowing to, when you enter the temple and bow, or when standing outside? When bowing to a Buddha image, or bowing to a monk, the object of obeisance is clear because it is right in front of you. Your bow is targeted. But what if there is nothing directly in front? What if you are bowing to the whole temple? I think the implied object is ultimately the Buddha, but the act is inherently vague. Physically, you can bow to nothing in particular, but conceptually there must always be an object, however remote or abstract.

A stumbling block

One distinctive feature of doors in traditional Chinese buildings is the doorsill (also called a bridge or a saddle) (Figure 1.1). The doorsill is a structural element, required by the three-part construction of traditional Chinese buildings: a heavy, tiled roof, held up by pillars, on a massive stone platform. The door frame is attached not to the foundation but the walls, and the walls

Figure 1.1 Doorsill or bridge of traditional Chinese doorway. Jingye Temple, near Xi'an. Photo by the author.

themselves might not hold it in place. So doors were constructed as rigid boxes, held in place with beams linking them to the pillars and anchored by heavy stone weights. Inside these boxy frames are the actual moving parts of a door. The doors do not have hinges in the modern sense (barrel hinges) but rather what's called a pivot hinge: the door itself is constructed with a round pole on one edge which rotates in sockets above and below. The saddle is therefore needed to keep the frame square, especially given the wear and tear of traffic and repeated operation of the sometimes very heavy doors.

Daoxuan gave a number of instructions regarding this distinctive architectural feature: "When going out through the door of the hall, ... lift the feet."[14] A doorway is primarily and fundamentally there to be walked through, and yet blocking the way at ground level is a large wooden beam which you are not supposed to step on. Daoxuan also instructs: "You must not sit on the doorsills"[15] [*menkun*], and then immediately, again, "You must not step on the doorsills [*menxian*]."[16]

I have heard different explanations of this prohibition, including the idea that stepping on the doorsill is symbolic of stepping on the Buddha's head. Or at least on someone's head: in Lu Xun's story "A New Year's Sacrifice" (1924), a destitute old woman worries that after death she will be sawn in half because she remarried, and she is advised, "Go to the Tutelary God's Temple and buy a threshold to be your substitute, so that thousands of people can walk over it and trample it, in order to atone for your sins in this life and avoid torment after death."[17] Here, the doorsill is a stand-in for the human body, and the twice-widowed woman hopes to be stepped on by proxy. The same effect would hardly have come with the purchase of a lintel. And clearly the rule against stepping on doorsills was not widely followed.

In fact, there are a number of similar prohibitions in Daoxuan's *Admonitions*, against stepping or sitting on other things: "When washing your robe, you must not let your hand press down on it, and also must not let your foot step on it."[18] "When folding robes, you must not put it into your mouth, and also must not let your foot step on it."[19] "You must not sit on robes."[20] And, in a remarkable rule, he writes: "Do not step on the shadow of the halls and stupas."[21] And, with a similar logic, "Do not step on the Master's shadow."[22]

So, feet and bottoms are marked as impure, contrasted especially to the head. The prohibitions against putting one's feet or bottom on the doorsill must be seen as examples of the larger set of objects identified in the same way: robes, books, tabletops, Buddha images. Even the places where the Master has sat must be treated as a distinct category: "Places where the Master often sits or lies, you must not unceremoniously sit or lie."[23] But the injunction against stepping on the doorsill is unique in that the doorsill is located precisely where you might think it natural (almost unavoidable) to step on it. It is rare that one has to deliberately avoid stepping on a book (because they're not usually on the floor) but doorsills are "in the way." (If they don't want me to step on the doorsill, why don't they move it out of the doorway!?) It is not just that one must not step on the doorsill but rather that precisely as one walks through a hole in the boundary, there is a construction which halts you, challenges the very nature of a doorway as a place to step through and draws your attention down to the act of crossing the boundary. And if it's a temple door, you are supposed to bow, before and after.

So the door is a good example of how the architecture, the material construction itself, imposes on bodies a certain pattern of behavior. In these practices and discourses, we see body and material objects articulated together in set patterns; the sacredness of the "Sangha-ground" consisted in part of a protocol or series of injunctions, like "put tab A into slot B." *This* (part of your body) must (or must not) touch *that* (object or point in space). There is a kind of DNA matching between building and body, far beyond the well-known uses of the body as an architectural metaphor (the temple as a body).[24] This isn't metaphor at all, it is a technology. Foucault called it "body-object articulation."[25] He went on: "Over the whole surface of contact between the body and the object it handles, power is introduced, fastening them to one another. It constitutes a body-weapon, body-tool, body-machine complex."[26] Foucault was writing of a soldier and his rifle here, but one could expand the scale of the object (as indeed he does throughout *Discipline and Punish*), to speak of a body-building complex.

The building doesn't just divide space, it structures space, according to different sets of prohibitions and jurisdictions. The monastery and the palace constituted "an architecture that would operate to transform individuals"[27] by its construction of spatial distinctions. This structure of authority is a kind of machine, and the product it makes is you—a new you, a refined and redefined person who comes in contact with the power of that monastery or palace. As Knapp wrote of the Chinese house, "Ethics-shaping messages were encoded in the very framework of the dwelling's layout, then reinforced by meaningful applied ornamentation."[28] The machine processes the (relatively) raw material of the public. So perhaps, the product is difference itself, a sense of different space, which means therefore a different subjective experience, a different sense of one's relation to power, a different body. The difference could be articulated in various ways: raw/cooked; unmarked/marked; public/private; profane/sacred. It is a spatial difference, and also cognitive, social, legal, and (so the claim goes,) ontological. In practical terms, the difference is marked by bowing.

When *not* to bow

Daoxuan wrote a lot about bowing, especially in his *Buddhist Rites of Obeisance* (*Shimen guijingyi*[29]), but before we leave the *Admonitions*, his guide for newly ordained monks, let's look at one section which deals explicitly with rules of when *not* to bow. Daoxuan made it clear that obeisance was necessary and integral to the Sangha, so the exceptions listed here are very interesting:

> Section 18. Norms for when you must not bow when you see (senior) monks and teachers. 11 items.
>   1. In front of the Buddha.
>   2. In front of the stupa.
>   3. When the assembly is gathered.
>   4. When ill.
>   5. When in a high seat.
>   6. When the Master is reclining.
>   7. When the Master is washing his bowl or having his head shaved.
>   8. When the Master is washing his feet.
>   9. When the Master is chewing a willow twig or rinsing his mouth.
>   10. When the Master is walking in a village. [Earlier in the text, he wrote: Meeting a venerable resident monk in front of the temple, you must not pay your respects.[30]]
>   11. When the Master is in the washroom or toilet.[31]

Normally, junior monks must bow to senior monks and especially to their Master, but there are exceptions. When ill; when the Master is engaged in a number of bodily functions (resting, head shaved, washing feet or mouth or whole body, excreting); when washing a bowl; and when in public view outside of the monastery. The junior monk is also not to bow before the senior monk while in the direct (frontal) presence of a higher symbolic object toward which a greater obligation of obeisance is due: the Buddha (in the form of an image, or a pagoda, which might include monastic ancestors or scriptures); and when the assembly is gathered (presumably also in front of a Buddha image).

In these rules, the body of the Master becomes the focus of attention and takes the highest position, canceling out even the hierarchical obeisance practice of two other unequally ranked monks: a monk may receive a bow but not while in the presence of the Master. If any bowing is to take place, it must be directed toward the highest-ranking monk and only then toward other monks in sequence. There is a prohibition on being first-bowed-to in the presence of a "higher" ritual object. The direction of obeisance always rises to a peak; the purpose of bowing is to create that peak.

The Buddha image ranks higher than any monk, although often the most senior monk, when giving a Dharma-talk, sits with his back to the Buddha, facing the bowing monastic community. When giving a sermon, or during his own funeral, the abbot—literally, the one in the "high seat" (*shangzuo*)—takes the position of the Buddha: facing toward the bowing disciples. So, there may be times when obeisance to the Buddha and to the abbot are, visually at least, indistinguishable.

Also, a bow is proscribed while the junior is in a higher place, on a porch or platform perhaps and when the spatial difference of the two bodies does not correspond to the prescribed ritual relation of the two bodies (in terms of a high-low distinction). When the ritually lower monk is physically higher than the Master, the junior monk should not bow to the Master, and the Master will not respond to a bow. So, an exception to bowing is made when there is what might be called a flaw in the physical/ritual topography: a mis-matching of the vertical positions of two bodies in physical space and in symbolic space. In these situations, the monk must descend before bowing.

If we reverse these prohibitions to see what Daoxuan was trying to avoid, we may imagine a number of uncomfortable situations: the senior monk receiving obeisance instead of the Buddha; a chaos of collective obeisance; the pathetic efforts of the infirm; a clash of height-as-space versus height-as-seniority; and obeisance to a man engaged in personal hygiene and who therefore cannot properly respond. Also prohibited is the *public* display of bowing between monks, which would perhaps disrupt the smooth and formalized movement of monks through the "village" and present the public spectacle of obeisance by junior monks, to whom laity were in turn expected to bow. "When before the Master, you must not greet people of the same class as you. When before the Master, you must not accept the greeting and bowing of other people."[32] Junior monks not bowing to senior monks when in public seems to weaken the hierarchy of senior monk/junior monk, but it strengthens that of cleric/laity. Outside of consecrated monastic space, the cleric/laity distinction "outranks" the senior/junior distinction.

We may compare these 11 items to the five of section 17, "Norms for when you should not stand up when you see Monks and Teachers."

1. When your illness is heavy. [cf. above, When ill.]
2. When having your head shaved. [cf. When the Master is… having his head shaved.]
3. At the time of the big meal.
4. At the time of the small meal.
5. When you are in a high place. [cf. When in a high seat.]

Again illness, shaving, and eating are specified, and the vertical distinction. Standing up when the senior monk enters the room or courtyard (the effective space), while less of a physical operation requiring floor-space and a temporary halt, can be considered also as a mode of embodying hierarchy. Standing up, of course, raises the body, even if it is only in order to then lower the body, in a bow. Here, paradoxically, the higher status belongs to the one seated, and so if the master is standing, the students should not sit. In the sutras, the Buddha sits while others sit or stand, but the Buddha never stands while others sit. Or perhaps, this is only paradoxical if instead of vertical distinction we look at the principal that the lower in rank has to expend more energy than the higher in rank. "In a ritual context, then, the chair embodies the political privilege of energy conservation."[33] Perhaps the sitting/standing distinction is subordinated here.

I once experienced a very specific moment when sitting/standing and up/down were inextricably linked. I used to teach English to large classrooms of monks at Mahachulalongkorn Buddhist University in Thailand. The students all sat, and I stood. Although monks are higher than laity, I was their teacher, and besides there was the practical fact that I had to be visible to them all. Though by standing I was higher than them, they were seated, and thus we belonged to distinct horizontal planes. But one day, weary from the heat, I sat on the edge of the desk at the front of the class. There was a subtle frisson among them, which I blithely ignored. But the following week, a monk I did not know approached me in the hallway and firmly, seriously, said: "When you are teaching, don't sit on the desk." The logic of it was instantly clear: I had sat at a higher level, like an abbot or the Buddha. My students were among the nicest people I ever met, and there was always good will toward me, but that shock wave was unmistakable. Fortunately, I was always forgiven for my lapses of etiquette, because I was a foreigner. My outsider status exempted me from the consequences of the blunder I would never have made if I were an insider. The ritual exemption of the outsider is a theme I will return to in Chapters 3 and 4.

Returning to Daoxuan, there is even a vertical logic to the direction of one's gaze. "When walking, you must look straight ahead at the ground seven feet in front of you. Do not step on insects and ants."[34] Daoxuan became famous for his care of insects. His biography in the *Song gaosengzhuan* (Biographies of Eminent Monks, Compiled in the Song Dynasty) states, "When fleas followed him, he carefully put them aside." And: "He would use a piece of cotton to put lice onto the ground."[35] He was also meticulous about saving insects that had fallen into the drinking water or that might be in among the firewood. Surely though, the avoidance of taking life was only one part of this injunction against looking up too much. With the lowered gaze we have a kind of obeisance performed with the eyes.

Other rules indicate a vertical distinction as a general ordering principle: "If there are words being spoken, you must modestly put yourself in the lower position, you must not take the upper portion."[36] "All who hang up their shoes must not [hang them] higher than a person's head, or higher than a person's face."[37] "Do not carry your bowl too high or too low, but at the chest."[38]

The *Admonitions* was a set of practical instructions, and as such its very genre precluded any richer discussion. But Daoxuan had much more to say on bowing, which we will sample in the next chapter, and on refusing to bow, discussed in Chapter 3 and 4.

An influential diagram

Even taken out of context and considered "in itself," a bow creates a space—a difference of front and back, of high and low. But there's not much to say about bowing in a vacuum. In fact, there is always some context. As the case of doorway ritual shows, the built environment of a temple or palace is the material substratum, frame, and guide to bowing. One of the most influential images for those of us thinking about Chinese ritual space is that of the imperial palace in Beijing, visualized as a pyramid.[39] Since movement toward the center of the ritual-architectural complex was spoken of as ascending and was the occasion for ever-more emphatic and more ritually controlled obeisance, the palace could be imagined as a pyramid, with a series of topographic layers. It is a pyramid suggested by language but also by physical architecture and movements of the body. The pyramid is a picture of a perception that the emperor was *highest*.

The ritual topography of temples and palaces is a mountain. Traditionally, monasteries are always in the mountains, even when they are, in fact, in the city or the plains. The entrance to a monastery is frequently called "mountain gate" (*shanmen*). When you speak of the physical site of the temple or monastery, the language you use expresses the site as if it were a mountain—you "go up" (*shang*) as you "go in" (*ru*), go down as you go out. Hence, the abbot "ascends the hall" (*shangtang*); one term for "abbot" is "high seat" (*shangzuo*). A similar linguistic pattern was the case with imperial sites of ritual, such as audience halls. The subject summoned to an audience approached in the middle of the night, from miles away, on a long North-South axis toward the Southern gate and was gradually admitted through a series of gates, "ascending" until finally face to face with the emperor. Higher than the Son of Heaven was Heaven itself.

The ritual space of temples and palaces is a symbolic pyramid, with the most sacred object/person at the peak. Partly, of course, it was physically true: halls were built on raised stone platforms, and the central image or throne would be raised further, on a platform—a dais or altar. Altars are always "pointing to" their principal image. Temples in turn "point to" the altars. They point *upward*. But verticality was also perceived on the horizontal plane: the *inmost* place was the highest, no matter what the empirical facts were. The pattern of gates and courtyards, and placement of altars (or thrones), gives a strong sense of frontal axis and a strong sense of passage upward through layers from the outside to the inside.

By lowering the body—by bowing—the object of obeisance is raised up in contrast. Obeisance makes a vertical distinction; it demonstrates the aboveness (superior-ity) of another object or person by lowering the subject's body. Directionality is produced by the frontal qualities of the body itself: faces, eyes, hands in frontal orientation; one always "faces" a particular direction. The direction of this obeisance can, of course, change, as the frontal plane of the body changes (as one moves). One can bow to one person, then turn and bow to another; in which case, sequence is crucial. But you can never bow behind you.

The pyramid has become a standard image for thinking about Chinese space. The palace space has been generalized to households and temples, based on a number of structural similarities.[40] To some extent, this is quite valid: even a small home of the traditional *siheyuan* (quadrangular courtyard) type was a miniature replication of the same structure: a South-to-North approach, an open central space, the most honored location in the North, facing South.[41] But inherent to the image's evocative heuristic power are some problems. The pyramid is a four-sided figure, but the South-to-North path is by far the most important. No one going up to bow before the emperor entered by the side doors. And yet, as an image of a perception, the highness of the emperor might also be perceived from the sides, although surely less emphatically so. Also, there are limits to how much the imperial example can be generalized to temples. Everyone who has been in a busy Chinese temple knows that as an image of obeisance, this pyramid is wildly inaccurate—in fact, even as an image of obeisance in a palace, it's a simplification, designed to make a point by screening out everything but one central path. When we move to consider actual temples, and how people actually bow in temples today, we get a vastly more complex and nuanced picture. Take for example the busy Longshan Temple in downtown Taipei.

Longshan Temple

Longshan Temple is, by the standards of most Buddhist temples, a fairly simple space. The main hall houses an icon of Guanyin (Figure 1.2). It stands in a courtyard surrounded by a rectangular building with a large front gate,

Figure 1.2 Longshan Temple, Taipei. Main courtyard. Photo by the author.

offices on either side, and a narrow year yard facing a line of altars for Daoist gods. While there are a number of gods behind, there is clearly one principal image in the single main hall. There is also an open courtyard space in front of the temple.

One feature common to Chinese Buddhist temples but lacking at Longshan is the large front gate containing pairs or quartets of images of the deva-kings (*tianwang*) and often an image of Mile, the so-called "fat, happy buddha." These deva images typically face each other in the gate, that is, they look at (rather than occupy) the central axis. Some pious visitors give these deva-kings obeisance as well, thereby performing obeisance in a direction which does not strictly cohere with the logic of the simple pyramid. They bow away from the axis. One might consider that each act of obeisance creates a mini-pyramid of its own. However, obeisance to these guardian figures is unlikely to be as deep or sustained as obeisance to the principal image of the temple. At Longshan, the front gate is a large ornamental gateway with orange tiles and dragons on the ridges, but it has no depth in which to place deva-kings.

There are pilgrims who start bowing—forehead down to the ground—before they enter the very first gate: they practice "one bow three steps" (*yili sanbu*), but this is rare. Later in this book we shall see a full range of obeisance, from a nod of the head through successively deeper postures down to a full prostration. I have seen full prostration at Longshan, but it is not common. There are always entirely idiosyncratic bows, but based on observation in 1999 and 2013, it is possible to generalize about obeisance at Longshan. The vast majority of the obeisance is relatively slight: palms together at the chest or forehead, slight inclination of the torso, nod of the head. There are twelve distinct zones of obeisance, each with its own human ecology (Figure 1.3).

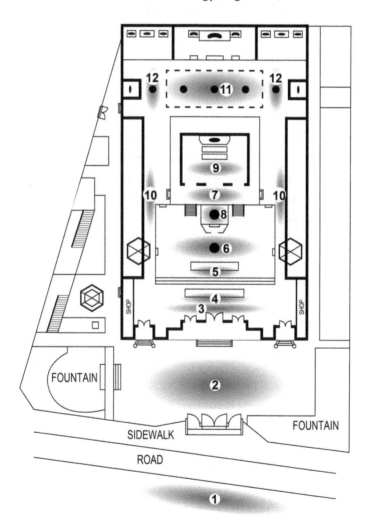

Figure 1.3 Longshan Temple, Taipei. Twelve zones of obeisance. Diagram by the author and Diana Fouts.

1. Outside the temple, across the street, there is a large open paved area, decorated with astrological motifs. Some passers-by stop, turn toward the Temple, and bow. It is impossible to say with any precision who they are bowing to, though the principal image (Guanyin) is most likely. In this public location no one lights incense, as there is no incense burner.
2. In the front courtyard, within the gates but outside the building itself. Most visitors will bow here. Because the temple is not wheelchair accessible, visitors who are mobility impaired bow before the front gate of the building, which is barred rather than solid, giving a slight sense of visual contact with Guanyin. Sometimes they are left there while their relative or assistant goes in to offer incense, on their behalf.

    A sign in this area announces the rules of the space, including rules against nudity, weapons, drugs, animals, spitting, advertising, camping, barbequing, begging, selling things, gambling, and political agitation. *Jitongs* (ecstatic mediums) are forbidden from entering the temple to consult deities through spirit possession. Already injunctions are invoked, but the space is ambiguous and transitional. To one side are the underground public toilets.

    So, you go through into the temple "itself," through the door to your right. You pass, or stop at, a booth for the sale of incense. Inside the compound, along the South edge of the courtyard is the spacious covered walkway, facing North. Here are two distinct rows of obeisance.
3. A fluid, public zone of obeisance, populated mostly with people who come, light their incense, bow and move on within a few minutes. It is a comfortable space for obeisance because with your back to the wall or closed middle gate, you are shaded from the sun and sheltered from rain, and as long as the temple is not too crowded, you're not in anyone's way. Some people in this area stay for some time, reciting scripture or some extended liturgy.
4. In front of these bowers but still under the covered walkway, there is a row of temple women in black robes, kneeling and reciting scriptures placed before them on tables. These women do not come and go but remain for extended periods. Though their main activity

is reciting scriptures, they remain in a kneeling position, using kneeling stands—low, square stools constructed on a slant and with cushions, called *baidian*.

The open courtyard, architecturally the lowest level inside the temple, has two patterns.

5. People kneel on *baidian* or stand behind a row of tables for offerings. Mostly, the people who bow here do so with their offering before them. The offerings are mostly food and flowers (Figure 1.4).
6. The general open space of the courtyard is the location of a wide variety of personal devotion, such as for people who wish to engage in an extended series of bows. This is also a space for people to gather when a dharma service is taking place. During these collective rituals, they stand in loose lines.
7. The highest point for most visitors is in front of the main hall, on the porch (but not inside the hall)—most directly in front of Guanyin. At Guanyin's door. Obeisance tends to crowd in the middle, where the icon is directly visible. On most days, it is physically awkward to remain in that central position for very long, because it is a busy spot.

Figure 1.4 *Baidian* in zone 5 of Longshan Temple. Photo by the author.

8. The porch extends outward in the center, where an incense burner is located. Here people bow to Guanyin but also to the cardinal directions, and they bow as they put their incense into the burner, making their offering to Tiangong. The title Tiangong means literally the "Duke" or God of Heaven. The title sometimes refers to the Jade Emperor (Yuhuang dadi). Some of the obeisance to Tiangong is done facing *away* from the main hall, with one's back to Guanyin.
9. Inside the hall, the monks, nuns or black-robed temple women perform obeisance periodically, for example when leading a service. They do so using kneeling stands. Otherwise the interior of the hall is off limits. Access to the interior is restricted because the temple is so popular. There would be serious wear-and-tear as well as crowd control issues. Also, there has been a concerted effort in Taiwanese temples toward reducing incense, especially inside buildings.
10. On either side of the main hall people sit reciting scriptures. Here is little explicit obeisance, but they may lean forward at the appropriate moments in the text, making a kind of seated obeisance. They are roughly facing the hall—looking toward the *front* of the hall, as if their obeisance could go up the stairs, turn a right angle and go through the door but not go through the walls—as if their obeisance had to approach Guanyin's face.

    Except for the obeisance to Tiangong before the incense burner in front of the main hall, all of the obeisance described so far can reasonably be considered as directed toward Guanyin.

    The space behind the main hall is given to a series of Daoist gods, aligned in two ways.
11. Nine gods are arrayed facing South, divided into three sections of three gods each. Obeisance to these gods may be uneven, depending on their popularity. Wen Chang is particularly popular; he is located on the Eastern side of the back wall of the temple.
12. Two additional altars have been added, facing inward, so that the worshiper has to turn at a right angle from the North-South axis. These two small halls have been squeezed in, so that the Northward obeisance to Wen Chang for example, may be muddled with the Eastward obeisance to that West-facing god, Huatuo. Also the construction of these two additional halls has impaired access to the two gods at the

far edges of the South-facing line. You can still bow before them, but the space is narrow, and undoubtedly many people skip those gods or conceive their obeisance as covering all three in a general way.

Did I say Longshan was simple?

Obviously, few people perform obeisance in all twelve of these zones. A fairly typical pattern is suggested to the visitor by the instructions posted on the wall near the booth for the sale of incense. There are seven incense burners: two in front of Guanyin and five behind. The instructions read, in Chinese and in English:

a. Light seven incense sticks.
b. Face the censor in front of the Main Hall and worship, introduce your name, address and birthday, followed by a request for His/Her blessing and protection. After worshipping all Main Hall gods, return to Guan-Yin censor and insert one incense.
c. Up to the Platform face the censor in front of the Front Hall and worship. After worshipping Heaven Lord [Tiangong], insert one incense to Heaven Lord censor.
d. Other 5 censors, please follow step b. and each censor inserts one incense.

Much of the obeisance is *offering*, mostly incense. Many temples in Taiwan have signs specifying the number of incense sticks required for full coverage of the available gods. Partly this is a response to health concerns and concerns with damage to the buildings from excessive incense. It is my strong impression that the volume of incense has decreased over the years. At Guandugong, a large temple complex on the edge of Taipei, the main hall's incense burners have even been fitted with an ingenious system for smoke removal: two metal pipes run from just inside the burner down to the ground, and underground to a chimney structure at the side of the hall, which houses fans, so that smoke from incense offered to Mazu blows out above the temple roof.

Temples display diagrams or charts for the correct number of incense sticks and locations and the direction of the traffic flow. At Longshan, the right-hand gate (as one faces the temple) is marked as the entrance, and next to it is trough-like sink for last-minute preparation of flowers to be offered. However, once inside, the left-hand stairway up to the porch in front of the main hall is the designated entrance to that zone; leaving on the right then, you turn left and head for the Daoist gods, offering obeisance to them from right to left. Some people leave by the exit in that corner, but most return to the main courtyard and exit out of the front left-hand gate, pausing perhaps at the shop which sells rosaries and charms. The dominant pattern then is a zig-zag (Figure 1.5).

It is hardly surprising to find obeisance in a public temple is not as neat and tidy as a highly controlled imperial ritual. The observation of the real

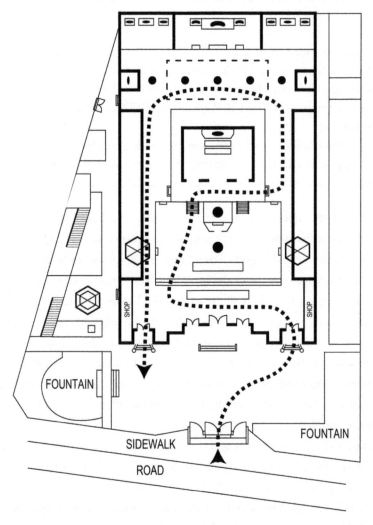

Figure 1.5 Longshan Temple. Pattern of traffic flow. Diagram by the author and Diana Fouts.

rather than the ideal also raises questions of methodology. One person bows and in doing so creates an implicit pyramid. But standing next to that person is another, smoking a cigarette. Old folks read newspapers, gossip, and doze off. What do we do about all this "static"—all the people mulling around, not behaving ritually at all? Screen them out? Do they not count? For Western visitors accustomed to Christian church services, the static is a little disconcerting, because Christian worship is highly coordinated in comparison—everyone sings the same hymn at the same time, and so on. I am also reminded of the pervasive depopulation of temples in Art History: photographers must go to great lengths to photograph the buildings without people in them. We can hardly blame Art Historians for being primarily interested in the buildings, but it does give the impression of temples as empty museums. This book is not in that sense Art Historical, yet the temptation is to ignore everyone who is not doing something recognizably "religious," most obviously, by bowing.

For example, huge numbers of photographs are taken, though the icon itself is difficult to photograph. Is photography a form of devotion? It's a form of attention, certainly—memorializing, the making of an artifact, the fixing of an image. Although people might offer incense and bow, and then take a photo or two, they don't do these things at the same time. They might have someone take a photo of themselves there in the temple but not usually while bowing—the memorial photo is definitely a more secular activity, putting the temple in the same category as the outdoor sculpture park, the sports event, and the beach. The bow is always directed at a deity or deities, whereas photographs are omnidirectional—directed here and there at the many architectural and decorative attractions and at the visitors themselves. Taiwanese are apparently unselfconscious about photography. In Mainland temples, you often see signs, "no photos," but in Taiwan the only injunction I ever encountered was, "no flash," and in another case a man asking me not to film him while he was participating in a Daoist ritual—this was a personal preference on his part, as the Daoist priest leading the ritual didn't seem to care.

Rain changes the pattern. This brings up Bourdieu's discussion of *langue* and *parole*—the abstract ideal of the ritual always differs from any actual performance, and the actual performance should not be taken as some kind of inadequate approximation.⁴² It rains a lot in Taiwan. Morning and afternoon patterns shift a little as well, because those who wish to sit on the side and recite scripture prefer the shade. Again, do we just pretend the weather is always the same? The pyramid moves around a lot during the day (Figure 1.6).

So what kind of body-space do we find? Obviously, we do not find a simple pyramid. We find a cluster of peaks—the highest being the most-deeply-bowed to image ("the principal image"), and many of these peaks positioned along a central axis, but with side-peaks, quirks of directionality. We also see that the obligation of obeisance is effected primarily "in front of" the principal image (even if the icon is not directly visible). Near the image and in front of the image, there is the deepest obeisance; of all locations this is the place to bow, even if one bows nowhere else. But *behind* the image, there is no

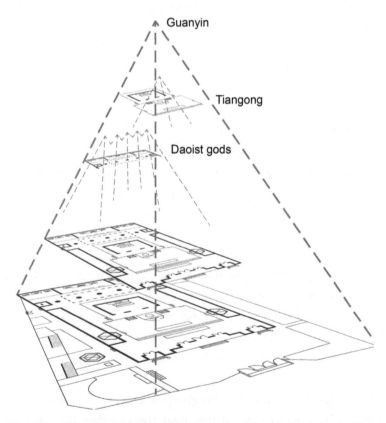

Figure 1.6 Simplified ritual topography of Longshan Temple. Diagram by the author and Diana Fouts.

prayer-cushion, no altar for offerings, and no one bows. The ritual topography of this image would thus be a rather one-sided pyramid.

Guanyin is in the middle facing South, but the axis before her is fairly broad, covering the whole of the porch, courtyard, and facing veranda, at least judging from the locations of obeisance. People feel they are bowing "to" Guanyin from almost anywhere in the front half of the complex and even outside across the street. She has a broad, inclusive gaze. Her gaze even goes around corners.

And yet, there seems to be no absolute obligation of obeisance and no ritual policing: even in front of Guanyin, people just stand up straight; take pictures, talk with friends, make phone calls. It is as if they are ritually off the hook, standing at ease, like the un-costumed stage-hands who come on to remove props in the Peking Opera. Resumption of the performance in the central axis involves ritual obligations (not facing away from the image) and a negotiation with any number of architectural forms and furnishings: stairs, incense burners, doors, and altars. And with other people.

If the structure of authority is a machine for processing subjectivities, it doesn't always work. Children are particularly dangerous to the system. At Longshan, I once saw a bizarre sight: a women had brought her four-year-old granddaughter to the temple, and grandmother wanted to bow to Guanyin. She stood before the hall and began a series of bows, of the type common in public temples: with her palms together, she put her knees onto the edge of the bowing stand and lowered her forehead down to the cushion. The little girl, however, was not in a pious mood, and skipped back and forth along the front of the temple. She found grandmother's behavior most amusing. She stood in front of her grandmother, palms together but looking back at her, mimicking obeisance. She positioned herself precisely so that when grandmother bowed, she bowed, and the old lady's head bumped the little girls' bottom, provoking further snickering. What do we do with a case like this? Do we just tune it out, because she wasn't doing it "properly?" Or "sincerely?" Any theory of obeisance has to take into account farce, parody, sarcasm, and insincerity. Any theory of obeisance must include the possibility of utter indifference.

Foreigners are also dangerous to the system, because they don't often have the internalized body-knowledge (what Bourdieu called *habitus*) that allows for smooth social interactions. And we have a well-documented example of a foreigner not doing the Chinese ritual right, namely the Macartney mission of 1793, discussed in Chapter 5.

So far we have seen that the difference between profane and sacred space was not only a matter of architecture but was also performative and cognitive and linguistic. In the case of Daoxuan's rules about doors, we can correlate the architecture with the performance, because the bows are explicitly linked to the site. Like a gateway, a Buddha-image doesn't move, so obeisance to the Buddha is relatively fixed—except that, as it turns out, not all obeisance to the Buddha was directly in front of the Buddha but might be performed from a distance, ambiguously. Obeisance to a more mobile object like a senior monk is still more complicated because unlike the Buddha he needs to eat and take a leak. He moves around, and he interacts with other monks with their own internal hierarchy, so it is not always clear to whom the layperson should bow first. When it comes to obeisance in an actual Buddhist temple, we find not only mingled Buddhism and Daoism (commonplace in Chinese temples) but also anomalies and overlapping layers, apparent discrepancies of direction, and ad hoc improvisations.

This book

In 662 CE, the Chinese emperor Gaozong ordered an imperial debate, which was held a month later, on this question: should Buddhist monks and nuns be commanded to bow to their parents and to the emperor? Confucian imperial ritual required that all subjects bow to their ruler, but Chinese Buddhist monks claimed the right to abstain from bowing to *any* laity. This claim to exemption from proper social interaction provoked persistent conflict between Buddhists and imperial ritualists throughout the Medieval period. There are a number of letters and writings prior to 662, but the 662 debate was particularly well documented, so the arguments are unusually vivid and varied.

One of the key participants in the arguments (if not the debate itself) was Daoxuan. He wrote on why monks should not bow to laity, but he also wrote in a more positive way about what bowing means to Buddhists. Daoxuan was the founder of what became the dominant school of vinaya (monastic discipline) in China, and beyond this issue he wrote extensively about monks' bodies. For Daoxuan, control of the body, and bowing in particular, were not incidental details but fully integrated into the entire project of enlightenment. The next chapter describes Daoxuan's teachings on the merits of obeisance. Chapters 3 and 4 explore the 662 debate.

Starting with the Hebrew Bible, the so-called monotheistic religions have condemned certain kinds of bowing which they named idolatry. Idolatry is the name for someone else's wrong obeisance. When Western missionaries went to China, starting in the sixteenth century, they brought with them a history of idolatry. In Chapter 5, I look at Christian refusals to bow in China—in one major case, a refusal to kowtow to the emperor, but beyond that, refusals (of converts) to bow to icons and ancestral tablets. The seventh-century Buddhist case overlaps with the later Christian cases in that both groups claimed the right not to bow—the objects of their disobeisance were not always the same, and certainly the arguments were very different. So at this point, it remains an open question, what can be gained by a comparison?

Given that the Medieval Buddhist case and the late Imperial Christian case come from such different starting points, what is it we are actually comparing? What is bowing? When do a nod of the head and a full prostration belong in the same category, and when do they not? In Chapter 6, I examine some of the attempts to explain obeisance theoretically and elaborate on my own definition: a bow is a performance of a vertical distinction. The last chapter is a thematic reflection on disobeisance, looking in particular at the refusal to salute the American flag. In the 1930s, thousands of children were expelled from schools because they were Jehovah's Witnesses, and they believed the salute to be idolatry. Saluting the flag is certainly performing a vertical distinction, even if it achieves this distinction by raising the object rather than by lowering the subject. While it may seem that bowing is much less common in modern times, the semiotic system survives. Hierarchy has not disappeared and for the most part we still express it vertically.

2

Buddhist Obeisance

The early Tang context

From the breakup of the Han early in the third century CE, the territory of China was divided into a series of smaller dynasties, some of them quite short-lived. It was under these conditions of political instability that Buddhism spread in China. Territorial unification was achieved by the short Sui dynasty (581–618) and consolidated by the more durable Tang (618–907). This unification was accompanied by an increasing emphasis on the single pinnacle of power. The emperor was the peak of a pyramid of power. Above him was Heaven, of which he was the "Son." The imperial cult of Heaven supported the notion of his singular status as the "one man" (*yiren*) above his empire, which "helped establish the cosmological grounds for an intensified absolutism."[1] Below him was, in theory, everyone. Of course very few of his subjects ever had the opportunity to bow to him, but all of them were theoretically included beneath him in a single hierarchy.[2] The sense of a single apex of imperial cosmology only increased during the Tang.

The monk Daoxuan makes reference to the singular absolutism which was increasing in his time, not to contest the notion but to insert Buddha as that "one man" instead of the ruler or any great sage.

> Just as there are not two suns in the sky, so there are not two kings in the same state. It is only Buddha who can be called the Great Sage. His light illuminates the myriads under Heaven. Therefore, his teachings daily spread. There is no state which does not look up to his influence. His precepts and principles are complete and refined; all who are learned partake of his feast [literally, his mat]. These teachings of Kongzi and Laozi, in name and status are equally common (*su*). [They are] no different from ordinary people.[3]

Throughout the early Tang, the state created numerous laws for clergy. In 637, for example, Taizong (r. 626–649) promulgated the *Daosengge* (Regulations for the Daoist and Buddhist clergy), which claimed jurisdiction over monks and nuns and claimed priority over the vinaya.[4] Gaozong (r. 649–683) tried to push imperial jurisdiction even further. In 655, he passed (and then had to retract) an edict putting monks under ordinary law instead of the *Daosengge*. The early Tang was a period of increased sponsorship but also control of Buddhism. Against this backdrop, the revival of the old complaint about monks not bowing to the ruler was not surprising. The whole business came to a head in 662.

The following two chapters deal with the bowing debate of 662. But first let us see what bowing meant, at least to one of the key lobbyists. In 661, just months before the debate, Daoxuan composed a treatise on monastic obeisance, *Shimen guijingyi*, "Buddhist Rites of Obeisance."[5] (I will use the abbreviated title *Guijingyi*.) Primarily addressed to Daoxuan's fellow monks, this treatise articulated a complex Buddhology of obeisance. At times, Daoxuan seems to be preaching in a very general way, apparently without direct relevance to obeisance, but the presence of general Buddhist themes in the discussion of bowing is not incidental. Rather, they demonstrate the doctrinal and spiritual importance of obeisance.

Ordering the bowing body

Daoxuan lamented the current state of Buddhist practice: "Nowadays the order is pitiful, and those without manners are only cheating themselves."[6] The correct ordering of obeisance ultimately derives from scripture. Among those who had an audience with the Buddha, physical posture was differentiated according to doctrinal and institutional categories. Daoxuan paraphrased the *Dazhidulun*:

> The *[Da]zhidulun* says: the outer paths [non-Buddhist teachings] use other methods; so when they come, they sit down of their own accord. The white robes (laity) use the guest's method, thus I command them to sit. The body and mind of all the five classes of those who have left the household (i.e. the

Sangha) belong to the Buddha, thus they stand and do not sit. If it is arhats who have attained the way, such as Sariputra, etc., all sit and listen to the Dharma. All those of the third fruition[7] and below do not sit when they listen, because their acts are not yet accomplished, the binders and fetters are not yet broken.[8]

So physical posture in the presence of the Buddha displayed one's status within the Buddhist cast of characters: outsiders, lay "guests," the ordained, and more or less advanced disciples. Continuing his scriptural citations, Daoxuan cites a ranked sequence from the *Dabeijing*:

> The *Dabeijing* says: After the Buddha has gone, practice the bodhisattva way. Seeing the Three Treasures, *sarira* (relics), or stupas and images, the master-monks, fathers and mothers, seniors, good friends, those on outer paths, the many sylphs (*xian*), [non-Buddhist] sramanas (monks), and brahmins, there are none who do not fall flat and humbly lower themselves to show respect and courtesy. Due to this reward, they have become Buddhas. Of people and animals of the mountains and forests, there are none who do not fall flat to show respect to the Buddha.[9]

The sequence places the Three Treasures, relics of Buddha and Sangha, stupa and images, master-monks, in that order, as objects of obeisance; then we cross the line between ordained and lay, going to parents, seniors, and friends; then follow a set of sectarian classifications: the heretics, sylphs (referring particularly to Daoists), (non-Buddhist) monks, and Brahmins. Even animals are said to acknowledge Buddha's superiority.[10] The listing of such categories in sequence from top to bottom is widespread, for example in the first chapters of most Mahayana sutras, which begin by listing everyone present, starting with the Buddha.

Daoxuan recounts one of several canonical stories of the institution of specified forms of respect:

> The Tathagata perfected the way on Gajasirsa mountain. After he ferried Kasyapa [to salvation], he recalled that in the past King Bimbisara had previously made an invitation. He led his mass of followers to that country. The King, together with the crowd of gentlemen and sramanas ... first asked, "when the Buddha comes, all come far to welcome him, not yet knowing

the proper forms of respect. Some bow to the feet and sit down. Some lift the hands, make polite inquiries and sit down. Some call your name. Some interlace the fingers and brings palms together. Some are silent and sit down. All have doubts." Kasyapa was a long-standing master. ... When Kasyapa knew [of Bimbisara's problem], he wished to resolve the many doubts. He ascended into empty space and got down to pay respect to Buddha's feet (*lijing fozu*). He laid his hands on (the Buddha's feet) and with his mouth he exclaimed: "The Buddha is my master; I am the Buddha's disciple." Then he took a fan, and waved it while standing behind the Buddha.[11]

The issue here is not only the confusion of ritual forms among the onlookers but also the relative rank of the Buddha and Kasyapa, the latter known as a venerable ascetic in his own right. To clarify the relationship, Kasyapa displays the contrast of hands and feet, verbally defining this contrast as signifying master/disciple. His ascent into empty space just before this act might be a magical display to signify his status as "higher" than laity, so that the message is: I am higher than you, and the Buddha is higher than me.

Daoxuan cites a story of the Buddha putting in order the rituals of respect within the monastic community. In response to confusion over correct terms of address, which he dismisses as mere pride, Daoxuan outlines the four basic rules of monastic obeisance[12]:

1. Those of the Way do not bow to laity. (Monastic over lay)
2. Monks do not bow to nuns. (Male over female)
3. Those who preserve the precepts do not bow to those who break the precepts. (Disciplined over undisciplined; orthoprax over heteroprax)
4. Those who received the precepts before do not bow to those who received the precepts after. (Senior over junior)

My use of the word "over" in the parentheses above is intended both figuratively and literally: in an immediate sense, bowing creates a vertical distinction of high and low. These four rules can be represented spatially in the form of a diagram (See Figure 2.1).

The four rules of monastic hierarchy present a topographic map of social difference. The following story of the bird, monkey, and elephant illustrates rather elegantly the shared logic of social order and obeisance.

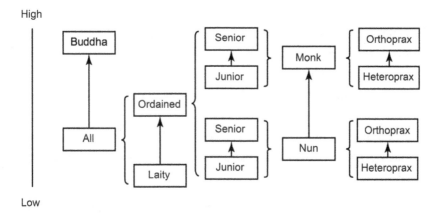

Figure 2.1 The vertical topography of monastic obeisance, according to the four Buddhist rules.

Of old, there was a mynah bird, a monkey, and a great elephant. Together they lived in a forest as friends. They said to each other: "the most senior of us should be respected with ritual form. How can we live together if we don't know the ritual of respect?"

The elephant said: "[I am so old that] I saw this [now tall] tree grow [when it was] even with my belly."

The monkey said: "[I am so old that] I have crouched on the ground and touched the top of the tree with my hand."

The bird said: "I brought the seed of this tree from a distant forest and let it fall, and so it grew. I should be the most senior."

So at that time, the great elephant carried the monkey on its back, the bird stood on the monkey, and they traveled all around.[13]

Here, seniority is the key determinant of ritual status, which is expressed in directly physical terms as senior = higher, junior = lower. The ritual meaning of seniority is directly embodied by the contact between senior feet and junior head, making a clear vertical line from top/senior to bottom/junior. It was certainly lucky for the bird and the monkey that the elephant was the youngest!

In practical terms (for human beings), this kind of correlation of vertical ritual space and seniority means that age is one criteria for determining who bows to whom, who places their body lower than the other. In the same chapter, Daoxuan distinguishes obeisance practice according to a difference of fewer or more than nine "dharma-years" (retreat seasons since ordination): "For the junior monk, there are five norms: 1. bare the shoulder; 2. take off shoes; 3. bow to the feet; 4. perform the *hugui* [a kneeling posture]; 5. put palms together. For the senior monk, it is different; there are four norms: you leave out the bow to the feet. Therefore know: the bow to the feet is not performed to one below one's station."[14]

The duration of one's monastic career is not the only way that time enters into the equation. Daoxuan discusses the ordering of the times of obeisance on a daily basis:

> In practice, one must consult others on the divisions and sequence, using the Dharma to calculate it. In regards to this, the *lun*[15] says: "three times a day, three times a night," the bodhisattva bows and chants to all Buddhas. The gentleman who transmits the texts [of the Dharma] reveres and venerates this teaching. Thus there is the division into six times, in order to purify the three (bad) karmas (of body, speech and mind), from which come the habits of forsaking [discipline] and laxness at the other times.[16]

But "although the words ['six times'] have a number, the meaning of the practice is inexhaustible."[17] Obeisance is thus not only a matter of an act, performed a measurable number of times at fixed intervals but also a kind of permanent meditational posture, a mental state: in a more literal sense than Foucault intended, a subject position.

Any ordering of obeisance is about the space of the body; but Daoxuan also gives attention to location, the ground upon which obeisance properly occurs:

> If the form is purified, the mind is clear and far-sighted. For this reason, one must be solemn and dignified toward the place of the Way (*daochang*) and setting up venerable images. This starts one on the correct path to spiritual illumination, and it also penetrates into the illuminating ferry of the sagely Way.
>
> First select the terrain (*fangtu*) of the Three Bodies.
>
> [small print:] The *Contemplation of Samantabhadra* says: "the Dharma Body of Vairocana is in all places. The dwelling place of Buddha is called the radiance of constant stillness."[18] The remaining Response and Transformation Bodies are listed according to their type and marks.
>
> Next, manifest the radiant transformation of the ten Buddhas.

[small print:] Such as in Nagarjuna's *Treatise on Ten Stages*, which completely lists the forms of the good virtues.[19]

Praise the many forms, for each has precepts and usages. When repenting and diligently requesting [the Dharma], distinguish among the locations.[20]

Here also, the physical site of bowing to monastic authorities is of concern. The importance of flat, level ground in obeisance to the monk's master is emphasized for example in the *Shangongjing jing* (Sutra on Properly Offering Respect), translated in the fifth century: "If the ground is level and proper, you should do obeisance. If the ground is not level or too confined, you should withdraw and stand, and then when the master has gone past, go to a level place and ask the Dharma."[21] Compare this to the emphasis on not bowing while physically higher than the master, discussed in the previous chapter.

Daoxuan notes that the sutras have some inconsistencies and deficiencies concerning the forms of respect, so he compiles a new list of twelve. This kind of re-editing is typical of Daoxuan's work, as for example when he went through the three available versions of the vinaya and picked out the best bits.[22] This section is the nearest Daoxuan comes in this text to any "how-to" guide. For some acts listed, he writes almost nothing, but under some of the headings, his remarks range far beyond simple technical instructions.[23] What follows is less a list of distinct gradations of obeisance and more a list of aspects of obeisance. Heng Sure calls them "twelve expressions of respect."[24]

> 1. *nanwu* (Sanskrit *namo*), which Daoxuan translates as "I bow" (*woli*) or "take refuge and bow" (*guili*). "In the sutras, when people came to the Buddha, they said '*namo*,' or 'the non-attached perfected one' or 'the correctly awakened one.' This is called the karma of the mouth, praising the merit of the Tathagatha." Daoxuan cites scriptural examples of obeisance. "It is just like among the laity within the Tang boundaries, those below the Son of Heaven praise and esteem his abundant virtue."[25] So for Daoxuan, praise counts as verbal obeisance.
> 2. *jishou*. ("reaches [the ground] with the head.")[26]
> 3. *fu zuoju* ("spread out the sitting cloth" or *nisidana*, a cloth for bowing on). Clearly, this is not a complete act of obeisance in the strict sense, but one element of the larger ritual context.[27]

4. *tuo gexi* ("remove sandals"). In India, Daoxuan says, this is very respectful. "In this land, the rites of the many ministers in the court are held in the palaces, so shoes are not taken off." In India, he notes, the ground is muddier than in China.[28]

5. *piantan* ("baring one's [right] side").[29]

6. *wulun zhaodi* ("five wheels touch the ground"). Also called *wutishedi*, "five [points of the] body touch the ground." The five points are the two forearms, two knees, and the head.[30] This form is widely cited throughout all the literature on bowing, approximately synonymous with a full prostration and with the kowtow (*ketou*).

7. *toumian lizu* ("head and face bow to the foot").

8. *youxi zhaodi* ("right knee touches the ground").[31]

9. *hugui* (胡跪 "foreign kneeling") Both knees are on the ground. "It is called foreign kneeling because it is the form for foreigners (*huren*)." It is also known as *hugui*, (互跪 "mutual kneel"). The monk performs the *hugui*, but the nun performs the *changgui* ("long kneel") because she is "weak and easily exhausted by lifting herself up."[32]

10. *yixin hezhang* ("single-mindedly bring palms together"). "It is the bringing together of the palms and ten fingers to make offering to Sakya's masters and disciples, as in the Vinaya."[33] Another term for this is *heshi*, "bringing together the ten" fingers.

11. *yourao* ("circumambulate with the right side" toward the object of respect, i.e. clockwise). "In the canonical Vinaya, the regulations order a circumambulation with one's right side [toward the object]. A leftward circumambulation of a pagoda is what the spirits belittle. [Unfortunately,] the leftward circumambulation is what the common people honor."[34]

12. *qushen zhanyin* ("bend the body and reverently look up").[35]

Under number seven, "head and face touch the feet," Daoxuan elaborates on the head-foot distinction.

> In the sutras and vinaya texts it often says "head and face bow to feet" or it says "head-bow to Buddha's feet" (*dingli fozu*). What is highest on me is the head, what is lowest on the other is the feet. Taking what I honor, to pay respect to what is lowest on the other is the extreme form of obeisance. It is rather like among the laity, when friends who have great respect for each other do not use their names, but rather they call each other "beneath the feet" (*zuxia*). The meaning is of this kind. It is also similar to how the Son of Heaven and the heir-apparent have their special terms of reference. Not

daring to refer directly to the body [of the emperor], some say "(one who) mounts the carriage," or "chariots and carriages" (*chengyu, chejia*). Or some say "beneath the stairs," or "beneath the hall" (*bixia, dianxia*). All rites of respect are one [in their purpose], but the styles of practicing respect in the center and in the borderlands are not the same. In this land, when we establish (the norms of) respect, we consider bowing from a distance respectful. In India, when they establish respect, the supreme bow is one in which they approach close to the body and place hands on the feet.[36]

This discussion moves freely between actual head-to-feet movements (as in a particular form of a bow) and linguistic obeisance, the use of some reference to what is underneath the feet as a respectful second person pronoun. One lowers oneself by presuming to address not the person but the ground beneath his feet. The same spatial structure is applied to a variety of objects: Buddha, friends, and the emperor.

Although Daoxuan provides some indication of physical technique, his goal in listing and commenting on these ritual acts seems to be terminological precision and a continuation of his general themes. More plainly descriptive accounts of obeisance technique are to be found, for example in his *Admonitions* (as noted above) and his *Xingshichao*.[37] At least within this treatise, details of the act take a second place to the doctrinal, mental, and spiritual dimensions of obeisance.

Ordering the bowing mind

In terms of mental attitude, probably the most pervasive theme of the *Guijingyi* is pride. "With foolish pride as the root, one increases the filthy fetters."[38] "Some who are boastful and haughty lift themselves up and shun others' names and hopes. Toiling in body and mind, they angrily insult beings, so that although outwardly they yield benefit, yet inwardly they are really just prancing around."[39] "Pride does not let in the reality of the Dharma."[40] Daoxuan repeatedly points out that obeisance is particularly efficacious against pride: "practicing respect is basically to get rid of pride."[41] Pride consists of placing oneself higher than one's low status warrants.

The mind's delusions are subtle and extensive; although one practices contemplation, yet they gather and arise in disorder. The body's forms are phenomenal and manifest; bending down causes the overturning of lofty pride. Pride is what the common people should be ashamed of, [but it is also] what all the low and backsliding sentient beings obey. Both the practitioners of the Way and the common people [should] reject it.[42]

Other bad attitudes are also criticized: "Covetous and angry glares, as soon as they are released, implicate one in the three [woeful] paths."[43] "Repeatedly giving rise to covetousness and anger clearly causes painful consequences. It is like how receiving a body which is short and low is due to objecting to the height of a stupa. A voice [that is loud and clear enough] to halt an army horse is due to promoting hand-bell offerings."[44] Here, we see how physique is supposedly determined by negative or positive attitudes toward devotion. The "low" body resulting from resentment of the high stupa, or perhaps a begrudging attitude toward making donations to build stupas (the symbolic body of Buddha or all Three Treasures) is certainly noteworthy. We sometimes regard this depiction of karma as simplistic or belonging to folk Buddhism, but Daoxuan includes it without any caveat. Of course, the (positive) height of the stupa or the monk is different from the (negative) "loftiness" of pride.

The necessity of increased attention to devotional activity and cultivation in general is due in part to the gradual degeneration of the Dharma, in which standards of morality and discipline grow lax.

> The times proclaim the dregs and the murky, trouble and delusions increase daily. When will it all collapse into debauchery? If one is not serious about study, how can one succeed in ferrying [beings to enlightenment]? Therefore I entrust this knowledge about the pure practices of bodily form. By being humble and yielding, self-pride is repressed. It must be that if one is lax and negligent, haughty pride will increase the old habits. This is called anxiety. Calamity cannot but be deep.[45]

Daoxuan refers in particular to those whose pride and delusion is so great that they refuse even to listen to the Dharma, and are thus like "overturned vessels"[46] (which cannot contain the rain of the Dharma—another vertical metaphor, since rain falls from above). On the same track, he also refers to the scriptural precedent of those who refused to listen: "In Buddha's age there were people who withdrew from the mat."[47] This is a reference to Hinayana monks, who, from a Mahayana standpoint, selfishly cultivate themselves and feel proud of their high meditational attainment. The stereotypical proud Hinayana monk is attached to his display of skillful technique in pursuit of purity. In response, Daoxuan asserts a characteristically Mahayana doctrine: the Hinayana practitioner reifies the distinction between purity and pollution, thinks of this distinction as ultimately real, and selfishly clings to the side of purity. The very act of letting go of attachment creates an insidious form of dualism. In fact, however:

> In the teachings revealed by the great Sage, boundaries are in one's own mind. The lower-than-stupid coldly hold that defilements are outside consciousness. [If this is] what you take to transform and guide you, there will be no way to part with them.[48]

Again, "opening and manifesting [Buddha-nature] does not come from the outside. Awakening enters through sincere causes and arises inwardly. When deluded, it is called bowing to the outer realm (*liwaijing*). After awakening, one returns to bowing to one's own mind (*lizixin*). Thus the sutras say: 'When the mind is focused on Buddha, this mind is Buddha.'"[49] The act of the bow itself remains the same, but the object of obeisance changes according to the level of enlightenment.

Having spent so much of his time working on vinaya texts, and insisting on the great value of scripturally validated discipline, Daoxuan acquired a reputation as a kind of crypto-Hinayana monk. Later stories circulated which represented him as obsessively insisting on keeping the rules while oblivious to true reality and the bodhisattva spirit. In stories about his encounters with the unorthodox monk Falin, or the Tantric monk Subaraksimha (Shanwuwei), and about his visit to Wutaishan, Daoxuan comes across as the literalistic pedant. "Falin passed by him, and the Vinaya Master did not show him ritual courtesy (*li*)." But a heavenly being tells Daoxuan, "his *bodhisattva-bhumi* [level of bodhisattva attainment] is not something you understand. So, when he comes again, treat him well."[50] Daoxuan never again objected to Falin's egregious violations of the vinaya. These stories are part of a dialectical process of differentiation in which Daoxuan is a stock figure standing for narrow-minded adherence to vinaya. But any reading of his works makes clear, while he viewed physical discipline as essential to enlightenment, he never viewed adherence to rules as something to be attached to. On the other hand, he criticized the presumptuous emancipation from rules that he saw in the Sangha of his time:

> Some say, "I am a Mahayana person, I don't practice the Dharma of Hinayana." People like this are many, not just one, two or three. Thus inwardly they deviate from the bodhisattva-mind, and outwardly, they lack the proper conduct of an auditor [disciple of Buddha]. The four postures (walking, standing, sitting and reclining) cannot be nurtured, so these people are called dead wood.[51]

The profundity and spiritual potency of obeisance varies greatly. Daoxuan attributes to Ratnamati "seven kinds of bowing to Buddha."[52] (This text, the *Lifo guanmen* 禮佛觀門 is no longer extant.) This list of seven is very different from the list of twelve given above. These gradations reveal a great deal about the inner spirituality of obeisance, even if we must take these mental states as prescriptive rather than descriptive. This sequence goes from mechanical acts through progressive internalization to a point where the "bow" itself disappears into non-duality. The sequence also rehearses a hierarchy of benefit: from no benefit (1), to a meager benefit (2), to a conditional benefit which at least erases bad karma (3), to a gradual transcendence of any thought of benefit at all (4–7). This sequence (from no benefit, to karmic benefit, to a transcendence of concern with karmic benefit) is also parallel to a customary hierarchy of lay and monastic: lay people primarily seek karmic benefit, whereas clerics are supposed to move beyond such selfish concerns.

> 1. *Womanli* ("the bow of self-pride"). "It refers to relying on order and status. The mind has no offering of respect. Highly venerating one's own virtue, there is no real intention of looking up to the Master. ... They labor in vain without benefit. Outwardly it looks like obeisance, inwardly it increases the delusion of pride. Just as if one is a wooden person, feelings are not abundantly respectful, and the hand does not touch the ground. The five wheels[53] are not all used. This is pride-karma, so it is called 'the bow of self-pride.'"[54]

2. *Changheli* ("the bow of chanting together", or "sing-along bowing" as Heng Sure calls it.[55] It is also known as *qiumingli* "the bow of seeking fame"). We might call this social bowing. "Even though there is no lofty pride, the mind has no calm thoughts. The demeanor is roughly correct, the body and mind are reverent, and rising and falling are co-ordinated, [but still,] … the blessing is thin and meager. It is not a true offering."[56]

3. *Shenxin gongjingli* ("the bow of offering respect with body and mind," also known as *shenxinli* "the bow of body and mind"). "Hearing and chanting the Buddha's name, you hold the Buddha's body in the mind, as if [the Buddha was] in front of you, [the Buddha's] form good and complete, dignified and solemn, dazzling and brilliant. When the form in the mind is complete, you really are face to face with the Three Bodies [of the Buddha]. [The Buddha] extends his hand to rub the top of your head to remove your sinful karma. This is using the body and mind to offer respect. You do not have any other thoughts. In offering respect, you do not feel weary. This is called the mind of bowing to Buddha within the boundaries of the world (*jingjie lifo xin*). Appearing before your eyes, you are absorbed [in the vision] without confusion. This person guides and benefits humans and gods ever higher and greater. [Yet,] although the merit is great, it is not yet the wisdom mind, and afterwards many backslide."

4. *Fazhi qingjing jieda fojingjie lifo* ("the bow to Buddha which emanates wisdom and purity so that one can penetrate into the Buddha's realm," also known as *fazhi qingjing li*, "the bow which emanates wisdom and purity"). Here, the entire experience begins to take on a cosmic quality reminiscent of the vision of Maitreya's tower in the *Huayanjing*, in which all facets of reality reflect all the other facets.[57] "If there is any thought, it is not obstructing thought. Now I penetrate [the realization that] my own mind is empty and pervading without obstructions. In this way, I practice bowing to the Buddha. In accordance with the mind's capacity, my bow to one Buddha is a bow to all Buddhas. All Buddhas are one Buddha, by way of the Buddha's Dharma-body, interpenetrating without obstacles. Thus a bow to one Buddha completely extends to all of them. In the same way, many kinds of incense and flowers offered are equal to this. As for respecting the Dharma and Sangha, the meaning is also equal to this. Because the Three Treasures are of the same nature, in principle there is no difference. [Although] the three vehicles have different names, the framework of enlightenment is the same. Thus we know: one bow is all bows, all bows are one bow. In this way the Three Treasures are able to fully interpenetrate."[58]

5. *Bianru fajie lijing gongliang* ("the offering of obeisance for wholly entering the Dharma realm," also known as *bianru fajieli*, "the bow of wholly entering the Dharma realm"). This bow elaborates the previous bow by projecting the bowing self into this vision of interprenetration. "The practitioner visualizes the dharmas [i.e. constituent parts] of one's own body and mind from the root. If you do not reside in the Dharma realm, Buddha's Dharma is outside the body. But know this: the dharmas of the body and mind of all Buddhas do not reside outside of my own body. Emitting wisdom and excelling in penetration, one's own body and all bodies wholly fill the Dharma realm.... I now bow to one Buddha, one Buddha's body fills the Dharma realm. In the Dharma realm [and] the existing three realms, for those who have reached the stage of no outflows, the Dharma body is entirely the Buddha's body. The Buddha's body fills all. Through the Buddha, my body also fills all.... In their causal conditions and in their results, the four postures (walking, standing, sitting and reclining) are not removed from the Dharma realm. Body follows mind, so [there is] release without obstructions. From the causal conditions of the Dharma realm, all phenomena arise into completion. It is like hanging a hundred thousand mirrors in a single room. There are some who only see the mirrors. In the mirrors are only images. The pure illumination of the Buddha's body surpasses these mirrors. All of the Dharma realm fully manifests in the body."[59]

6. *Zhengguanli zishenfo* ("bow of correct contemplation that one's own body is Buddha," also known as *zhengguan xiushengli*, "bow of correct contemplation and cultivating truth"). Having asserted the unreality of the phenomenal world outside of the Buddha-mind, there remains the possibility of still thinking that Buddha is a real thing, an external thing outside of one's own mind. "How is it that all sentient beings each have Buddha nature, equally and fully? According to the causal conditions arising in the Dharma realm, it is only in a false awakening that there is an "outside" that can be contemplated. Therefore false delusions constantly engulf one in death and birth. If you are able to reverse the reflection (*fanzhao*), then there will be an occasion for liberation. If one faces another realm and says "there is something which can be contemplated," [this is] the false practice of false people. The teachings of the sutras do not allow it. So they say: Do not contemplate "Buddha," do not contemplate "Dharma," do not contemplate "Sangha" [as external objects], because [instead you should] see your own true Dharma nature. It also says: Seeing the self in form and sound is called practicing a false path. So when the practitioner

constantly practices bowing, only seeing body and mind, if there are [still the mental constructs called] "bowing" and "respect," you are not yet able to penetrate into liberation. Constantly despise the common practices. After, at the moment you penetrate, you know mind has no outside. And you know the pure original nature of your own mind. This is simply that your own nature dwells in Buddha nature. According to the effort to cultivate illumination, you draw out [a realization of] Buddha nature. The result of the three *asankhyeyas* [innumerable years of practice] are perfect, the ten stages are ascended. In the end you attain the fruit of Buddha nature. This awakening is subtle and wonderful. It is only the sage who reaches it."[60]

7. *Shixiang sanbao zita pingdengli* ("the bow of the true form of the Three Treasures, with self and other equal"). "The main idea is the same as above. But above, there was still "the bow" and "the contemplation [of the bow]," the dual difference of self and other. Now, in this [bow], there is no self and no other. The Buddha and the ordinary person are a single thusness, there is no difference between past and present.... The sutras say: "contemplate the body's true form; contemplating the Buddha is also thus."[61] Because one cannot use the mind in order to attain the true form removed from thoughts. One cannot use form to seek it. One cannot use obeisance; [and yet] one cannot but do obeisance. Bowing and not bowing are the same. Offering and not offering are the same. With the calm mind silently extinguished, it is called the equal bow (*pingdengli*). Thus the Manjusri Ten Bows[62] says: "Because of no arising and no passing away, obeisance has nothing to contemplate." Practicing these latter two bows, silently one can penetrate them, and with blessings one can practice the Way. This [practice] causes stopping and contemplation (*zhiguan*, i.e. the mind as empty and still, and the mind in its analytic mode) to roam in tandem, true and common (or clergy and laity) to move in unison. The mind is empty and boundless, [even while] the body truly is still bound to causes."[63]

These seven states of mind illustrate well the doctrinal richness of obeisance in Buddhist tradition. Performed properly, obeisance is enlightenment in this very body. In the "bow of self-pride," the pride is directly correlated with the hand not reaching the ground—the body not lowered enough. In the third type of bow, you retain the self-other distinction ("Hearing and chanting Buddha's name, you hold Buddha's body in the mind, as if [Buddha was] in front of you."), but as you progress, you gradually erase any sense of boundaries, thereby creating increased stores of merit by practicing obeisance to all Buddhas simultaneously: "bowing to one Buddha is bowing to all Buddhas." In this mental state, bowing to a monk is also the same as bowing to all Buddhas. Then the identification of self and Buddha takes place through the realization of non-duality: "the dharmas of the body and mind of all Buddhas do not reside outside of my own body;" "there is no self and no other. The Buddha and the ordinary person are a single thusness." Whereas one might argue that obeisance reifies the hierarchical difference between the bowing monk and the superior Buddha, here the act of obeisance is interpreted as a moment of absolute non-duality. This motif of non-duality unifies Buddha, Dharma, and Sangha: the Three Treasures.

The object of obeisance

At least that's the lofty principle. Backing up a little, a bow by definition must have an object. In the 662 debate, the problem was not the practice of bowing as such but the appropriate object of obeisance. So what exactly is it that the monk bows to? In order to rationalize obeisance, Daoxuan must define the objects of obeisance, namely the Three Treasures (*sanbao*). He discusses four understandings of the Three Treasures.[64]

First, "One Body Three Treasures" refers to the nonduality or non-differentiation of Buddha, Dharma, and Sangha. Second, "Contemplation of Principle Three Treasures" refers to five aspects of the Dharma body, complete only in the Buddha, namely: precepts, meditation, wisdom, salvation, and knowledge of salvation.[65] Third, Daoxuan outlines the "Transformation Three Treasures," the Three Treasures in their unified salvific aspect.[66] The emphasis here is on the salvific power of the Three Treasures, set in the narrative of decline. After Sakyamuni Buddha is gone, beings must rely on the Dharma he taught, as recorded and transmitted by monastic institutions, the "sons of Buddha," the "guests who have received the Way."[67] So far these are more or less doctrinal and relate rather indirectly to the question of obeisance.

The fourth understanding, however, seems more directly relevant. The "Tangible Three Treasures" (*zhuchi sanbao*) refers to the material Buddha images, to the books and words of the scriptures, and to the bodies of monks and nuns.⁶⁸ As we will see in the next chapter, those who wanted monks to bow to the emperor drew attention to the observable physical presence of monks in China. They hoped that emphasizing their physical presence would make it harder to claim any transcendence of the obligations of subjecthood in the imperial domain. Daoxuan writes that the monastic institutions bear the burden of maintaining the tangible Treasures: "Those who labor to announce and explain true and false, with the power of sincerely relying on form and appearance, are called the Sangha-Treasure."⁶⁹ He goes on to Dharma and Buddha, both in terms of their perceivable manifestations:

> In speaking names and sentences, the most important thing is to reveal principle. Principle is not just texts and words, which do not [of themselves] cause awakening. Thus, according to the names and teachings, the conditions of teaching and hearing are called the Dharma-treasure. Here principle is dark and mysterious; if one is not a sage, one cannot know it. Although the sage is said to have disappeared, the shadow-image is set up, which is called the Buddha-treasure.⁷⁰

Dharma is ultimately beyond words, but the words and texts are the "tangible Dharma;" Buddha is gone, but the Buddha-image is the "tangible Buddha." Daoxuan makes it clear that although the Three Treasures in reality transcend material form, these tangible objects are still the holy manifestation of the Buddha, and furthermore, if one is sufficiently advanced in spiritual cultivation, one can perceive the real principle in these material objects. Sadly, the dull-minded masses see only the material aspect. The irony of this position is that in later historical memory, Daoxuan himself is depicted as a quasi-Hinayana monk of dim perceptions, unable to perceive Wutaishan, for example, in its radiant splendor as a divine realm, seeing only rocks and trees.⁷¹

Daoxuan remarks on the material Buddha image in particular. "The Sutra⁷² says: 'Building an image is like [growing] wheat,' the merit gained does not run out, because it is the vessel of the Dharma-body. The *lun* says: 'As for metal, wood, earth and stone, the substance (*ti*) is not sentient. Regarding constructed images, those who respect or break them gain blessings or sins.'"⁷³ The great merit of constructing Buddha images was known among Chinese Buddhists from the earliest period of translation, in particular from the *Zuofo xingxiang jing* (Sutra on the Production of Buddha Images), which tells of the wonderful benefits and rebirths of those who build images.[74]

And yet: "Today there are those who sit peacefully before an image, with feelings lacking respect and courtesy. This can be referred to as idly receiving sin, uselessly piling up on body and mind."[75] The comments here not only link the Buddha to his image but also posit the negative effects of disrespect for images. They also suggest the negative effects of "mere" form, ritual actions without interior attitudes of respect and trust. His point is reinforced by a quotation from the *Zengyi ahanjing*, relegating the disrespectful to the level of reptiles (dragons and snakes) who, as Daoxuan says, "have no respect and who spit out much foolishness."[76]

Numerous references throughout the text say trust (or faith) is the supreme virtue, particularly in the early stages of cultivation: "In taking refuge, and spreading and protecting [the Dharma], if one does not have trust, respect will not succeed."[77] "To have trust in dignified manner is the start of entering the way."[78] "Trust is the origin of the Way (*daoyuan*), the mother of merit and virtue."[79]

"In principle," trust gives rise to the outer forms of respect. And yet: "In practice (phenomena, *shi*), it must be that establishing forms of respect and founding usages initiate the method of the first act of trust."[80] This circular logic, that trust is the root of respect but that forms of respect gives rise to trust, appears throughout the text. At least initially, salvation takes place in rites and forms, because it is through these that the first moment of deep trust, the *bodhicitta*, occurs.

It is interesting to compare these remarks with the assertions about "respect" (*jing*) in the bowing debate. Here, interior attitude is all-important: lack of such sentiment even in one who "sits peacefully before an image" leads to bad karma. In the bowing debate literature, there is an attempt by the monks and their supporters to disassociate respect (the interior feeling) from respect (the exterior enactment). We will also return to the relation of mental state and physical performance when we look at Protestant views of bowing, in Chapter 5.

Remarking on the dangers of disrespecting the tangible Three Treasures, and on the correct attitude of reverence, Daoxuan borrows from ancestral cult practice and from the *Analects* in describing the emotional state of one who sees the "bequeathed traces" of Buddha:

> It is like approaching the pure temple (*qingmiao*),[81] naturally one is sad and respectfully lifts up the eyes. One has grieving feelings, as if [the spirits were] present,[82] with no doubts. Now I am like this.... One must bend the head and bend down to reach to the feet and practice obeisance, as if the training in the true rites speaks the Dharma to me.[83]

The performance of obeisance "as if" the spirit was present suggests more than a kind of reverential pretense, but the living presence of the spirit in the icon. Rituals such as the "eye-opening" ceremony show that icons were not only, or not primarily, didactic, but thought of as living. As Robert Sharf comments: "Such ritual consecrations are intended to transform an inanimate image into a living deity... icons thus empowered were treated as spiritual beings possessed of apotropaic powers, to be worshipped with regular offerings of incense, flowers, food, money, and other assorted valuables."[84] Many miracle stories vividly demonstrate the animation of the icon.[85]

If the assertion of the living presence of the spirit in the icon contradicted the observer's perception of the icon as a mere chunk of wood, Daoxuan recalls the characteristically Mahayana notion that our experience of objects is determined by the purity or impurity of our perceptions. He writes: "All Buddhas constantly emanate radiance and teach the Dharma. The sentient beings, due to beginningless sins, meet them face to face and still do not see. It must be that one image is like this, so the other images are as a rule also thus."[86] Daoxuan's point here is that Buddha images may appear to be merely inert material objects, but they and indeed all forms can be perceived as the salvific manifestations of the Buddha. The difference in perspective is classed in terms of the Two Truths, true and common.

Trust in and obeisance to the Three Treasures is superior to trust in any other object of obeisance, such as the indigenous deities:

> Thus the *sutra* says: "one who takes refuge in Buddha is truly named a gentleman of pure trust (*qingxinshi*). In the end he does not falsely take refuge in the various other celestial spirits (*tianshen*)."[87] Why is this? Because the true Three Treasures in nature and in form constantly reside, they are

worthy to be relied on by beings. From the other celestial emperors come suffering and vexation in body and mind. They have action [as opposed to the non-action of a Buddha], they have outflows, they do not have power. Not able to save themselves..., how could they be able to save beings? It is only the Treasures which have left the world that have the power which can be relied on.[88]

Here, Daoxuan reproduces the conventional Buddhist discourse on non-Buddhist deities, acknowledging their existence but placing them firmly in the realm of samsara.[89] Since deities themselves have not transcended birth and death, they cannot be reliable. Daoxuan asserts the singular veneration of the Buddha as highest of all orders of beings:

> The *Benqijing*[90] says: When the Buddha first came down from Heaven and was born, and traveled in all directions, he lifted his hand to point to Heaven and Earth, and said: "Above Heaven and below Heaven, it is only I who is venerable." According to the ninety-six (heterodox) teachings which people of that age considered weighty, he was named the great sage, master of humans and gods. In order to cut off heresy and return to the correct, he showed this form. It is only Buddha who alone is venerable surpassing all heterodox paths. Thus we say he has venerable dignity.[91]

So what is it we're supposed to bow to? The Buddha, obviously. That includes Buddha images, because if your perceptions are correct, Buddha images and Buddha are non-dual. In the bowing debate, there were snide comments on monks liking to receive obeisance, and bowing to each other, but very little objection to bowing to Buddha images. Was there any kind of Medieval Buddhist equivalent of idolatry or a concern to avoid such an accusation? Idolatry has a specific Western history, which I don't intend to invoke yet, but will try to tackle in Chapter 5. Still, clearly there was some need to articulate what the physical object was, and how bowing to the object was ultimately bowing to Buddha. Hence the non-dual argument, and in ritual practice, the consecration ritual. The labor expended on consecration and explanation surely demonstrates that the materiality of Buddhism was a vulnerability.

How does this discussion of duality and non-duality relate to obeisance? Daoxuan needs to establish firmly the non-duality of multiple phenomena such as Buddha-images and Sangha-images and a single principle (the ultimate truth and enlightenment taught by Buddha). The goal is to demonstrate that obeisance to an image or a monk—manifestly tangible, objectifiable, producible, material objects—is the same as obeisance to the highest abstract principles of Buddhism—that bowing to this, that, and the next thing (as long as they are within the Three Treasures) is always only bowing to the One. Of course, this is tricky ground, and Daoxuan has to juggle. Perhaps also Daoxuan wants to attack a perception of obeisance as an obsession with particular forms. Despite the valuation of non-dual wisdom, Daoxuan clearly values "principle" over "phenomena"; even if they are ultimately one, this is only perceivable by sages (who see principle in phenomena) and not perceivable by common folk (who for the time being have to "rely on" phenomena). Principle is formless, universal, and totalizing; phenomena is local, specific, and in forms.

The subject of obeisance

The question of what we bow to takes us to the first of the Three Treasures, and the heart of the entire Buddhist project—what is a Buddha, what is truth, and what is enlightenment? And yet, what exactly is it that bows? This question takes us to the core of Buddhist anthropology—the examination of the self. Daoxuan repeatedly emphasizes the pain, corruptibility and impermanence of the physical body, specifically the body as bequeathed by parents: "When, in time, liver and gall spread on the ground and the body-form and bones break apart, you should know that respect for the universe's highest venerable one [the Buddha] exceeds [the respect due to] the father (literally, that which belongs to Heaven)."[92] Here we get into the contemporary politics of bowing: why monks should not have to bow to their parents. The small print comment adds:

> By a father and mother one is born into a body: repayment is made in one lifetime. Buddha gave rise to the Dharma-body: our appreciation[93] ends [only] far in the future after many kalpas. High merit is hard to reward, deep virtue does not fade, deep wisdom has substantial benefit. It is not something our appreciation can reach.[94]

Chapter 3 of *Guijingyi* begins with an allusion to the *Xiaojing*—and hence a reference to filial duty of obeisance to parents, but Daoxuan immediately follows it with a Buddhist qualification: "Ritual form is conduct (lizhe liye, 禮者履也) It is simply respect.⁹⁵ It is what the [Lotus] Sutra says: 'pay respect (*gongjing*) to the stupa-shrine; humbly lower yourself to the bhiksus.'"⁹⁶ The highest "filial piety" is thus obeisance to stupas and monks. One implication of this placement of the Three Treasures above parents is a belittling of the role of parents in producing the physical body, consistent with the emphasis on forgetting or despising the body, and leaving the household.

Indeed, an antagonistic relationship to the physical body is required, since "Form is tied up with common custom. The suffering body constantly binds you. Thus one should break free and oppose [this bondage] by taking refuge.... The mind is blocked with delusion and perverted views. Perverted views reside in the norms of beings⁹⁷ (*shengchang*)."⁹⁸ The mind too, then, is an "ethical substance,"⁹⁹ in that the entire world of the material body—the body as conditioned by culture—is the source of delusions. Monasticism is thus a technology for instituting a para- or anti-society, a social order defined by alterity.

Ultimately, in principle, "the Buddha's Dharma takes mind as the root, and body as the branches."¹⁰⁰ But for Daoxuan, the training of the body has a practical priority: "first you make your body comply and then in the end remove the mind's delusions."¹⁰¹ The body can be manipulated and constructed like any material object: "The body is like wood and stone; if engraved and polished, it successfully becomes a vessel" (for the Dharma).¹⁰² This metaphor of the body as the product of the artisan's skillful labor bears a striking resemblance to the production of an icon. The image of the body as raw material, subjected to skilled labor in the production of an object of capacity, a vessel of experience, suggests in turn Harpham's remark: "We look to a work of art for evidence of a will seeking expression by imposing itself upon alien matter. The ascetic body is in this sense an exemplary artifact: what the ascetics displayed to their audience was precisely their *form*."¹⁰³

Conclusion

When Chan master Shengyen visited the University of Iowa in the 1990s, someone with a literal understanding of "Zen iconoclasm" asked him if

Buddhists are still supposed to bow to Buddha images. "Of course," he said. "Why shouldn't we?" He moved onto the next question. For the most part, obeisance to the Buddha is learned early on and then becomes a constant activity for laity and clergy in Asia. Bowing is by far the most common religious act. Buddhist sutras and masters have not necessarily taken the time to articulate the reasons or spiritual dimensions of bowing. Medieval monks, or for that matter modern scholars, mention bowing all the time but rarely focus on it. Daoxuan did take the time to show bowing was, or can be, the heart of Buddhist practice. He was undoubtedly provoked by contemporary criticism of the monks' refusal to bow to laity. Arguing against monastic disobeisance, the Eastern Jin ruler Huan Xuan wrote, "Though the doctrine of the Buddha is so broad that it extends beyond what can be seen and heard, it is not different from secular doctrines in the importance that it attaches to veneration."[104] The monks never trivialized bowing as such. Perhaps the fact that Daoxuan had emphasized the importance of bowing in a lengthy treatise was especially galling to those who objected to their refusal to bow. Like bowing, the grumbling about monastic disobeisance was in the background for much of the time, surfacing for extended discussion in particular texts during the fourth and fifth centuries, and then, reaching the heights of an imperial debate.

3

The 662 Debate

Imperial ritual said everyone must bow to the emperor, and everyone should bow to their own parents. Buddhist monks said they could not bow to any layperson, not even to the emperor or to their own parents.

Earlier cases

The first recorded instance of conflict specifically over monastic bowing practices took place in the Eastern Jin, in 340.¹ The two sides were represented by pro-bow Yu Bing (296–344) and anti-bow He Chong (292–346). (By pro-bow I mean specifically, saying the monks *should* bow to rulers.) Behind the conflict was strong clan rivalry between the Yu and He clans.² Yu Bing spoke for the then-dominant Yu clan and was backed by among others Cai Mu, who later made the "black list" of wicked persecutors in Daoxuan's *Guang hongmingji*.³ In policy terms, the proposal came to nothing and was squashed even by the state ceremonialists, who cited the weight of past custom.⁴

I briefly extrapolate the main themes of the 340 conflict as twofold: first, the pro-bow side claimed everyone in the emperor's territory was his subject and had to bow accordingly. In response, monks posited Buddhism as a parallel realm, with its own law codes. So this was a question of the legal significance of physical presence in a given location. A second kind of issue involved the idea of a total social order. If the king's supremacy is not acknowledged, the whole hierarchical system was in danger of collapse. In the words of Yu Bing, "It is not so that the Lord of Ten Thousand Carriages (the emperor) desires to be venerable [*haozun*, likes to be venerated], nor is it so that the common people of the countryside desire to be low [*bi*]. But if (the distinction between) high and low [*bizun*] is not clearly exposed, the ruler's civilizing (activity) will become confused. For there can only be one (principle of government[5]); if one makes it two, disorder will be the result."[6]

The second instance was in 403–404. As in 340, the emergence of what was presumably a latent problem, and the reasons for its limited impact, have much to do with the unstable fortunes of different factions contending for imperial power. Before taking the throne of the Eastern Jin, Huan Xuan proposed making monks bow but abandoned the proposal when he was ruler. He, and his proposal, died in military conflict soon after.[7] The 403–404 debate consists primarily of two sets of correspondence: Huan Xuan with Wang Mi and Huan Xuan with the distinguished monk Huiyuan, who also wrote a treatise on the matter, *Shamen bujing wangzhe lun* ("Treatise on the fact that sramanas do not pay respect to kings").[8]

Again there were questions of territoriality and the relations of body and place. Does the presence of the body within a territory necessarily constitute the individual as a subject? Under what circumstances is the body exempt? What can one do to the body, if anything, to constitute the body as a distinct category in legal practice? The analogy of the monk's realm with statehood is still central and so are the strong assertions of territorial exteriority (living "beyond the limits") versus interiority (the monk as a subject of the Jin). The role of the ruler in the maintenance of social hierarchy also remains a critical issue.

There was also an appeal to natural sentiments. What is the correct method of embodying those supposedly natural virtues (such as reverence and gratitude) associated with parents and rulers? Throughout the pro-bow statements, there was a pervasive appeal to filial piety. Not bowing to parents was not the only body-practice which provoked the accusation of unfiliality; there was also cutting off one's hair and not producing heirs. Neither side rejected the value of filial piety, but Wang Mi drew a line between respect in the mind and the physical enactment of that respect. Indeed, monks claimed to fulfill filial piety better than even a householder, because they could aid their parents in future lives.

I have moved rather briskly over these two cases, because they have already been discussed by Hurvitz, Zürcher, and Tsukamoto, and because I see the 662 debate as a culmination of the debate, with these earlier arguments in the background.

Pre-debate lobbying

In 657, Emperor Gaozong issued an edict which forbade monks from receiving the homage of their parents. This is not exactly the same as telling monks to bow to their parents, but it brought up the whole question of bowing once again. Then on the fifteenth day of the fourth month of 662, Emperor Gaozong ordered a discussion of the bowing issue to take place one month later. The effect on the Sangha was "electrifying."[9] The monk Weixiu[10] and two hundred other monks went to Penglai palace to present a memorial but were rebuffed. They assembled at Ximing Temple (of which Daoxuan was then the abbot) to plan their campaign.[11] They composed and delivered several messages from monks to high-ranking laity. The mood of this pre-debate lobbying is alarm. Wang Yarong's 1998 novelization of Daoxuan's life depicts the mood as fiery and radical, with monks loudly proclaiming their willingness to die for the Dharma and Daoxuan as the solemn voice of reason.[12] The imperial order calling for the debate tried to reassure those who "fear and mistake" the idea of forced obeisance:

> Now I desire to order Daoist priests and nuns, and Buddhist monks and nuns to be made to bow to the Imperial Lord, to the empress and princes, and to fathers and mothers. There are some who fear and mistake the constant sentiments. It is appropriate to hand down to civil officials the task of carefully debating this issue, and reporting to the throne.[13]

Daoxuan presents the imperial debate as a welcome opportunity to set things straight: "Being considerate of our very anxious hearts, [the emperor] has arranged the court debate. Monks are grateful for this brilliant order [to allow debate], and feel afflicted with tears."[14] Of course, it was conventional to attribute great mercy and wisdom to even the stupidest emperor; we cannot be entirely certain if the clerics thought this debate was a valuable opportunity or a threat. Probably it was some of each. Weixiu indicates the affronted hostility of his opponents: "Spreading the reputation [of monks] for disturbing lay custom, some people show an attitude of being slighted and slandered."[15]

Daoism gets lumped in with Buddhism, in the imperial order for example, but it is clear the real focus is Buddhism. In general, the sectarian divide is less significant than a division of foreign (Buddhism) versus native

(Confucianism and Daoism), as for example in Yanzong's introduction to the arguments for not bowing:

> The sagely supreme Teaching of Feelings [Daoism] and Teaching of Names [Confucianism] both order one to bow to lords and parents. Anxiously and cleverly they found a way to open up the Court's debate, even to the point where outspoken gentlemen in great numbers offered up a tally. The ministers of the state (*sheji*, altars of gods of soil and grain) contended and made statements, and openly discussed it.[16]

Direct involvement in matters of state was a delicate matter for a group that claimed a permanent condition of being outside worldly concerns and transcending self-interested desire. Weixiu had to remark on the apparent contradiction of lofty non-attachment and the practice of engaged argument:

> Although it is said that a stream of words in the end binds one up in the appearance of debate, yet how could we [Buddhists] come to China and suddenly be ordered to bow? [We] draw upon ourselves the anger of Heaven Above [i.e. the emperor]...Monks offer respect (*fengpei*) in trepidation, casting [their eyes] up to the screen.[17]

Looking upward to the "screen" indicates an audience (real or rhetorical) with the emperor. Daoxuan to Rongguo: "Handing down the rule at the palace gate succeeds in clarifying [the difference of] the clergy and the laity."[18] There are repeated references to monks at the gates and steps of important laity. Daoxuan:

> We monks called the doorkeeper, but it is difficult to reach to the journeying crane [polite reference to Prince Pei]. I look to the nine-leveled heavenly steps.... In the end I lay up a store of time wasted in a hundred anxieties. This is why I come forth with concern and state these points, to explain.... I hereby reverently hand over [this document] and enjoin [you]. May a clear wind blow within the Nine Boundaries [China], the true image become flourishing, and great happiness radiate over the four seas. Do not allow any tiresome obstruction. I prepared this statement of explanation.[19]

There were monks at gates, knocking on doors. At the beginning of Daoxuan's message to Lady Rongguo, Yanzong inserted a note indicating problems at the gate:

The Lady was the mother of the empress [Wu Zetian]. She respected and venerated the correct teachings, and did a lot to support the [Dharma-] gate of merit. She built images and wrote out sutras. Her support for building construction was continuous, as she went in and out of the imperial apartments. Rong[guo] inquired, but she did not know the monks had reached the gate [of her residence], [so they] sent in a document as follows.[20]

The fact that Rongguo did not formally meet the monks is presented as an accident of miscommunication, so that the failure to meet was due only to poor communications between outer gate-keepers and Rongguo's inner entourage. Understandable. There were many representatives from palace guard units among both the pro-bow and anti-bow speeches—perhaps there was a deliberate miscommunication. Or it may be that Rongguo, while sympathetic to the clerics, did not want a formal audience with monks at a time when formal audiences with members of the imperial family were precisely the issue under debate. In Guisso's judgment, although she had pro-bow leanings, her influential daughter Wu Zetian "made no public expression of her view" and remained relatively passive on the issue.[21] Daoxuan ends his message to Rongguo: "If you treat this statement lightly, then I sigh in deep fear."[22]

For a month, no doubt, the issue was debated in various ways among members of the imperial house, officials, literati, monks, and nuns. This month was also perhaps occupied with determining the positions of various powerful people, deciding who would draft the presentations and who would read them. On the fifteenth day of the fifth month (June 6, 662), more than one thousand officials assembled at the Department of State Affairs (*Zhongtai dutang*) for final recommendations. A large crowd of monks presented petitions at that time, but were excluded from the discussions. The formal presentations made during the debate are discussed below; but first let me tell you what happened.

The tally was 539 anti-bow, 354 pro-bow.[23] That is 65 percent anti-bow. While it may seem like a numerical victory for the monks, even the three-to-two advantage might not have been particularly decisive. Less than a month later, Gaozong issued an edict, allowing the monks not to bow before the throne but asserting that they must "kneel" (*guibai*—torso erect) before parents, because their parents' "merciful nurturing was extremely profound."[24] As Weinstein comments,

> In fact, he had retreated to the position that his father, T'ai-tsung, had taken in 631. Although one might suppose that the Buddhists could find comfort in the fact that their long-standing privilege of being exempt from bowing before secular authorities had been upheld, it was soon evident that the monks felt themselves to be arguing from a position of strength.[25]

Thirteen days later, new petitions were submitted against bowing to parents, together with more appeals to lay supporters. For example, Daoxuan's letter to Wu Zetian of the thirteenth day of the eighth month 662, protested the requirement to kneel to parents.[26] Soon, Gaozong "decided to end the confrontation completely and nullified the offending edict."[27]

The 662 debate articulated the issue of bowing more fully than previous cases of the debate, but the question persisted, such as in 714 during Xuanzong's reign, when he ordered monks to bow to parents and withdrew the order two months later. The issue came up again in 733. According to Weinstein, after 755, clergy were formally exempted from bowing to the throne.[28] However, according to Zürcher, "it became the subject of heated controversies and conflicts for centuries, until, in late imperial times, the Buddhist clergy had to abandon its claims, and lost even the semblance of independence."[29] The argument that came to dominate was already present in the 662 debate: the emperor is a great bodhisattva, and therefore by supposed Mahayana logic, the relatively unenlightened monks should bow to him, lest they be accused of a Hinayana self-pride and attachment to their own purity. I suspect the ultimate resolution of the problem was not any imperial order but a diminishing power of Buddhism in elite circles, so that the issue ceased to be relevant.

Who took part in the debate?

Each debate participant is listed with his institution and rank. Analysis of the institutional affiliation of the debaters shows some distinctive patterns, but we can't generalize too much from this information. Some officials were presumably relatively free to vote according to their own inclinations or the inclinations of their superiors. In many cases the speaker was of relatively junior rank, an aide or administrator. We might reasonably assume that lower-ranking officials mostly represented the positions of their superiors. Only in a few cases were there officials from the same administrative unit arguing on opposing sides. For example, an erudite (*boshi*) from the Court of Imperial Sacrifices (*Fengchangsi*) argued for bowing, and an aide (*cheng*) and a recorder (*zhubu*) from the same unit argued against it.[30] There were three cases of disagreement between the Left and Right of the same units, such as with a General-in-chief (*dajiangjun*) of the Martial Guard of the Left (anti-bow), disagreeing with an administrator of the Right of that unit.

The clearest difference between the pro- and anti-bow representatives of military units is the predominance on the pro-bow side of representatives from military units associated with the Heir Apparent Li Hong (Prince Pei, eldest son of Wu Zetian). These are: Left and Right Military Guard, Left and Right Office of Protectorate Guard, Left Police Patrol Guard Command,[31] Left and Right Guard Honoring the Inner Apartments, and the Left and Right Good Fortune Guard. Also there are four non-military units associated with the Heir Apparent on the pro-bow side: Household Administration of the Heir Apparent, Left and Right Secretariat of the Heir Apparent, and the Court of the Watches. On the anti-bow side are no military units assigned to the Heir Apparent. In other words, there seems to have been a strong pro-bow lobby coming from the Heir Apparent or from his assigned bureaucratic and guard units.[32] Since at this time, Li Hong was only nine years old, this strong lobby must surely indicate his mother Wu Zetian, active behind the scenes.

I will leave to an appendix the details and some additional remarks on the institutional picture that emerges from this list. Any conclusions based on this institutional data are limited by the nature of the source: an anti-bow text by a Buddhist monk. It is always possible the editor, a monk named Yanzong, neglected to include some pro-bow speeches. But on the other hand, he had his own way of dealing with pro-bow speeches: point by point, he interjected his own small-print refutations. In broad strokes, though, the pattern that emerges from the institutional affiliations of debate participants is this: (a) a pro-bow lobby from the Heir Apparent (and Wu Zetian); but (b) otherwise mixed pro and anti positions in the military, although the Ministry of War sided with the monks; (c) perhaps stronger support for the monks among provincial officials; (d) stronger (but not unanimous) pro-bow support among Courts related to the emperor's ritual body and imperial guest ritual.

The 662 debate was documented by Yanzong in *Jishamen buying baisu dengshi*, (A Collection on the Matter of Why Monks Should Not Bow to Laity.[33] I'll refer to this as *Jishamen*.) Yanzong went to Chang-an to study under Xuanzang (who returned to China in 645).[34] He completed a biography of Xuanzang, started by Huili,[35] and wrote a biography of the Buddhist hero Falin.[36]

The *Jishamen* is divided into three chapters. The first, *Gushi pian* ("Chapter on Old Matters"), is a summary of previous debate on the issue. Chapter 2 is *Shengchao yibubai pian* ("Chapter on the Arguments for Not Bowing, from the Sagely Dynasty [i.e., the Tang]"). It includes: (a) the imperial order of 657, ordering debate on the issue of bowing, (b) letters from the monk Weixiu, and from Daoxuan, to Wu Zetian's son Prince Pei, the governor of Yongzhou (i.e. the area of Chang-an), and to her mother, Lady Rongguo, (d) quotations from historical and scriptural sources, compiled by Daoxuan, and (e) a series of anti-bow speeches presented at the debate itself. Thirty-two speeches are recorded.

The last chapter is *Shengchao yibai pian* ("Chapter on the Arguments for Bowing from the Sagely Dynasty"). Three "compromise proposals" are recorded, followed by twenty-nine speeches in favor of bowing. And the last fascicle contains "follow-up" documents: (a) an anti-bow statement by the monk Xuanfan; (b) a tally of anti-bow votes, followed by a concluding anti-bow argument from Linghu Defen of the Directorate of Education; (c) a tally of pro-bow votes, with a concluding statement by Yan Liben of the Ministry of Works; (d) an imperial order allowing monks to abstain from bowing to lords, dated the eighth day of the sixth month; (e) an anti-bow statement from Cheng Shiyong, emphasizing the separateness of clerics and laity, with an assertion that in joint rituals Buddhists clerics should stand in front of Daoist clerics; (f) a further letter from Daoxuan to Lady Rongguo; (g) a further anti-bow statement from Weixiu, with some scriptural citations; (h) a letter from the monk Chongba of the Hongfusi on parents and rulers not receiving the bows of the ordained; and (i) a general summation (*zonglun*) by the compiler Yanzong. This last document is examined in detail in the next chapter.

Arguments

We turn now to the speeches in favor of ordering monks to bow (*yibai* or pro-bow) and those opposed (*yibubai* or anti-bow) as well as the memorials by Daoxuan and Weixiu.

Many of the pro-bow speeches are punctuated in the text by Yanzong's editorial interruptions in small print. It is perhaps here that we come closest to a kind of "conversation," though sometimes the argumentation consists of simple contradiction. Rather than a connected series of statements intended to establish a proposition, sometimes we find the automatic gainsaying of any statement the other person makes. The statement by Li Chunfeng, Director of the Astrological Service of the Orchid Pavilion (the Censorate, Palace Library), is a good example, and I quote it in full with Yanzong's additions:

> Of the levels of the three crimes (punishable by death), there are none higher [worse] than coercing the ruler.
> Reply: Monks receive favor and enter the Way. It is not called "coercing the ruler."
> Of the extremes of [the crimes covered by] the five punishments, nothing comes close to unfiliality.[37]
> Reply: Parents allow [monks] to leave the home. How is it unfilial?
> Thus, going against virtue and being contrary to etiquette are the basic sources of great disorder.
> Reply: Monks act on and follow the canonical teachings. It is not going contrary to virtue and etiquette.
> Only reverence and loyalty are the correct ways of the well-regulated country.
> Reply: Although in their physical form monks abstain from honoring parents, yet inwardly they cherish filiality and reverence. In etiquette [they are] contrary towards the principal person (*shizhu*) [i.e., the Emperor], yet their minds are full of mercy and loyalty.
> Turning to Laozi's teaching of empty quietude, it depends on yielding in order to be accommodating. As for the Buddhist scriptures' [notion of] yielding harmony (*chonghe*), constantly not treating [others] lightly is universal respect (*pujing*).
> Reply: this matter is as replied to in [the item by] the Awesome Guard of the Left. [Chen Xuanming][38]
> I have not heard of any arrogant lord or parent, nor a boastful assembly.

Reply: Monks' bodies make complete [or actualize] (*ju*) Buddha's precepts; their forms make complete Buddha's rites. Humans and celestial beings look up to [monks], rather than [monks] being "boastful."

May I, [Li] Chunfeng, encourage the people, pacify the nation and calm the households. Now, ordering Daoist priests and nuns and [Buddhist] monks and nuns to do obeisance to lords and parents is no loss to the Dao [of the Daoists] or to Buddha.

Reply: The sutras say, bowing to lords injures lords, bowing to parents injures parents, practicing reverence [in this way] offends against the teachings. How can one say there is no loss?

Following the correct norms (*zhengfa*) of the nation's ruler greatly removes the former evil practices, deeply eliminates demoralizing falsity.

Reply: To think obedience to the Dharma is a false evil practice, or [to think] disobeying the teachings will do away with [bad things], this is called the confused head falling into transgression. Turning one's back on the Way is a serious transgression.

May the ways of obedience be known forever, and the importance of natural instincts.[39]

In this speech and the argumentative annotations, we see many of the themes of the pro-bow arguments: disobeisance is unfilial and subversive; it contradicts the Buddhist teaching of egolessness; the emperor's great virtue warrants a visible demonstration of respect. Aside from the rather mechanical rebuttals, probably the most interesting remark by Yanzong is his location of Buddha's teachings in the body: "monks' bodies actualize Buddha's precepts; their forms actualize Buddha's rites."

I will discuss three broad themes in this chapter: the immutability of natural feelings, the transcendence of social distinctions, and uses of history and canonical texts. From there I will structure the discussion around Yanzong's general summation of the arguments.

The immutability of natural feelings

The 657 order begins by asserting the supremacy of certain sentiments associated with the relationships of ruler and ruled (respect) and of children and parents (love). "The rites of lords and parents are the most important of the three instructions; the way of love and respect receives first place of all the hundred practices."⁴⁰ The same kind of assertion is made in various forms throughout the pro-bow speeches. These relationships are frequently paired to Heaven and Earth, in homologies which give them broad cosmological or ontological significance. Respect for the ruler is not just a human construct, but inherent in existence itself. Li Yifan (pro-bow) says:

> The father's benevolence and the son's filial piety arise from Heaven's rule; the lord's righteousness and the minister's loyalty depend on Earth's proper ritual. Of the weightiness of the three venerations, the lord is first. Of what the five teachings venerate, the father resides at its head.⁴¹

We should not see this Heaven and Earth rhetoric as mere literary flourish. Ritual (*li*) had cosmic power. Variously translated as rites, rituals, propriety, and sometimes more specifically as bowing, *li* refers to an embodiment and performance of correct social distinctions, a "psycho-physical dispositioning"⁴² which sustains social order because it corresponds to cosmic order: the vertical relationship of Heaven and Earth, *yang* and *yin*, which in turn correlate to male/female, father/son, indeed to virtually any binary pair. It is not sufficient to simply think these differences; you must act them, so that good virtues and the fate of the dynasty depend on good ritual. At the "head" of filial love sits the body of your father (or ancestor) and at the pinnacle of a subject's loyalty is the body of the emperor. Ideally, you have one father, you have one emperor, although of course (other peoples') fathers are many and the emperor is still only "one man."

On the pro-bow side, the sentiments of love and respect were also considered to be fundamentally human, natural, and unchanged by any act such as an ordination ceremony. Dou Lujian:

> The highest veneration and awe belong to lords and parents. As for the source of the natural ability to feel respect, what difference is there between ordained and lay?⁴³

Dou simply brushes aside any relevance of the ordained/lay distinction to this issue. Similarly, Neng Xuanyi (pro-bow) trivializes the external markings (in this case, clothing) of the ordained. First, he asserts the fundamental supremacy of these devout emotions:

> Only the love of those who themselves bear children and raise them is truly deep. The rites of the One Man (*yiren*), supremely venerable, dignified and

respectful, these are indeed weighty. How can they [Buddhist monks] wrap their bodies in black robes and then not bow to lords and parents? They [Daoist priests] put a yellow hat on their heads, and then they discontinue the rites of sons and ministers!⁴⁴

One might call this pro-bow argument "clothes do *not* make the man." Distinctive features of clothing refer synecdochically to the ordained, to the clerical institutions: for example, in the expression "the black robes and yellow hats."⁴⁵ Buddhist clothing and paraphernalia appear, in these hostile voices, as tricks or stage props in the proud theater of self-promotion.

However, robes (*jiasha*) also appear in anti-bow arguments:

As for the labor of one bow, this ritual act would display the downfall of the Three Robes. So this is something that cannot be allowed, and how could it be? If a king has no father, he serves the Three classes of Old Men. If without an older brother, he serves the Five classes of Experienced Men [Or, Five Classics].⁴⁶ The lord's veneration also has an object of respect.⁴⁷

The Three Olds refers to the three (classes of) old men: men over eighty, over ninety, and over one hundred. They and the five (classes of) experienced men are discussed in the *Liji*, where it is said that when feasting these old men, the emperor himself cut up the meat and presented them with the food, using the rituals appropriate for his father and elder brother.⁴⁸ Here, we have a classical reference to an inversion of hierarchy, when the ruler/subject hierarchy is momentarily set aside to perform the older/younger hierarchy. This kind of analogy, along with others to be discussed, seems to chip away at the absolutism of the "one man," showing that even within the Classical canon obeisance to the ruler was not absolute. The inversion is of course only within certain circumstances, when the emperor's identity changes during the ritual.

The monk's robes are not merely clothes but ritualized clothing, a kind of wearable performance. The robes stand for an anomalous identity, a special case. The individual monk is a bearer of a persona. The persona is wrapped around the monk. The representatives of the Ministry of War describe some of the doctrinal and ritual ramifications of the monk's robe:

We cite the Sangha's Vinaya. Respect the monk's robe just as you respect the Buddha-stupa. One refers to the robe as the garment of the field of merit (*futianyi*). The robe is called "[the robe which] puts to an end" (*xiaoshou[fu]*), because using it one is able to put an end to suffering. Their armor is called the garment of endurance (*renruyi*); using it one is able to make the demon-generals submit. It is also analogous to how the lotus blossom is not polluted by the muddy filth.[49]

On the one hand, a fundamental change of status is associated with the change of clothing. Ordinary filial piety and respectful subjecthood are superseded by a kind of "meta-filiality" or "meta-subjecthood," consisting of the monk's heroic efforts toward universal salvation.

On the other hand, the change of clothing is trivialized and the relevance rejected. No change of clothing or hairstyle, no ritual on a high platform, can change the inherent subordination of ruler to ruled or parent to child. Dou Lujian: "They only rely on the cloth (of robes) and bowl, in order to venerate themselves."[50] Quite a nasty accusation. How do we interpret this Confucian remark that the monks "venerate themselves" (*zizunchong*)? These terms (*zun* and *chong* separately or together) are not necessarily specific acts, so it is possible that Dou meant this remark figuratively, as referring to an arrogant attitude. Or it might be taken more physically, as an objection to monks bowing to other monks or to monks encouraging lay people to bow to monks. Though criticism of the continued obeisance of monks (to other monks and to Buddha images) does not feature prominently in the debate record, Dou may be highlighting the fact that monks never for an instant rejected the practice of obeisance as such. Dou might have even been aware that the prominent lobbyist monk Daoxuan had just the previous year composed a whole treatise on the subject, insisting on the importance of bowing.

The accusation of self-veneration appears in various forms, all using the vertical homology of pride as high and humility as low. To be proud (in the negative sense) is to make oneself higher than one should be. Self-inflation and haughty ways are repeatedly attributed to monks. Yang Sixuan and Yang Shouzhuo say that monks "reject true human feelings and then become indulgent and boastful," and: "they themselves occupy the higher-up (*gaoshang*) place."[51] Dou Lujian: "How can they esteem themselves, and make themselves higher? (*weigao*)"[52] Verticality is clear in the discussion of the pride of monks who do not bow, here in the negative connotations of the perceived act of raising-oneself-up.

Transcending distinctions, or not

The imperial edict of 657 cites the essential scandal: despite the irrefutable priority of these natural relationships, monks still do not bow.

> As for the two gates of the Buddha and Laozi, their principles are beyond the common boundaries. But as for the footsteps of reverence and filial piety, the phenomena (*shi*, i.e. their observable manifestation) should harmonize with the ferry of the *ru* (Confucians) and comply with the most venerable and supreme [ruler] in the land. [Yet] they do not practice the ritual of obeisance, behaving like this from long ago until today.[53]

Some of the pro-bow officials offered qualified praise for Buddhism, particularly its doctrinal and meditational aspects. Buddhism's contemplative spirituality is commended, and there are general references to its profundity. There are acknowledgments of the transcendent alterity of the monks. Even the 657 edict says Buddhism is "beyond the common boundaries." Yang Sixuan and Yang Shouzhuo (pro-bow): "The two gates of Buddha and Dao basically esteem the empty and the mysterious (*xuxuan*), extending the expedient means of the three vehicles, adopting forgotten words to a single purpose, which is only stillness and solitude."[54] Jiang Zhenzhou (pro-bow) notes the spiritual compatibility and harmony of Buddhism and Daoism, in that they share the virtue of respect: "The two gates of Buddhism and Daoism both hold to mysterious transformation. Although the black and yellow [Buddhists and Daoists] have their differences, the will of reverence is not different. [Therefore,] proclaim the order to bow in order to extend the respect of ministers and sons."[55] The mystical vision is all very well but simply irrelevant.

Still, as one would expect, explicit praise for Buddhism and the attribution of transcendence are stronger in the anti-bow speeches. Gao Yaoshang says: "in the two clans, of Sakyamuni and Laozi, as for the manners of the outstanding great sages, their wisdom radiates beyond defilement, transcending the surfaces of things."[56] The great wisdom of Buddhism can survive any textual criticism because it is precisely formless, amorphous, claiming to have no fixed words to explain it. Gao continues:

> The Dharma is basically quietude and silence, it is not something with names and words. The greatest Way is unseen and unheard, and thus, there

is no stated teaching. Regarding the great multitude of three thousand realms, [one with] small wisdom cannot calculate their source. In the midst of dim confusion, [even] the worthies do not have the means to understand its principle.[57]

The assertion of the transcendent wisdom of Buddhism is also an assertion of the lesser wisdom of non-Buddhists, which is tied to specific forms. One of the common polemical strategies in the debate is to accuse the other side of pedantic formalism, of excessive emphasis on mere outer form, thereby positioning oneself as speaking from within a transcendent source, having understood the inner essence. And there are ways of acting in accordance with that transcendent view. Of course, an opponent might in turn see insistence on those forms of transcendence as obstinate formalism.

Li Yifan: "Even granting that Buddha's way is venerable and awe-inspiring, Heaven's rank is completely weighty."[58] Here, Buddha's *way* (a metaphor of travel) is lower than Heaven's *rank* (an image of vertical stratification). The ruler was associated with the importance of the very idea of rank, which was granted by his harmonizing Heaven and Earth. The 657 order reads:

> We state Heaven's norms by spreading filial piety, we aid Earth's usages and spread proper ritual form…. Heaven unites the transformation (or, salvation) of the joining rivers, and hands over to the nation's king the justification to apply force. Faithfully return to this![59]

It sounds like one-up-manship. Yan Liben waxes eloquent on the emperor's virtuous influence: "the imperial, wise course of action is distantly far-reaching, spreading the morality of Earth like a broadcasting wind. The [moisture of the] sagely marsh moistens [i.e. bestows benefit] far and wide, soaking Heaven's norms [into the world] and cleansing and enriching [the world]."[60] Here, the metaphors are basically territorial, that is, horizontal, like the weather and the water table.

So monks can no more evade the emperor's authority than keep wind from their monasteries. The monks are subjects just as they draw water from the empire's wells. Li Yifan asserts the compromised status of the monks, relying as they do on the ruler's power. He even asserts the difficulty (or impossibility) of enlightenment but for the existence of the ruler: "Holding fast the precious mirror needs the presence of the Lord."[61] (The mirror is how they see their own

Buddha-nature.) Without Heaven's higher rank, there would be no Buddha's way. Pro-bow Ma Dashi makes rank and jurisdiction clear: "The governance of bequeathed teachings [such as Buddhism] resides with the nation's king."[62] He also asserted the necessity, or at least compatibility, of obeisance to parents (and lords) to spiritual cultivation: "How could respecting (*jing*) parents hinder the esteemed Way? How could bowing to lords destroy the seeking of the Real?"[63] How does this one good deed harm your great quest?

In response to this kind of argument, Daoxuan had conceded the value of the Teaching of Names (Confucianism) as the means to establish the "dignified rituals of the laity" and cultivate the virtue of the True Man (*zhenren*). This admission does not weaken Daoxuan's position on the distinction of monastic and lay but rather assigns to each a jurisdiction. And yet, he says, "the legal policies give protective shade to the [Buddhist] Way."[64] This might be taken as a concession, but it is also a mandate for the aspiring Cakravartin (ideal virtuous Buddhist ruler) to sponsor and protect the monasteries. The clerical lobbyists were quick to credit the Tang house with peaceful rule and generous aid. Daoxuan: "I bow and consider the great Prince [Pei], ruling and holding together the capital city and imperial domain, pacifying and administering the motion of the latitudes. As [monks of the] Way and laity become plentiful, the many affairs are peaceful."[65]

For Daoxuan, the ruler should support the Sangha for the sake of universal benefit. Yet, the monk's non-membership is supposed to be unaffected by any sponsorship or protection. For Li Yifan and others, on the other hand, the ruler makes monastic practice and enlightenment possible. The physical presence of the monk within the ruler's territory, and dependence on the ruler for the maintenance of law and order (of the entire "order of things") necessarily constitutes the monk as a member of the imperial world, under imperial jurisdiction.

At times, the arguments seek to erase the social distinction of ordained and laity: as in the passage by Neng Xuanyi quoted above, which says in effect: changing your clothes or putting a hat on—marks of ordination—do not exempt anyone from proper expression of fundamentally natural feelings. The non-recognition of the distinctions created by ordination and monastic training is clear in other pro-bow speeches: no matter what monks have done to themselves, they are subjects of the ruler because their bodies remain within his territory. The inability of the monks to truly disentangle themselves from the sphere of lay power is repeatedly cited as a reason for them to bow. Chang-an District Magistrate Zhang Songshou said:

> Outwardly they elevate themselves by not bending (*qu*); inwardly they turn their attention to private interests. The disciples have the name of entering the Way, but actually they do not have the reality of leaving the laity.[66]

This is a direct repudiation of any valid distinction of laity and clergy. Yan Liben even uses a Buddhist argument against the monks. He invokes the idea of ultimate non-duality, rejecting ordination and referring to the monks as "gentlemen" (*shi*). He claims these strange-robed gentlemen are blinded by dualistic egoism:

> Principle does not divide into dark and bright. The great Way embraces all sides, thus it is not divided into "true" (*zhen*, ordained) and "common" (*su*, lay). Those gentlemen who disobey [the norms of] this place are emptily astray in thoughts of the mere forms of things. These followers who are engulfed in the common are tied up in the knot of ego.[67]

At this point in the text, Yanzong inserted a small-print reply:

> Now, of the monks, there are none who do not consider the court sagely, for it acts as the savior of the nation. By aiding and serving in the imperial tombs and temples, we assist [the court] and benefit the ranks of the masses. And so, saying [things like] "disobey [the norms of] this place" and "engulfed in the common," how could this not harm the blessings of the imperial house?[68]

Here Yanzong seems to ignore any argument from non-duality. Monks participated in imperial funerary rituals. Non-Buddhist funerary specialists, at least at the imperial level, were mostly Confucians (even if they were also Daoists). Yanzong brings this "joint venture" out into the open, arguing the public benefit of the imperially sponsored Buddhist ancestral cult (as well as, more generally, all sponsored Buddhist ritual). Here we see one of the material stakes in the debate, corresponding roughly to a competition of Buddhists against Confucians.

Yan Liben's point is that the distinction between cleric and laity, and the labor needed to maintain it, shows a false dualism which is not consistent with the idea of a single, unified Principle. Still, despite some conciliatory rhetoric and such appeals to ultimate non-duality, on the whole the pro-bow arguments defend the notion of hierarchical social difference. For Confucians, generally *li* (true principle) was considered non-dual (and therefore admitted no possibility of difference), but *shi* (phenomena, things) can be numbered, distinguished and discriminated. *Li* and *shi* were considered not in contradiction, however, but ultimately one. And yet, principle is "higher" than phenomena. The contradiction was dispelled by acting in accordance with principle; one did this by scrupulously following the correct discriminations of phenomena. To say that the monks should bow to the ruler puts monks firmly in phenomena, in the specific form of a body and land. The Buddhist claim to have transcended the "world" (phenomena) is thus a claim to non-duality, localized in the monk's body.

Still, the majority of pro-bow arguments say that the monks' disobeisance corrodes the legitimate ordering of social difference, which defined "the rites of lords and ministers, fathers and sons; the order of venerable and low, of noble and base."[69] Ma Dashi (pro-bow), who spoke also of the final sameness of Buddhism and Confucianism, explains the metaphysics of social hierarchy:

> Radiance divides into two sources.[70] These manifest as the [respective] manners of the venerable and the low. Rank can be explained as the Three Powers (*sancai*–Heaven, Earth and Man). Therefore it shows us the nature of the father and son relationship. How illuminating is the ritual form of love and respect, born together with Heaven and Earth, and the morality of the lord and minister, established together with creation and transformation![71]

The sentiments of love for parents and respect for rulers were present from the very first moment of duality. All duality involves differences in power, and love and respect are simply the appropriate virtues of the less powerful. Following the yin-yang logic so evident in these remarks, the first moment of differentiation was yin-yang, which correlated in turn with all observable phenomena. Between yin and yang there is always a difference. Fundamentally, yin/yang *is* difference.

The Buddhist monks also used these concepts of difference and unity in this debate. Daoxuan: "the teachings divide into three Dharmas,[72] handing down the imposing [rites] of ten thousand years, putting the four classes [monk, nun, layman, laywomen] into ranks, and displaying the pure rules of the five [Buddhist] vehicles. Of course, the great expanse of the Dharma-ocean is difficult to divide into classes."[73] Daoxuan shifts abruptly between Buddhist teaching as multiple (three, ten thousand, four, and five) and the Dharma as a vast unity incapable of distinction. Weixiu uses the *li-shi* distinction to point out the limitations of Confucian-imperial rule: "phenomena are not just the statutes of the Classical domain; principle exceeds the usages of Heaven's norms (*tianchang*)."[74] In other words, there is more in Heaven and Earth than are dreamt of in your rituals.

Anti-bow speakers said the reality of the cleric/lay distinction offered a departure from the ocean of suffering, from "this shore," and from family, but it is also a change of clothing. The question is: what is the meaning of that "change of clothing"—if by that we mean all the alterations to the displayed body?

The produced nature of the monastic body is clear in Daoxuan's message to Lady Rongguo, which includes a remarkable correlation of the manufactured Buddha image and the monk's body:

> [While] the Sage stays hidden, the monks must keep disciplined. If not for the self-discipline of later generations, who could have revealed [the true teachings]? Thus, metal, stone and plain mud display the appearance of the true image. The dharma-clothes and cut hair determine the form [*xiang*, marks] of the whole Sangha. To trust or to slander the [Dharma] clothes result in two different fruits of retribution. Turning one's back on this cultivation is not the correct way at all. In addition, it is difficult to know the true and the false, the raw and cooked of monks. The shallowness and depth, the stupidity and wisdom of the practice of virtue are misleadingly alike [i.e., easy to confuse]. Thus the sutras explain at length and give evidence throughout, like the inexhaustibility of the sea. The vinaya regulations create a different class, like the boundary of the shore.[75]

These remarks correlate the building materials which go to make Buddha images and the clothing and hair-style which are used to create a complete Sangha. A monk can be built like a Buddha image is built, as long as the correct rules are followed.

We've seen the non-duality of the Three Treasures in Daoxuan's treatise on obeisance. The particular basis of their non-dual claim was the idea of transmission, something quintessential which is "passed down," like a father passes down his seed to the son. The Buddhist monk receives the transmission from his primal ancestor in the ordination ceremony, and becomes the legitimate heir to Buddha. All this is accomplished by the rule-governed stylization of the body.

So Daoxuan draws a parallel between the manufacture of an icon and the production of a monk. We see the direct association of monk's body and Buddha-image, here in the association of the raw materials of Buddha-images with the clothing and hairstyle of monks. Recall also Yanzong's reply to Li Chunfeng: "monks' bodies actualize the Buddha's precepts."[76]

The unity of Buddha, Buddha image, and monk is clear in the speech of Wang Xuan and Cao Xiaoguan (anti-bow). Playing the Devil's advocate, Wang and Cao object to clerical disobeisance by negating the effects of the outward changes effected on the monk's body:

> I once contended with a monk, saying: "These servants began to cut off hair and put on the black [robes], I can't see the difference. And yet, they order lords and fathers to bow to them! That is truly far from having proper human feelings!"
>
> The monk replied: "Even if one has just begun to shave the head, the form is already the same as Buddha. [This ritual act] is already able to make the demon palaces quake. Although plaster and wood are called insentient, how is it not like them? Plaster and wood, as soon as you set them up [on the altar], become the main image."[77]

The immanence of Buddha in the monk's body is derived from the doctrine of inherent Buddha-nature; it is broadly diffused in ancestral cult practice, in funerary ritual, and in the configuration of altars. The monk's body is placed in the highest ritual position and identified with the ancestor. Actually, there was a fair bit more to making insentient stuff into an icon than just "setting it up," unless by that phrase is meant the entire process of manufacture, consecration, and daily maintenance.

These remarks assume as self-evident that Buddha would not bow to a ruler. As far as I can tell, no one ever suggested that the Buddha himself should have bowed to the emperor of the Zhou if he had visited China. The analogy of monk to Buddha (via the Buddha image) places the identity of the monk at the highest apex. A lay-person does not have to bow to a Buddha image, but one could hardly expect a Buddha-image to bow to anyone.

We can see the soteriology of the markings and rituals of the body in the speech of Gao Yaoshang (anti-bow), who mingles discussion of hair and cosmology, robes and purity, bowing and transcendence:

> [Those who] respectfully accord with [the Buddhist teachings] roam freely in the six migrations. [If you are] disdainful and remiss, then the ocean of suffering flows for a long time. Thus [monks] get rid of facial and head hair, become *sramanas*, cast off their lay clothes and fasten on black robes. They desire to climb onto the other shore, to leave this stream of desire. Fathers and mothers honor their appearance, the five Marquises consider weighty their precepts. This distinguishes those of the [Buddhist] Way from lords and relatives, as [the monks] leave the lay world and cut off defilements. They do not adhere to the rites of the many. They do not covet the ranks of the five Marquises. One should not insist on this lay instruction, urging [the monks] with customary usages. As for bowing the head (*baishou*) in private halls, and bowing the forehead (to the ground, *jishou*) in public rooms, please follow the old custom. Grant it upon a foolish one.[78]

Histories and canons

We see extensive quotations, citations and allusions to the Classics, to official Histories and Buddhist narratives. Yanzong's collection of documents on the debate devotes the first two (out of six) fascicles to a "Chapter on Old Matters" (*Gushi pian*), reproducing the correspondence of Yu Bing, Wang Mi and He Chong, and the early fifth-century statements of Huiyuan and Huan Xuan.

Ma Dashi, who thought monks should bow to the ruler, describes the beginnings of Buddhism in China: "When the man with a golden appearance was seen in a dream [by emperor Ming], the wisdom sun first opened [in China]. A purple mist floated through the Pass, a mysterious wind began to blow. Flourishing in middle antiquity, the teachings began to gradually change."[79] Buddhism's movement over vast expanses of territory suggests fluid or atmospheric metaphors, to Daoxuan as well:

> Since the silver river shifted its tracks, the Jade Pass[80] has flourished and transformed. The brave sages of the past gave exceedingly good support [to Buddhism]. There were none who did not bow their heads and ask

the Way, taking refuge in knowing the ferry. Thus were created a series of Buddhist monasteries and benevolent ancestral halls spread out [over the land]. Heavenly beings rely on this road to the field of blessings, the living and dead cherish the rites of the correct path. The pure believing gentlemen flourish like a forest, the highly-esteemed guests [*bin*, i.e., monks] gather like a cloud.[81]

Again that word *bin*. What is interesting about the term is its "fluid" relationship to place. Buddhism is also described here as a "silver river," as a "purple mist," "mysterious wind," images which again suggest an ease of movement over space. Daoxuan elaborates further:

> It has been more than six hundred years since the Three Jewels flowed East. The Four [classes of] laity establish the preconditions of taking refuge in the vows. The Five Masses [of the ordained] open the matter of the field of merit. A hundred kings handed down the transformative influence of the Way; the wind [*feng*, influence] of the sages blows for ten thousand years. Thus it is that [all beings within the] encircling oceans know refuge, and living beings' spirits transfer merit. That being so, the wisdom-sun has been hidden for more than a thousand years. Correct practice is hard to ascend to, strict rules are easy to break.[82]

The rosy images of Buddhism in China are none the less under a cloud: the gradual loss of wisdom in the world since the Buddha's parinirvana. Buddhists divided time into periods of True Dharma (*zhengfa*), Replicated Dharma (*xiangfa*), and the Decline of the Dharma (*mofa*), followed by the absolute End of the Dharma (*miefa*). In various allusions, the degenerative narrative recurs in the debate literature. Gao Yaoshang (anti-bow) notes: "Short is the *kalpa* of the three robes."[83] Daoxuan had written to Rongguo: "when the norms of the time are muddied, people crossing the ford get exhausted and deluded."[84]

Daoxuan explains:

> Because we are practicing at a time of diminished radiance, complying with the order from above [to bow] would bring us grief and suffering. Moreover, since the Dharma teaching flowed East, it has been deeply involved in both success and failure. Thrice [Buddhism] has been persecuted, and five times faced [the issue of] bowing. All these cases were not in periods of peace and brilliance, but rather under the rule of violent and harsh lords. Thus they

issued commands unlike the standards of the previous states, opposing the norms, even to the point of [receiving] the blame of good historians.[85]

The past history of debate was also recalled by Weixiu: "Of old, when the Jin emperor Cheng was young, Yu Bing falsely issued edicts. Huan Chu was deceptive and false. Wang Mi spoke words of resistance. Then, in his later years, emperor Wu of the Song ruled harshly, and ordered monks to bow to the lord, but subsequently restored [the old rule] and desisted."[86]

Both sides make extensive use of scripture. Many pro-bow speakers referred to the Daoist classics. Lu Cai: "I respectfully examine the *Laozi daodejing*, which says that of the four great things within the boundaries, the king is one of them."[87] This remark refers to the *Daodejing* Chapter 25: "the way is great; heaven is great; earth is great; and the king is also great. Within the realm there are four things that are great, and the king counts as one."[88] Lu Cai goes on:

> In the Daoist canon, it says: for one *daoshi* [Daoist master] to attain the Way, then he must pursue honor for the seven generations (of his lineage Patriarchs) and his father and mother. This is to establish the body and complete the Way. One holds in honor and pursues the illustriousness of the previous generations. In the present time, those who have not yet attained the Way are born of a father and mother. As a matter of principle, they should bow in respect.[89]

Weixiu and many others borrowed the authority of Buddhist scripture to argue the anti-bow case: "Now, if we revert to bowing to lord and father, it would pervert and go against the many sutras."[90] Daoxuan to Rongguo: "We are well prepared to list the sutras of the past [if you] ask to see and hear them."[91]

But the 662 debate also shows the use of Buddhist scriptures to argue against clerical disobeisance. More than one speaker said that the pride of disobeisance was contrary to the teachings of the Buddha. Ma Dashi: "I have not heard of a sutra of proud boasting. The five thousand teachings, how can they contain the morality of boastful self-promotion?"[92] There were also those who made use of Buddhist texts to present an argument about the ruler as bodhisattva—and therefore worthy of obeisance. Lu Cai:

> In the *Renwang banruojing*, it says: [those of the] rank of bodhisattvas, prior to the first stage and during the three states, are the rulers beneath the four

heavens. The Buddhist scriptures also say: if the bhiksus attain the fruit of *srota-apanna* [first stage of arhatship], after 80,000 kalpas, they begin to be seen in the land before us. Now, ordering Daoist monks and nuns to bow in respect, and the great monks and nuns within the boundaries to bow in respect to the bodhisattvas before us, this does not pervert the basic teaching. It is correct to disseminate it.[93]

Yanzong conceded at least part of the argument: "Allowing that the bodhisattva of the three virtuous positions are the rulers beneath the four heavens, it is only that at present he has wife and child, and does not forsake the family status."[94] In other words, even a ruler who is a bodhisattva is still a layman, and monks still do not bow to laymen. Were it not for the bodhisattva's marriage and family, he would undoubtedly become a monk.

Lu Cai goes on:

I also cite the *Wuliangshou guanjing*, which says that one who desires to be born in the wonderful land of bliss must first filially serve father and mother.[95] And then it says it [filial service] is completely sufficient for the practice of the precepts…. If one does not bow to father and mother, how could one complete one's filial service? Now ordering [Buddhist] monks and nuns, and Daoist priests and nuns, to bow in respect to father and mother is also not opposed to the fundamental teachings.[96]

Wang Xuan and Cao Xiaoguan recount a discussion with an unnamed monk, in which further Buddhist scriptural examples seem to undermine the anti-bow position. (In fact, Wang and Cao were anti-bow, so in their assertions to the monk they are playing the part of straw men.)

I, your subject, further contended with that monk, saying: "In the *Weimojing*, monks bowed to Vimalakirti's feet. In the *Fahuajing*, monks practiced universal respect (*pujing*). In the texts of these two sutras, [monks] bowing to laity is clear. Why do monks then manage to not bow and venerate [laity]?"

The monk said: "Buddha's regulations of the Vinaya sutras are the constant rule of monks and nuns. The monks bearing the Dharma in the *Weimojing* momentarily practiced a bending of ritual form (*zhanxingquli*). As for the great gentlemen of the *Fahuajing* [it was just] one moment of different practice (*yishibiexing*). Why should we take a temporary different practice to disorder the constant law-code?"

I deeply conceded it. I have heard that when a wife dies, [people] drum on pots, surround the corpse and sing. This is also a temporary different practice, but how could one then be lax about the rules of mourning garments?[97]

Pro-bow debate participants used Buddhist scripture against their opponents; anti-bow arguments in turn made use of Confucian canonical texts.

More could be said about the speeches in the debate, but from this point, I will use the Summation to cover a number of points.

4

The Editor's Conclusion

Yanzong concluded his documentation of the bowing debate with his own *General Summation* (*zonglun*). This final statement from the principal archivist of the debate is somewhat more than a digest of the previous anti-bow arguments. Perhaps they were the ten points Yanzong thought most effective. It certainly gives us a convenient way to structure further discussion. He highlighted a number of analogies, revealing a larger field of disobeisance. Each of these points has a distinct logic and intertextual reference. The refusal to bow was based on the assertion of the reality and ultimate validity of a boundary, created by ordination and monastic training, between Sangha and state, between ordained and lay. Opposing arguments tried to belittle or erase that boundary. My question here is: In asserting the special prerogative not to bow as a representation of that boundary, what legacies of disobeisance could Yanzong draw on? Who else did not bow to the ruler?

The principal arguments are as follows, in order:

1. Monks are like the spirits that the ruler bows to.
2. Monks are like the impersonator of the dead, who stands for the ancestor, and who is bowed to even by people who otherwise would not; monks stand in the place of the Buddha. (Indeed, monks are Buddha.)
3. Monks are like descendants of previous dynasties, treated as state guests according to Classical ritual.
4. Monks are teachers, and the emperor's teacher does not have to kowtow.
5. Monks are like soldiers in armor, who according to the Confucian canon do not kowtow.
6. Monks are like one who has just been capped, to whom his mother and older brothers bow, because his performance shows he assumes the ancestral inheritance; the monk assumes the Buddha's ancestral inheritance.

7. Monks are ascetics and hermits, like the hermits praised by Confucius for not obeying the emperor.
8. Monks are like convicts, who cannot be forced to bow.
9. Monks stand for the Buddha like imperial representatives stand for the emperor, and who thus receive obeisance based on the emperor's authority rather than their own personal status.
10. Monks have supernatural influence. If they become like everyone else, they will lose that beneficial influence.

    In additional remarks at the very end of the entire text, he makes two additional points:
11. In the Classics, they emphasized the inner state of respect, not merely the external expression. So making monks bow will go against the Classics. Following from that point, he adds:
12. Not bowing with the body does not mean not respecting in the heart. (And presumably, monks indeed respect the emperor in their hearts.)

These analogies reveal complications in the ritual topography. The vertical logic of the Confucian-imperial ritual system seems to point upward and converge on a single body (the emperor's), so that the emperor is at the apex (or he *is* the apex) of a pyramidal social order. This pyramid was considered all-inclusive; ultimately, all obeisance was directed at the emperor, even if mediated through a chain of one's superiors. The monk's disobeisance disturbed this inclusive chain; the monk's obeisance did not point to the emperor, even indirectly. Monks were fractures in the pyramid. But clerical disobeisance was far from the only disruption of that apparently neat pyramid. From the discussion of that pyramid in Chapter 1, it is obvious that the image makes a good point about the overall concept but is not a depiction of reality.

The monk's body, here and not here

Again we find the motif of alterity, diplomatic immunity, the outsider's status. Yanzong begins with an assertion of the great merit and profundity of Buddhist monasticism. He wrote: "Their feelings transcend the world, but their traces [phenomenal selves, literally "footprints"] reside in the imperial domain. This is the reason for resistance in the matter of etiquette in the imperial residence, and why they turn their backs on the merciful family members."[1] Monks' bodies were mere "residual traces" or "evidence" (*ji*) residing in imperial territory. This belongs to a long history in Buddhist rhetoric of claiming the physical body is unreal and not the first time the unreality of the body had been invoked in a confrontation with imperial might.[2] The "trace" is a rhetorical strategy which diminishes the importance of the monk's physical body and locates the real identity of the monk elsewhere. Or nowhere at all (following the logic of no-self), but in any case, not here.

What kind of person could be here and not here? Or, within the territory but free of the ruler's power? Yanzong's point number seven claims "They come from outside the country."[3] Monks are outside of "the world" of worldly things, outside of the very concept of subjecthood. The monks came from outside the country? I wonder if any Confucians at the debate, taking that statement literally, rolled their eyes at this patently false claim?

You can see the belittling of the observable body in an argument made about the ambiguity of the very idea of respect (*jing*). In his remarks at the very end of the text, making points I have numbered eleven and twelve, Yanzong says:

> Ancient and modern treatises all say *bujing* (not respect). Just examining this word, I presume to doubt it. What is *jing* (respect)? It penetrates into the heart (*tongxin*). The *Quli* chapter (of the *Liji*) says, there are none who do not *jing* (respect). *Bai* (bowing) is only the body bending. As for the rituals of the Zhou Chen Nine Bows, if the lords and fathers are dignified then the mind respects them, and none would be allowed to do anything inconsistent with Dharma and vinaya. To worship and over-emphasize the body bowing is to err in your understanding of the Classics. Using *bai* (bow) instead of *jing* (respect) is the proper usage. Therefore this book says *bubai* (not bow).[4]

So a purely interior attitude of respect for the ruler is already present in the monk, *if* "the lords and fathers are dignified." It is the outer, physical enactment of respect which Yanzong says is forbidden by Buddhist scripture, and obsessing about the merely external is not in the spirit of the Chinese Classics. He makes a point about the terminology of the debate, counseling against saying, monks do not *jing* (respect) the ruler but rather saying, monks do not *bai* (bow to) the ruler. Huiyuan's treatise was on why sramanas do not respect (*bujing*) rulers. Yanzong is saying, *bujing* is a framing error. If you start by trying to defend not respecting the emperor, you've almost lost the debate already.

For me, there's something vaguely modern about this distinction and Yanzong's conscious strategizing about it. He's telling us how to tell the story right. As for the propaganda hint there about avoiding certain words, Yanzong must have known the majority of his readers through the ages would be other monks. There is an insider quality here—a bureaucrat compiling a legal brief for other bureaucrats to use the next time anyone tries to sue them.

So, on the one hand, the body is insignificant, and real identity is elsewhere or nowhere. And yet, of course, they had bodies right there, Chinese bodies, breathing the emperor's air. They were not born monks. They were born subjects of the emperor. What kind of authority can sever that obligation? What ritual could override that fact? What made a monk so qualitatively different from anyone else?

Monks as gods

Are monks actually *gods*?

Yanzong's tenth point comes close to saying so.

> Furthermore, the merit [of the monks] moves the living and the dead, their teaching touches dragons and ghosts, calms the sea of suffering of humans and celestials, and purifies the misery and evil influences of all ranks of the multitudes. The merit of it is widespread, the benefit is also great. How could we transcend the people of the dusty world who bow to lords and parents? [We would] become broad-minded people of leisure just like Confucians.

A direct appeal to the supernatural power of monks. On the surface it seems to say, we're so supernaturally useful, surely we can have this one exemption? But maybe underneath it is a threat—if you force us to bow, we'll just be ordinary people and have no more supernatural power, so the dragons and ghosts might run amuck.

Monks are not gods, but can put in a good word with them, as long as monks remain a separate kind of human being. Yanzong's first point nudges the analogy a little further:

Offering sacrifices to mountains and rivers, offering state sacrifices to Heaven and Earth, desiring its benefits, the lord exhausts himself and is sincere. Now when the Three Treasures are supported, taking refuge in the precepts is very beneficial. The living and the dead are assisted and transformed, to put it briefly.

Here he is saying, the ruler bows to Heaven and to spirits, because they benefit the people and the state; monks also benefit not only the living but also those in the spirit realm, so rulers should bow to monks. The analogy imputes supernatural power to the monks.

Here's another way that the authority of the spirit-world could be assumed by a ritualized body. Monks are like the impersonators of the dead. Within the Chinese pre-Buddhist ritual canons, there were cases where certain individuals became entitled to the ritual treatment proper to someone else, for example in funeral practice. Fan Yijun (anti-bow) had made the point in the debate: "When a grandson is the impersonator of the ancestor, and when the descendants of the legal wife are on the capping seat, father and mother then bow to their son. It is transmitting the weighty."[5] Making his second point, Yanzong also compares the monk to this ritual actor in ancestral cult practice:

Playing the part of the impersonator of the dead, one harmonizes the two rows of spirit-tablets. One who divides up the sacrifices and offers up the cooked [meat], at that time he behaves not as a subject [i.e. he does not bow to his superior, but is bowed to]. Now [according to doctrine of] the Three Treasures Are One Body, one bows to monks as if they were the Buddha. It is all there in the scriptures, in no time I could find many such words.[6]

So the monk is like a performer of sacrifices, who harmonizes the spirits of the dead. The reference to the two rows of spirit-tablets (*zhao* and *mu*) derives ultimately from the Confucian *Liji*.[7] Ancestral temples were arranged with the primal ancestor in the center, with the *zhao* on the left (2nd, 4th, & 6th generations) and the *mu* on the right (3rd, 5th, & 7th). With the passing of time, generations of ancestors were moved up toward the first position of the primal ancestor (*taizu*) who remained in the central highest point. The ancestor harmonizes the descendants by occupying the correct position, much like the emperor is said to harmonize the two sides of government (*wen* and *wu*) and the whole world in general, merely by "facing South." This ritual arrangement dates from the Shang, but like many ancient things it was codified in the Han.

Yanzong then says that monks should be treated just as one would treat the Buddha himself. The Buddha was the founding ancestor of the Sakyamuni (*Shi*) clan, represented in Buddhist temples in that same spatial configuration. Lineage was the fundamental structure of Buddhism in China. Monks were sponsored to engage in ancestral cults of lay patrons. Buddhist temples had by then taken on some of the features and functions of ancestral temples. The representation of monks as lineage members preserving the inheritance of the Buddha is consistent with an increasing Sinification of the monastic institution in this period; and the image of the monk as center (or object) of sacrifice reflects the role of monks in the media of exchange between the living and the dead. The predominant metaphor of transmission from the Buddha to monk was *zong*, a descent line from a patrilineal ancestor. (It is very misleading when a term like *chanzong* is translated as "Chan school" or "sect.") The ideal was encoded with particular emphasis in mourning ritual. To follow the image of the ancestral cult with an erasure of the ritual distinction between Buddha and monk suggests an attempt to place the monk's body on the altar, in the ritual position of the founding ancestor of an ancestral hall.

The identity of one who has taken the ritual position of a dead person temporarily disappears in the ritual form, and the body that remains is invested—"en-clothed"—with the identity of the dead. If that dead person was a father, the mourning son performed prostrations to the impersonator as if it was really the father, no matter who their body normally belonged to.[8] The blurring of the distinction between the observable living body and the intangible other identity is echoed by the erasure of the distinction between the Buddha and a specific monk. The argument here is: the ruler bows to— and does not expect a bow from—the ritual actor impersonating the dead. If orthodox, canonical ritual provides exceptions to the pyramid of obeisance, so too the monk's position exempts him, because like the impersonator, the monk is ritually identical to his ancestor, in this case the Buddha.

Despite having "left the household," the monk's disengagement from the family was simultaneous to his placement in a new pseudo-family, in a pseudo-genetic vertical lineage with ancestors, patriarchs, and sibling-like generations of disciples. The filial distinction between master and disciple in some sense replaced the father-son distinction. The rhetoric of lineage appears in other several places. For example, in response to a speech by Yang Sixuan and Yang Shouzhuo, Yanzong interjects: "Shaving [the head] is receiving Sakya's lineage (*zong*)."[9] Yanzong also says: "Monks are the Dharma-king's heirs."[10] The assertion that "the Three Treasures are one body; one shows respect to a monk as if he were the Buddha"[11] suggests the monk's body as simultaneously trivial and the site of supreme authority: trivial, because merely the external trace or evidence of a greater but invisible authority elsewhere; and authoritative, because in some sense the monk is the Buddha. The monk's body is the Buddha's body, and yet, the Buddha is elsewhere. One shows respect to the monk as he enacts the ritual persona of the Buddha, no matter what feelings of disrespect the ruler might have toward any specific, individual monk.

The use of the discourse of lineage in the bowing debate counterposes the family to the state and relies upon a tension inherent in the social structure, between the father-son relationship and the ruler-ruled. This tension arises in historical narrative when someone's father commits a crime against the ruler, and loyalties are put in conflict. When put to the test, loyalty to one's father generally overrides loyalty to the ruler but not without ambiguity and tension. Confucius said he preferred the son who covered up the crime of his father to the son who testified to his father's theft of livestock.[12] The adoption of genetic ancestry as a model for the Sangha exploited precisely this tension.

And here's another ritual actor whose performance allows him to embody divine or quasi-divine ancestor, which exempts him from the dominant norms of obeisance. His sixth point:

> Using the yarrow plant, the diviner respects the elder, and caps [the young man] on the *zuo* (eastern steps of the hall where the host stands to welcome guests). Mother and older brother come to bow, considering that the ritual completes the man. Now sramanas take the great Dharma as their responsibility. Saving the many beings from mire and hot coals, reverence is continued and the ancestor transmits to the heir. This is the point about transmitting what's important.[13]

According to the capping ritual, when a man is twenty and has been capped, his family—even his mother and older brothers—bow to him, on the eastern steps at the side of the hall, which is a location normally appropriate to the host (most likely, the young man's father). This shows he is an adult who can receive and continue the ancestor's inheritance. Monks receive and continue the inheritance of their ancestor the Buddha. The point is to analogize monks to a case in Confucian ritual where the normal hierarchy of mother/son and elder/younger is suspended, because the son/younger brother represents the ancestral transmission at that moment. Again we have the idea that an invisible, somewhat remote power is momentarily present in the body of the young man, and the incarnation of that authority justifies an inversion of normal obeisance. So this example relates to the theme of incarnation of divine authority.

Not all the analogous authorities are divine, however. The monk is also like a teacher, specifically the emperor's teacher. Though not reliant on actual foreignness, the teacher enjoys a rather different form of alterity, because his status as transmitter of wisdom puts him into a different category. Confucius himself claimed not to innovate but merely to transmit the wisdom of the ages.[14] Yanzong could have cited the case of the emperor's deferential treatment of the "three classes of old men" from the *Liji*, mentioned in the last chapter. In Yanzong's fourth point, there is again an appeal to the Classics:

> Stressing the way and honoring one's teacher, [the emperor] does not treat him as a subject. Even though he is instructing the Son of Heaven, he does not face North. Now sramanas spread the Buddha's supreme teaching, lead the common people and guide the beings. It's about respecting the teacher and respecting study. This is the point about Confucian practices.

The first line is a paraphrase of a passage in the *Liji* which describes the honor due to a teacher. "There are two among his subjects whom the ruler does not treat as subjects. When someone is impersonating (his ancestor), the ruler does not treat him as a subject. When someone is a teacher, the ruler does not treat him as a subject. According to the ritual of the Great College, although [the teacher] is instructing the son of Heaven, he does not face North."[15] The hierarchy of teacher/student overrides the hierarchy of ruler/subject, according to the Confucian veneration of teachers. The teacher is allowed at least some degree of exemption from the normal imperial ritual. Monks are like teachers, so it's obvious they should not have to bow. Teachers could be said to bear the authority of the past, though "the past" is not quite the same as the Buddha, ancestral spirits, or gods, who presumably have some kind of continuing consciousness.

The extraterritoriality of monks

At times, the foreignness of Buddhism was not a stigma but advertised: monks described themselves as *fangwaizhibin*, "guests from outside the boundaries" who "come from outside the imperial domain." Two and a half centuries earlier, Huiyuan wrote: "He who has left household life is a lodger beyond the limits [*fangwaizhibin*], his traces are cut off from those of the beings. The Doctrine by which he lives enables him to understand that woes and impediments come from having a body, that by not maintaining the body one terminates woe."[16] The distinction between clergy and laity was the absence or presence of the body. Not from any particular domain, the monk's body was existentially alien. The monk's body was other: "the sangha is and must remain a brotherhood which is not of this world, a group with its own ideals and its own code of conduct."[17] And further, "the clergy has its own Rites, its own *li*. It is a world in itself, not even Chinese, and it must maintain its isolation, for any contamination between the two worlds is undesirable and nefarious."[18]

Yanzong brings a Classical reference to this rhetoric of alterity in his third point:

> The lords of the states of Qi and Song were descendants of the two kings [Yu of the Xia and Tang of the Shang]. The King [of Zhou] respected them as state guests (*guobin*). Now the monks are the Dharma king's heirs. As for the [Dharma-] King, [the monks] receive the Buddha's charge, to arouse ourselves through the four stages of enlightenment[19] and to advance their cultivation of the three practices [good, bad and neutral karma]. This is the point about the state guest.[20]

So, the King of Zhou gave fiefs to descendants of the two previous dynasties, the Xia and the Shang, even though those dynasties were long gone. The King of Zhou therefore gave respect, and indeed domains, to the descendants of (chronologically) remote kings. They were treated as "state guests" (*guobin*).

Similarly, monks are descendants of the (Dharma) king, chronologically and geographically remote. So monks should also be "state guests" and have some leeway in the required imperial rituals. Buddhism here is like an imperial domain.

What does it mean to be a state guest? In the *Sangdaji* ("greater record of funeral customs") section of the *Liji*, the phrase *guobin* is used three times (22.8, 22.9, 22.13). According to Legge's translation, *guobin* refers to "a visitor from another state," or "a minister [or commissioner] commissioned from another state."[21] When a parent of the emperor dies, the principal mourner is told to come out of the hall and descend the stairs to greet the visiting "state guest." The *Liji* specifies:

> Having gone down by the steps on the west, if a ruler, he bowed to a refugee ruler, or a minister commissioned from another state [*guobin*], each in his proper place.... The (young) ruler (who was mourning) bowed to refugee lords, and to ministers, commissioners from other states. [*guobin*][22]

The "state guest," then, was a high-ranking representative of another imperial order. If taking the role of principle mourner, the ruler does not wait for the state guest to ascend the hall and pay respects but rather goes out to greet him. This is another case where the normal ritual order is momentarily suspended or inverted, because it would be unseemly to insist on his own high status while grieving.

Yanzong's ninth point is a variation on the theme: "Also, those who proclaim [the imperial edicts], although they are humble, yet they bear [the authority of the Son of] Heaven, and are thus respected. Sramanas, even though they are humble, act on the behest [of Buddha], and so should be respected." Here again, we see the analogy of Buddha as emperor and the appeal to diplomatic immunity. Just as the emperor's servants are treated with a respect not for their own person but for the authority they represent, monks should be treated like the Buddha. But surely this kind of appeal is limited, because if the Buddha is by analogy the emperor of a vassal state, surely his representatives should kowtow to the Chinese emperor? But we should not be too literal about what is after all an analogy. This is a variation of: the Buddha as emperor of a foreign state. Monks are the Buddha's "crown princes." Monks should, by analogy, have some kind of diplomatic immunity or extraterritoriality. The Dharma-King is that other emperor, and monks (his "heirs," i.e. princes) are the authoritative embassies of his words, and carriers of his full authority.

The issue of Buddhism's foreignness involved questions of sovereignty and subjecthood, and inevitably Buddhists adopted some terms from the discourse of territoriality. The Buddhist claim to allegiance to an Elsewhere created a parallel realm, with its own law codes (Vinaya). And yet the "state within a state" was actually a "state outside the state." Xuan Fan remarks: "Buddha's Dharma is outside territory (*quyu*); it surpasses the veneration of the Four Greats."[23] The "Four Greats" (*sanda*) refers to: Heaven, Earth, Man, and Ruler. So Buddha is even higher than Heaven.

Against this virtual reality of the monk's subjecthood, anti-Buddhists in turn argued that physical presence within a territory was sufficient to constitute the body as an object of legal control. The body was included within a legal-territorial domain, irrespective of any ritual distinctions. Putting on the "black" (robe of a Buddhist monk)—or the "yellow" (hat of a Daoist priest)—does not change anything. The conflict is over the relations of body, territory, and sovereignty.

China had already a long tradition of principled withdrawal from and passive resistance to imperial power. Yanzong's seventh point quotes the chapter on recluses in the *Houhanshu*:

> "Yao called upon Heaven [i.e. none but Heaven was above him in power], but [the recluses Chao Fu and Xu You] did not come down from the heights of Yingyang. King Wu was perfectly beautiful, but in the end [the recluses Boyi and Shuqi] perfected their purity in Guzhu." Now the sramanas send their service on high, do not serve kings or feudal lords. They shed the mortal frame [literally, cicada shell] in the midst of clamor and dust. They come from outside the country. This is the point about withdrawing from people.[24]

Yingyang and Guzhu were the locations where these famous gentlemen had withdrawn and refused to obey the reigning emperor. Emperor Yao offered Chao Fu the throne and the hermit was so disgusted he went to the river to wash his ears out. Xu You was so disgusted by Yao's offer of power he wouldn't even let his ox drink downstream of where the filth of his words had been washed from Chao Fu's ears. Even though Yao was an exemplary ruler, Chao Fu and Xu You ignored his requests and Yao could not simply force them to obey. Similarly, King Wu could not make Boyi and Shuqi come down from their mountain, even though they were starving. They were exemplary hermits. Monks are exemplary hermits too and so should not have to obey the rulers in matters of principle. Here we have a case of principled men directly disobeying the commands of two of the great rulers of old and those rulers not only accepting but respecting their disobedience.

Violence

Among these Classical proofs, one stands out as rather unusual. The monk is like a soldier. The use of martial rhetoric in the self-representation of Buddhist monks had much scriptural precedent. For one example from a multitude, chapter thirteen of the *Miaofalianhuajing* (The Lotus Sutra) has the gathered bodhisattvas describe how "in a muddied kalpa, in an evil age,/We, venerating and believing in the Buddha,/Will don the armor of forbearance."[25] But Yanzong's point is more specific:

> The *Li* [-*ji*] says, "An armored man does not bow." Because this would be a loss to the integrity of his good appearance (*rongjie*). Thus, Zhou Yafu only performed the long salute (*changyi*) to [Emperor] Wen [of the Han]. Now the sramana's body bears the armor of endurance, he exterminates the generals of desire, holds the sword of wisdom, and destroys the mind's delusions. This is the point about armor.[26]

In the debate, Fan Yijun (anti-bow) cited the same reference from the *Liji*, adding: "The body of the man who has left the laity bears the armor of endurance. To order him to bow along with the laity is to overturn and diminish the court's usages."[27]

The *Quli* section of the *Liji* reads: "the armored one does not bow (*bai*); to do a bow, he squats down." (1:43) And at 17:17, we read a series of similar cases:

> the military charioteer does not bow [forward to the front bar of a carriage]; the armored one does not bow. A wife at an auspicious affair [i.e. a wedding], even if a lord bestows [something upon her], performs the "respectful bow"

(*suanbai*) [which is less than the full prostration]. Sitting in the role of impersonator of the dead at a sacrifice (*shi*), then one does not do a hand-bow (*shoubai*), but one performs the "respectful bow" (*suanbai*). Acting as the chief mourner, then you do not do a hand-bow.

In the context of the *Liji*, the expression "an armored one does not bow" might be explained by the desire to avoid the unseemly spectacle of a man attempting prostrations while encumbered with armor. One might also speculate on the need for military leaders to avoid being seen in subservient positions by their troops; or even on the possibility of the danger of asking a heavily armed military general to lie down on the floor, precisely at the point when his skills are most essential—before a battle.

Another aspect of the basic analogy is suggested by the biographical reference, also mentioned by Zheng Qintai and Qin Huaike (anti-bow, Ministry of War): "[Zhou] Yafu gave a long salute (*changyi*) to [emperor] Wen of the Han. Is not armor called "butting scales" (*chulin*)? Thus, people should not make an entangling net."[28] (The meaning of this latter remark is, I think: when a soldier puts on these "scales," people should not try to catch them in a net of ritual; armor gives the soldier and the monk the right to special treatment.)

Zhou Yafu was an enfeoffed military commander during the second century BCE who led successful campaigns against the Xiongnu and other forces. His biography is included in Sima Qian's *Shiji* section 57, along with that of his father, Zhou Bo. Indeed, Zhou Bo was known for his mastery of military strategy and gruff anti-intellectualism, as well as his paranoia, as when visited by a representative of emperor Wen, he "wore armor wherever he went."[29] His son Zhou Yafu was enfeoffed to succeed his father as marquis, and when the Xiongnu invaded in 158 BCE, he was made a general. The most important episode here is the emperor's tour of inspection. First, the emperor and his entourage galloped straight into two other camps, but they were unable to gain entry quite so easily to Zhou Yafu's camp. The officer at the gate said: "The general says that as long as we are in camp here we do not listen even to the edicts of the Son of Heaven. We take orders only from him!"[30] Soon, Zhou admits the emperor, with the proviso that the horses must not gallop.

General Chou Ya-fu appeared bearing his arms and bowed curtly [*yi*]. "Since a soldier in armor is not required to make the customary prostrations [*bai*]," he said, "I trust I may conduct the interview according to military etiquette."

The emperor, much impressed, straightened up in his carriage and bowed in return from the crossbar.[31]

Zhou Yafu thus stood in historical memory as an exemplary military figure who, at least on that one occasion, did not prostrate himself to the emperor, citing military ritual (*junli*). His father wore armor even when not facing battle, perhaps as a physical protection but perhaps as a ritual statement. In normal court ritual, the military leaders bowed to the emperor, but when their bodies displayed the adornments of warfare, the ritual topography shifted.

Yanzong and others capitalized on the polarity of *wen* (literati, civil) and *wu* (martial, military) as ritually and institutionally opposed arms of the imperial government. Those who promoted the virtues of *wen* in the ritual production of the emperor's body and environment often had "an anti-military viewpoint."[32] The opposition of *wen* and *wu* was most clearly marked by left and right, respectively. Aligned along the central approach to the throne, civil officials (and offices) were generally on the left, military officials on the right. As the *Daodejing* remarks: "The gentleman gives precedence to the left when at home, but to the right when he goes to war. Arms are instruments of ill omen, not the instruments of the gentleman."[33] "Left" here means the Emperor's left; taking the ritual position of "facing South," the left is thus the East side. Hence, maps of imperial capitals reveal military-related offices located on the West side of the road leading to the South gate of the palace. *Wen* and *wu* were also sides of a street.

In the early fifth-century Huiyuan had used the *wen-wu* dichotomy as an analogy. The 662 discourse elaborates on this analogy more extensively and provocatively. Absolutism would seem to represent a single sphere of power containing both *wen* and *wu*, but in the relatively peaceful mid-seventh century, these "sub-spheres" of power became increasingly distinct, with the more ideologically-laden *wen* becoming more valued, so that by 662, the analogy assumed a greater rhetorical weight.

Despite this analogy, there seems to have been no particular pattern to military support for the monks. Although the representative of the Ministry of War made an anti-bow speech, military units are represented with mixed pro-bow and anti-bow positions. In terms of the pro and con sides of the issue, the *wen/wu* distinction is not particularly evident in the debate record. Given the predominance on the pro-bow side of representatives from military units associated with the Heir Apparent, a tally which followed cliques within the palace is more likely. Thus, in comparing monks with armed soldiers, Yanzong was probably not trying to appeal to the *wu* side of the street, as if to make an ally against the practitioners of *wen* who controlled imperial ritual. Rather, this "armored man" reference highlights another case of partial disobeisance, comparable to the impersonator of the dead or the foreign ambassador. Here though, the soldier and the monk are not channeling any god or ancestor, and the foreignness is purely internal—branches of government rather than different states.

The case of the armored man seems to be an acknowledgment that the emperor is better not to insist on the full ritual from bodies prepared for violence—on others, or on themselves. With the analogy to an armed soldier, and the hermit, we seem to be coming close to a bare, brute fact: What are you going to do if we still say no? Have your guards grab us and force us to our knees? Monks would then be much like prisoners. To use direct physical force on monks' bodies in order to make them show respect would not only be scandalous, but also practically impossible. Yanzong makes point number eight:

> One who violates [the law and is punished with] the Five Punishments, is locked up in the Three Woods [cangue or manacle set connecting head, hands and feet], suffers severe beating, is restrained in iron, and yet all this does not control his complete ritual behavior. Now, sramanas cut off their body- and head-hair, they have no progeny, they injure their appearance and they change their clothes. This is the point about extreme punishment.[34]

Yanzong states simply the practical impossibility of directly *forcing* monks to bow. Even when the state puts someone is chains, it is still not possible to fully control their ritual conduct. Indeed, the gallows was sometimes the site of a last-minute display of disrespect for the ruler, the execution of a bound criminal an occasion for momentary symbolic inversion of the social order.[35] In any case, Yanzong argues, monks are already quite accustomed to hardship, (even to the point of cutting off their hair!) and would not fear any threat of physical punishment. One of their opponents in the debate, Ma Dashi, seemed to think it absurd that such stoical people cannot accept one little bow: "even being flogged and beheaded, still they do not complain about the suffering; but respecting lords and loving fathers, why is there such complaining about the burden of it?"[36] Asceticism shows that the state did not after all have a monopoly on legitimate violence.

It was perhaps from Zheng Qintai and Qin Huaike (anti-bow, Ministry of War) that Yanzong drew his argument: "[One who is] confined due to the [crimes worthy of] the Five Punishments, one who is in the Three Woods does not bow. How can those who have completed the Five Virtues and living in the Three Robes bow? Guilt does not oblige [the criminal] to offer respect in reverence."[37]

Some of the previous analogies were such as to raise the monk up by association with the Buddha, gods, ancestors, ritual actors, exemplary hermits, great generals even. But the monk is like the convict for different reasons: in a specific sense at least, when it comes to gestures of respect, physical coercion has its real limits. A convict is, of course, very low of the pyramid of rank, almost by definition at the bottom, but *even there*, obeisance can only be voluntary. Even at the lowest reaches of the imperial ritual order, there was a capacity for non-participation.

Describing a psychiatric ward patient strapped down on a bed, Erving Goffman remarked: "When the individual is subject to extreme constraint he is automatically forced from the circle of the proper. The sign vehicles or physical tokens through which the customary ceremonies are performed are unavailable to him."[38] Goffman points to the irony of the man who has been physically restrained due to his anti-social behavior, denied thereby the possibility of free social behavior, and thus the possibility of a social self. By comparing convicts to monks (under hypothetical duress), Yanzong reaches downward for still one more location of alterity—underneath the pyramid. There is also the irony of a man "outside the circle of the proper" uniquely free to disrespect the highest authority.

Buddhist disobeisance considered

Many of the themes of the 340 and 403–404 arguments over monastic disobeisance continued into the 662 debate, partly because the earlier documents were included in Yanzong's dossier, and consulted and referred to by the lobbyists. The relationship of body and territory remained an issue, with efforts made to define the body, territory, and their relationship, in ways which suited either the pro- or anti-bow perspective. The body's relationship to social order, sovereignty and law was also under debate. In all of this, the body was the crucial means of negotiation. Beyond the bowing or not-bowing body, this negotiation extended to all signifiers of monastic difference: clothing, hair, ritual, ancestry, sexual practice, ritual, (quasi-) legal codes, and sites of residence. The anti-bow voices asserted that these techniques were relevant to the processes of legal and ritual discrimination. The pro-bow voices brushed aside these markers of difference as trivial. The bowing debate was thus a debate about the monk's body, or better, the monk's habitus—about the means by which a distinct monastic body is produced, about the meaning of those techniques of difference, and about how posture and gesture are defined.

The imperial body and the monastic body were objects that could be made, and images of these bodies were also made in discourse. These bodies were made *different*. Certain patterns of physical posture and gesture served to mark boundaries between ordained above and lay below, or between ruler above and ruled below. The basic physical strategy of ranked differentiation was the bow, and its performance displayed and embodied hierarchy. One set of distinctions was within the category of the ordained—nuns bow to monks, for example. But the key distinction in this debate was between ordained and non-ordained. Confucians and Buddhists, everyone in fact, bowed to something, so there was no categorical rejection of the bow as such. But the two distinguished bodies (emperor and monk) clashed precisely at the moment of their mutual approach. Yet the topography of imperial ritual was not a monolithic pyramid, even in its classical canon. The constant re-negotiation of rank between institutions suggests multiple and diverging sets of distinctions of rank. The images of the emperor's encounters with monks, soldiers, ambassadors, and certain ritual actors, suggest a complex, fractured pyramid.

In many respects, the central issue was the physical production of legitimate social distinctions. The emperor was the ritualized figurehead of imperial institutions which produced and constantly revised law codes, which claimed compatibility with the past (of the Classics). The emperor was perhaps the single most powerful force for defining social difference. The monks had their own law codes and canon, the Vinaya, which defined the differences not only of ordained and lay, but also of monk and nun, novice and monk, senior and junior. These distinctions were all systematically embodied in obeisance practice. Many of these distinctions accorded with the principles of the secular law codes—most distinctions of gender and seniority, for example, were considered natural and were not contested in this discourse. What the Confucians considered a violation of natural feelings was disobeisance to parents and to rulers—a rejection of the parent–child bond and the ruler–ruled bond. Monks did not contest the "natural" respect due to parents and rulers, as long as "respect" referred only to an interior emotion. Hence, they had a stake in controlling the ambiguity of "respect" (*jing*) as something you *feel* or as something you *do*. What, then, is the relationship of interior emotion and physical action? The Confucians argued that there is in fact a necessary relationship, that the "natural" welling-up of interior respect must be enacted, that obeisance embodies the truth of difference, and that bowing is the sign which verifies the body's relation to the fundamental truth of hierarchy. In his last years, Foucault was looking for "the techniques, the practices, which give a concrete form to this new political rationality and to this new kind of relationship between the social entity and the individual."[39] Surely one such fundamental technology was bowing, including all the complex details of distinctions and stipulations, the timing and the spacing, that make up the field of obeisance.

Foucault also asked, "How had the subject been compelled to decipher himself in regard to what was forbidden? It is a question of the relation between asceticism and truth."[40] The monk faced a forbidden gesture—bowing to any layperson—and when this was challenged his whole identity was up for grabs, at least according to the anti-bow rhetoric. In terms of Imperial ritual, the monk defined himself by doing what was forbidden (or rather, by not doing what was compelled). My examination of the 662 debate shows that the Buddhist truth depended on that ascetic practice, and that monks could bring the greatest truth down to their knees.

5

Christian Objections

Comparative idolatry

Buddhism and Christianity were both missionary religions in China. Both were strongly associated with a geographical elsewhere (India or Western Europe). Both were stigmatized by, and also benefited by, their alien origin. We can certainly say both religions exerted significant cultural influence, but we can't speak of any Buddhist empire nor of any territorial colonization, except by an analogy such as in the title of Erik Zürcher's *The Buddhist Conquest of China*. Much like the early Buddhist missionaries, the first major wave of Christian missions to China (the Catholics of the sixteenth through eighteenth centuries) came with new knowledge but no armies. But in the nineteenth century at least, Christianity came backed by imperial powers.

One way to compare Buddhist and Christian missions to China is to consider what problems they had. There were historiographical issues, to start with. When Buddhists and Christians came to China, they brought with them historical narratives which did not fit with Chinese chronologies. If Buddha or Jesus was born in such-and-such a year according to Chinese chronology, and if it was such a cosmic event of universal significance, how is it the Chinese annals contain nothing about it? And there were conflicting canons: the Bible or the sutras versus the Classics. Some of the adherents of both foreign religions tried to justify their teachings in terms of the Classics, asserting some underlying compatibility while nonetheless superseding them.

Both foreign missions had to confront ethnocentrism. Beyond the inevitable bias we find in all cultures, Chinese imperial ideology always had a strong sense of the center-periphery distinction. The Jesuit Mateo Ricci did all he could to fit in, even (ironically) presenting himself as a Buddhist monk for a time. After shedding that identity, he could simultaneously pander to Chinese chauvinism and anti-Buddhism: "India is a small place, and is not considered to be a nation of the highest standing. It lacks the arts of civilization and has no standards of moral conduct to bequeath to posterity."[1]

There were many textual and terminological problems: how do you translate "God"? or "Buddha"? There were questions of the moral worthiness of the founders of the two religions. From the earliest times, there had been challenges to the status of the Buddha: he abandoned his father, wife, and child? And then, Jesus was an executed criminal! Neither the Buddha nor Jesus presented very inspiring models of good citizenship. As a seventeenth-century anti-Christian wrote, "the Lord of Heaven, Jesus, was nailed to death because He broke His country's laws. This was no case of recognizing the relationship between ruler and subject."[2]

There were various problems of their foreign bodies, related to celibacy for example. Jesuits tried to evade the issue of their celibacy because they knew of the anti-Buddhist rhetoric against celibacy as unnatural. But celibacy always seems to provoke the accusation of sexual excess. The accusation of sexual impropriety was less of a problem for Buddhists, though there were usually scandals or stories about monks breaking their vows, at least in popular story-telling. The image of communal Christian worship (male and female together, and different classes mingling) evoked a common theme in anti-heterodox discourse: the erotic mingling of male and female, the desirous transgression of social and gender boundaries. Or what about diet: the Buddhists criticized those who ate meat, but in general the Chinese felt the Europeans ate too much meat.[3] A popular Chinese perception that Westerners/Christians had an excessive taste for meat was one reason for the image of the vampiric missionary, removing the eyes or other body parts from Chinese converts as they approached death, or from orphaned or abandoned children, in order to make medicinal potions. Their most important ritual apparently celebrated cannibalism.

And of course, in both cases, they had to deal with obeisance. The Buddhist case examined in the previous two chapters was quite focused: members of the Sangha bow or don't bow to their own parents and/or to the emperor. When we move through the history of Western contact with China, we find first, the Catholic missions of the sixteenth and seventeenth centuries objecting to idolatry in general (no one should bow to non-Christian icons) and then a more specific sentiment: Christians in particular should not have to bow to icons, though some tried to make an exception for tablets of ancestors and of Confucius. Whatever private misgivings they might have had, Catholic missionaries and other foreign visitors seemed not to have raised any objections to bowing to the emperor. But in 1793, the diplomatic mission of the British Lord Macartney resulted in an extended back-and-forth because Lord Macartney would not kowtow to the Qianlong emperor. Soon after, a renewed trickle and eventually a small flood of Western missionaries, both Catholic and Protestant, entered China. Then the most pressing issue was again the prohibition on idolatry, namely: in general, no one should bow to idols; Christians in particular must never bow to idols; and Christians should not be forced to bow to idols. These objections to bowing sometimes reached the level of local government offices, when minor disturbances took place, but for the most part, the emperor was uninvolved. The sectarian divide is a little ragged: many Protestants considered images of the Virgin Mary and the Saints as idols.

As for these foreign bodies not bowing to the gods, a high degree of religious laissez-faire was common in China. You have your gods, we have ours. But when Chinese converted to Christianity, and acted in sometimes provocative ways toward the old icons and ancestral tablets, there was more at stake than a matter of personal choice. Families were scandalized by their sons refusing to honor their ancestors or even hauling the ancestral plaques out onto a bonfire. Iconoclasm was a form of extreme disobeisance. People resented the way Christians would try to exempt themselves from contributing to "pagan festivals." In contrast, Buddhists may have claimed their gods better than any others, but there was very little objection to Buddhist laity bowing to ancestral plaques or Daoist gods.

Christian disobeisance forms a parallel to the Buddhist case, in the strict sense of claiming exemption from certain acts of obeisance. Yet so many aspects of the two cases were different. Christianity arrived in China with an already rich tradition of refusing to bow, starting in the Iron Age. The second of the Ten Commandments—the *locus classicus* of Christian notions of idolatry—states: "You shall not make yourself a graven image ... you shall not bow down to them or serve them."[4] The Bible is filled with elaborations of the theme. In one particularly sarcastic attack, God is presented as describing an image-maker who cuts down a tree; he uses half of it as firewood, enjoying the warmth as he bakes bread, and from the other half he carves "a god, his idol; and he falls down to it and worships it; he prays to it and says, 'Deliver me, for thou art my god!'" (Isaiah 44.17) It is possible to discern two distinct rhetorics of idolatry: first, that the idol is merely an insentient lump of matter, so at the very least the idolater is engaged in an entirely pointless ritual; and second, that there is a demonic presence inside the idol, which makes the ritual not only misguided but dangerous.[5]

Long before Protestant missionaries arrived in China, obeisance had been extensively debated in Europe, particularly in anti-Catholic polemics. In the mid- and late-seventeenth century, obeisance was an object of interrogation in at least three areas: (a) does it have a sound *scriptural basis*? (b) Does it insult *human dignity*? And (c) is it possible to disconnect the act from its *historical associations* with idolatry and the Roman Catholic Church?

In anti-Catholic polemics, Chinese paganism was compared to Romanism. The specific connections included a similarity in obeisance practice, the great multitude of objects of obeisance, the presence of monastic institutions, and the devotional practices of women. In the hostile stereotype, the Catholic was quintessentially prostrated before the priest, the Pope, images of Jesus, Mary and the saints, or by extension the Golden Calf. Through this postural stereotype, Protestants were able to freely associate Catholics with other non-Protestants, including the Chinese.[6]

The rejection of certain icons during and since the Protestant Reformation is well known, and this iconoclasm of material objects went along with an iconoclasm of the body: religious ritual was significantly modified to exclude obeisance to broadly conceived "idols."[7] But with very few exceptions, even the most radical anti-Catholic iconoclasts bowed in church, even if the torso remained erect (i.e. kneeling). While they attacked the obeisance of Catholics, Chinese, or other "idolaters," British Protestants of course bowed during certain rituals (such as funerals or communion) and to their King and Queen. Actors bowed at the ends of performances. Gentlemen doffed their hats. To avoid any hint of idolatry, they made a sharp distinction between religious and civil obeisance, so that bowing to Queen Victoria was certainly not considered idolatry. And in church, if the thought arose, they affirmed that their obeisance was not directed at a material object such as a cross but directed at what this object symbolized, namely God. For many, this doctrinal caveat for their actions was deemed sufficient to justify at least the more erect forms of obeisance (lowering heads, kneeling). Those who bowed much more deeply appeared to many Victorian Protestants not as more pious but as inordinately focused on material devotion, especially when the objects of obeisance were maintained with great care, given offerings, spoken to, kissed, and treated as great treasures.

The Western legacy of arguments over bowing is too extensive for anything but a few points here. As a movement which attacked priestly power and in particular the efficacy of the Mass, the Reformation problematized bowing in church. Is kneeling in church Biblical? Is it idolatry? Some claimed that any form of obeisance was idolatry and must be rejected.[8] Catholics and indeed many Protestants asserted the possibility of obeisance directed only at what the symbols pointed at (God), despite the visible fact of bowing to a material object. This distinction was, however, routinely ignored by the most radical anti-obeisance preachers, who returned, bluntly and plainly, to the observable act, as if that were the only relevant datum. A late seventeenth-century "Fanatick Chaplain" says: "To worship the Bread is Idolatry; But to kneel at the Sacrament is to worship the Bread."[9] Such a radical rejection of devotional practice was undoubtedly a minority view. For most Protestants, kneeling was quite acceptable. After all, Paul had said that "at the name of Jesus, every knee should bow" (Philippians 2:10).[10] But the torso remained erect. Moderate voices also claimed that one can kneel to a cross and it is not idolatry as long as idolatry is not in your heart.[11]

In a certain abstract sense, the question was: what role does the "heart" play in defining the body's acts? This is a little reminiscent of the 662 arguments that the performance of the bow was (or was not) sufficient evidence of a state of mind—the Buddhists generally saying, monks respect the emperor in their hearts but can't perform that respect; and Confucians saying, no, if you don't do it, that means you don't feel it. The Fanatick Chaplain refused to distinguish between different acts of obeisance—"It is all one to me"[12]—and denied any significance to mental states. The moderate Divine, in response, asked "do you think that bowing down is meant of the Mind or of the Body?"[13] This line could almost have come straight from the 662 debate, such as in Yanzong's assertion that the state of mind determines what the body's action means. The extreme iconoclastic/anti-idolatry position could also be regarded as excessively fixated on mere bodily form (bowing *itself* constitutes idolatry). In the 662 debate, I noted the strategy of accusing the other side of pedantic formalism.

Idolatry was not merely bowing to an icon that can't help you, or to a rival icon, but bowing as a moral error—a sin. Idolatry is other peoples' wrong obeisance. The concept does not necessarily imply an objection to bowing as such, because it depends upon what is being bowed to. The Fanatik Chaplain represented the idea that bowing to *anything whatsoever* is wrong. He was undoubtedly something of a straw man in that text, but still, the idea was on the table. Or the floor.

Was there anything like "idolatry" in pre-modern China? Well, yes and no. While Buddhists sometimes had to deal with a Chinese dim view of India, as far as I know they did not have to respond to an accusation of their similarity to some kind of "paganism," like Catholics responding to Protestants nor to anything equivalent of a rival Sangha within China like Catholicism was to Protestants—Chinese Buddhists had an earlier, inferior form of their religion (Hinayana), but there were no Hinayana Buddhists in China who might object. And while some analogies could be made, I don't see the Mahayana/Hinayana divide as particularly akin to the Protestant/Catholic divide. For one thing, whatever differences the Mahayana and Hinayana had, they all bowed to the Buddha. One point of similarity, rather out of context, would be the accusations by reform movements that the previous forms of their religion were dominated by the narrow interests of monastic institutions. But Mahayana was if anything more actively devotional than the pre-Mahayana Buddhism.

The nearest we come to a concept of idolatry in pre-modern China is when elites viewed a religious activity as belonging to the ignorant masses—a primarily class-based objection. Even then they were just as likely to remark that, after all, these cults taught simple morality to peasants, who could not be expected to understand anything deeper. Or perhaps, there is some sense of idolatry in the elite views of heterodox cults and secret religious societies, though there was again little objection to obeisance as such.

I have written elsewhere how Protestant writers repeatedly asserted the resemblance of Chinese religious practice to the "the holy mummeries of the Romish Church."[14] The similarity of Chinese Buddhist and Catholic ritual was widely noted, and various explanations circulated: perhaps the Nestorians gave the Chinese a fragment of Medieval Christianity, or perhaps Saint Thomas had proselytized in China, or perhaps Satan was playing his evil games. In his influential book on China, John Francis Davis brushed all this aside: "To those who admit that most of the Romish ceremonies and rites are borrowed directly from paganism, there is less difficulty in accounting for the resemblance."[15] The ease with which Protestants could compare Buddhism and Catholicism was important because the primary frame through which they understood Chinese Buddhist obeisance was a combination of Biblical injunctions and this analogy to Catholicism. There was nothing comparable in the early Tang debates: no anti-obeisance diatribes in the Five Classics like the Bible's many objections to idolatry, no commandment from Shangdi or the sage-kings or Confucius against bowing to icons, and no major case of religious disobeisance (like the Reformation) for the pro-bow side in China to invoke. In 662, nobody had any problem with bowing per se; the debate was far more narrowly focused.

The controversial rite

The religious history of China was conceived by many Jesuits as beginning with a primordial monotheism available to the most insightful of the ancient Chinese through the workings of natural theology and then falling into degeneracy due in large part to the introduction of Buddhism. Protestant narratives of Chinese history often agreed. William Burder in 1870 described Confucianism as an ancient Chinese "primitive creed," the simple worship of a moral supreme being, which degenerated into "a multitude of superstitions," so that "the people forgot the simple worship of the Shang-tee [Shangdi] and embraced every new invention of idolatry with the utmost avidity."[16] Karl Gützlaff noted the similarity of ancient worship of Shangdi and the practices of Noah; but so much time had passed, it was impossible to be sure how pure the ancient Chinese religion was: "idolatry gained ascendency at a very early period." Hence, "we believe that the records which come down to us were greatly and purposely mutilated by the transcribers, and even modeled according to the prevailing customs of later ages."[17]

Confucianism, the least obviously theistic of the Three Teachings, had an ambiguous status in missionary discourse, especially since many saw Confucianism as an ally against Buddhism and Daoism. And yet, Confucianism had its distinctive religious aspects, and more to the point it endorsed the ancestral cult. Despite some efforts to sanitize obeisance to ancestors (as merely a natural gesture of remembrance), most Protestant opinion was against it.

The renowned Jesuit Matteo Ricci (1555–1610) knew the importance and legal obligation of obeisance to Confucius for Chinese officials. In order to avoid the charge that the Jesuits were condoning idolatry, Ricci argued that these rituals were gestures of respect, psychological rather than spiritual, secular rather than religious. The elite Chinese were not "worshiping" Confucius. It was no more "idolatrous" than kneeling before a king or a grave. Ricci picked up on certain voices of the more secular-minded literati class, who themselves defined these rituals in psychological or sociological terms, and claimed that bowing to the plaque of Confucius was no more than bowing to one's ruler or to one's parents—only an expression of respect. Respect—both the emotion and the action—was in turn the fundamental building-block of the entire socio-political order. Thus, one effect of the Jesuit position was the attempted emptying of religious meaning from what otherwise would have been seen, fairly unambiguously, as idolatry: bowing to an object other than a representation of Christ, Mary, or the Saints.

The Rites Controversy was extended and complex. In 1704 and 1715, and finally in 1742, the Vatican declared the debate over: such rituals were incompatible with Christianity. Only in 1935 was this policy amended to allow a qualified and explicitly "civil" veneration of Confucius; in 1939 a bowed head in veneration of ancestors was permitted. This revision to long-standing orders against obeisance to Confucius was impelled by the newly established Manchukuo and its ideology of Wangdao (Royal Way) requiring all citizens to bow to Confucius. Church leaders were assured by the Manchukuo regime that the cult was strictly civil. Pope Pius XI allowed a head bow, a decision further endorsed in 1939 by Pius XII. At the same time Pius XII allowed the bowing of the head toward ancestral altars, with a further clarification and consolidation of policy in 1941.

There is a wonderful irony in the position that the Rites Controversy forced Rome to take prior to 1935. On the one hand, some of the more radical

Reformation critics claimed that no matter what the mental state or intention, obeisance even to most Christian images is idolatry, and in response, Rome affirmed the orthodoxy of its own obeisance practices by asserting the importance of mental state—despite appearances, we are bowing to God, not the icon. On the other hand, faced with the arguments of Ricci, Rome denied the orthodoxy of Chinese obeisance, arguing that no matter what the mental state or intention, obeisance to Confucius and ancestors was idolatry. Meanwhile, of course, the vast majority of Chinese devotion, to Buddha and so on, was unproblematically condemned. Many of the accusations found in Protestant critiques of Catholic "idolatry" can be found in the Jesuits' critique of Chinese "idolatry." Idolaters are always someone else.

Here is Ricci explaining why bowing to tablets and even images of Confucius and ancestors is not, despite appearances, idolatry:

> Their piety towards parents and relatives consists in serving them when dead as if they were still alive. However, this observance does not mean to imply that the dead actually come to eat these things or that they need them; but they say that they do this because they know no other way of showing them their love and gratitude. And some people told us that this ceremony was instituted more for the living than for the dead, that is, to teach children and ignorant people how to honor and serve their living relatives, by seeing that persons of authority fulfill towards them even after death the duties they used to perform when they were alive. Since they recognize no divinity in the dead, since they beg them for nothing, all this is devoid of idolatry and perhaps it can be said that there is no superstition.[18]

So according to this argument, bowing to these objects is not idolatry because no one actually believes there is a real spirit present. The offerings are only didactic and symbolic, and no one asks for anything. He described the Confucius temple, typically next to the magistrate's building, which enshrined a statue or tablet of Confucius. He said the magistrates and others go before this altar and "give reverence to Confucius with the customary genuflections. They light candles to him and place incense in the censer which stands before the altar. On his birthday and certain other occasions during the year, they offer him in a very solemn manner dead animals and other edibles to show him their appreciation for the good doctrine left to them in his books through which they attained their magistracies and degrees. However, they recite no prayers nor ask any favor of him, as we have already noted in the instance of their dead."[19] And yet Ricci's own report betrays him. "Offering" and "showing" imply a persona receiving and seeing, and in any case Ricci admits there are other spirits like the City God to whom the officials offer.

In the educated elite among whom Ricci moved there were no doubt some who held this purely didactic view. The Confucianism that Ricci saw (and wanted to see) was probably relatively free of anything resembling idolatry. As an example from slightly later shows, in his "Instructions to the Missionaries" of 1720, the Kangxi emperor himself endorsed a non-supernatural view: "In China ancestral tablets are exhibited and revered so that the sons of men may remember their parents who brought them up."[20]

The Rites Controversy involved many arguments, over terminology, ancient Chinese religion, and the status of the Chinese Classics. It was also mingled with questions of trade, imperial toleration, and the legal status of foreign missionaries. Much of the subsequent debate was somewhat removed from the direct question of obeisance. Perhaps it is reductive to say that any such complex phenomenon as a full-blown "controversy" is *about* any one thing. But the most practical question was always there: can converts bow to Confucius and their ancestors? If these bows were no more than "secular" gestures of remembrance and respect such as one might feel toward any wise philosopher or any of one's ancestors, then there might be no problem. But Ricci's views were not supported by common practice, in which the ancestors did indeed have power and consciousness, and in which people asked them for favors. The more normal thought was that the spirits do come and consume the offerings (at least, the scent of them). The Dominican friars in China looked at the evidence and saw these rituals as simply religious. At a 1643 conference in Rome on problems with the China mission, of the seventeen points raised, we find: contributions to pagan festivals, the Chenghuang (City God) cult, the Confucius cult, ancestor worship, serving the dead as if they were alive, ancestral tablets, and funerals.[21] The Church in Rome was not having any of it, and a series of decrees ended the debate.

During the eighteenth century, the missionaries were subject to increasing control and even persecution. In this context, the Kangxi emperor's "Instructions to the Missionaries" of 1720 argued that not bowing to one's ancestors was beneath not only humans but even animals, whose young show signs of grief when their mothers die. "Even you who practice asceticism must also mourn and grieve should your parents depart. Should you treat their passing with indifference, you would not be equal to animals; how then can you be compared to the Chinese?"[22] I hear an echo of 662 in this remark. You are always a son, no matter what asceticism or monasticism you practice. As the Tang commandant Neng Xuanyi said, "Only the love of those who themselves bear children and raise them is truly deep.... How can they wrap their bodies in black robes and then not bow to lords and parents?"[23] The feelings a son has toward his parents are immutable, and failure to act on those sentiments is an abomination. The passage of a thousand years had not changed that argument.

Some Protestants accused Catholics of actually worshiping the material object, and a similar type of argument was presented in China by Cardinal Carlo T. Maillard de Tournon as a reason not to worship the sky (*tian*) while claiming to worship "Heaven" (*tian*). Kangxi responded:

> Take for example his contention that Heaven is a material thing and should not be worshipped. To speak my mind in simile, when one renders homage and gratitude to the Throne, one must address the Emperor as Pi-hsia [bixia] or Chieh-hsia [jiexia] "under the steps to the Throne," and similar terms. And when one passes the Imperial Throne one most certainly hastens to pay proper reverence towards the ruler. It is the same everywhere. Could one take Pi-hsia as a "seat under the steps," something made by artisans, and fail thus to show proper respect to it? The same idea underlies China's worship of Heaven.[24]

Here, addressing one's respect to the stairs should not be taken as showing respect to the stairs themselves but to what the stairs point to. The fact that there is a certain materiality to the sky (*tian*) does not make worship of Heaven (*tian*) wrong. As discussed in Chapter 2, Daoxuan mentioned the custom of referring to the ruler as *bixia*, "under the stairs," but there he was explaining the verticality of head-foot distinctions—the phrase was a discursive equivalent to the head touching the feet. Kangxi brings it up here for an entirely different purpose, to show that obeisance toward the throne or the stairs is not reverence to the material object but to he who sits above. Again, the distinctive notion of idolatry—of sinful obeisance to a mere material object—was almost non-existent in the debate of 662.

Debating ancestors

The one act of obeisance that virtually all Chinese practiced was to their ancestors. The proper degree of toleration of the ancestral cult was the most contentious issue of the General Conference of the Protestant Missionaries of China, held at Shanghai in 1890, and this topic was left for last probably for that reason. While most participants condemned obeisance to the dead, the most provoking paper was "The Worship of Ancestors—A Plea for Toleration" written by William Alexander Parsons Martin (1827–1916) and read in his absence. Martin was an American Presbyterian missionary and educator who had been appointed first President of the imperially supported Tungwen College in Peking. He argued for toleration and for only indirect attacks. He praised the moral effects of the ancestor cult and in contrast found the strict Protestant refusal to pray for the dead very "dreary."[25] Here, we might have come close to some parallel to the rhetoric of natural filial piety that was so common in the 662 debate, since Martin seems to suggest the Protestant lack of an ancestral cult is ungrateful to one's deceased parents. But "dreary" is hardly "unfilial," and no such argument was made. Simple kneeling at the grave was already sufficient manifestation of filial piety, whereas the Chinese ancestral ritual went far beyond that. Most controversially Martin denied that obeisance to ancestors constituted idolatry:

> The posture is always that of kneeling, alternating with prostrations … but it does not in itself form an act of idolatry, because the same posture is employed to show respect to the living. Children fall on knees and face before their parents; subjects before their sovereign; officials of every rank before those above them; and common people before their magistrates. Beggars in the street assume that attitude in asking alms.[26]

In other words, the physical act does not automatically constitute idolatry because it is identical to many acts of clearly secular or civil courtesy, in which the object of obeisance is not assumed to be divine. A British subject kneeling to Queen Victoria is not thereby an idolater. The beggar who grovels does not take you for a god. Martin thus replicated some of the arguments of Jesuits who had tried to persuade the Vatican and others that obeisance to Confucius and ancestors was not a *religious* action *in itself*. Martin concludes that the three parts of the ancestral cult—posture, invocation, and offering—are not necessarily idolatrous. "Considered as a mode of salutation, it merits our contempt as a fit expression of the abject condition of most oriental nations, but it is not sinful... Whether the invocation is an act of idolatry depends on the attributes ascribed to the deceased."[27] While it was widely felt that Chinese non-Christian idolatry was at the root of their "abjection," Martin thought that a prostrated body expressed abjection but not necessarily idolatry.

Henry Blodget's paper, which followed this, took care to distinguish between idolatrous and non-idolatrous expressions of natural grief for deceased parents. After describing the ritual of installing the spirit in the tablet, he concluded that it was neither "graceful" nor "innocent," but unambiguously idolatrous.[28] In reference to the history of debates between some Jesuits and the Vatican, he sided with the Pope. The conference proceedings include responses to the papers, and most of the speakers disagreed with Martin, denouncing the practice and rejecting his compromise position. High church liberalism would not yet have its day. Martin had argued that the idolatrous elements of ancestral practice could be removed and the remaining practices would be fine; others argued that it is all idolatry or tainted by idolatry. Y. K. Yen (Yan Yongjing), the only Chinese speaker, argued that one cannot remove the idolatrous element.[29] Harriet Noyes argued that the ancestral cult is indeed idolatrous, "for the same Chinese word is used to designate this worship and the worship of idols; the same forms of worship are observed; the prostrations, the burning of incense and candles and the offerings of food."[30] (The "same word" is probably *bai*.) Yet Noyes could also agree that the kowtow to officials is not idolatry: "While more abject than is usual in Western lands, it does not seem to be of the nature of religious worship."[31]

Hudson Taylor suggested that all who "wish to raise an indignant protest" against Martin's view should *stand up*. "Almost the whole audience did so."[32]

Bending bodies

By highlighting Chinese obeisance and judging it as idolatry, Protestant writers could both debunk Jesuit images of China, invoke anti-Catholic sentiments in depictions of Chinese religion, and implicate Catholicism with idolatrous heathenism.

Reports in the Anglican *Church Missionary Gleaner* frequently present acts of obeisance as comical or absurd. In "Praying for Rain in China" (1874), Arthur Evans Moule reported seeing a procession in which the principle object was not an idol but a toad. It was taken to the yamen office, where the magistrate "is obliged to come out with his secretaries and attendants, clad in mourning, to bow down to this toad in the broiling sun."[33] Or: "Here was 'a devotee beating his head with fearful violence upon a doorstep'; there 'a Buddhist priest walking on his knees'"[34] Such devotional behavior was seen as the "debasing domination of grovelling superstition".[35]

British Protestants, however, didn't do that sort of thing. On occasions, they physically pulled Chinese up who had bowed to them as they had bowed to Buddhist monks, rulers, and ancestors:

> Some Christian Chinese discovered themselves to us at Wan, and, taking Mr. Schereschewsky for a padre, they prostrated themselves before him, but he raised them up and quickly gave them to understand that such was not the fashion in our religion.[36]

The *Gleaner* and other sources reproduced many pictures of bowing and bending Chinese bodies, often contrasted with erect Protestants. For example, Thomas M'Clatchie stood benignly over a native convert who was bowing repeatedly and exclaiming "Ah, Jesus! Jesus! thus I worship Jesus!" M'Clatchie was clearly pleased at his earnestness but gestured toward the other man, telling him to stand up, in words and with his hands: "I raised him up, and placed him on a chair."[37] In the picture, the convert is bowing not at M'Clatchie but at an angle, presumably toward Jesus.

Perhaps the most preposterous representation of Chinese obeisance to an Englishman was in a popular novel of 1901, *A Flower of Asia: An Indian Story*. Though set in India, it features a representative Buddhist priest, called "John Chinaman" with a pig-tail. One night, the priest stumbles out of an opium den, and mistakes our hero, Dr O'Dowd, for an idol: "His unfocused eyes saw in the Doctor a statue of Buddha, and he salaamed profoundly before him."[38] Of course, O'Dowd was having nothing of it: "'Up with you, for a fool,' said O'Dowd. 'What do you mistake me for? I'm none of your idols, but a plain

Christian man.'"³⁹ As O'Dowd retreated, the priest pursued him, on his knees, touching his head to the ground. His devotion reaches the stage of actually grasping O'Dowd's legs and crying "Buddha! Buddha!" This idolization incenses the Briton: "'Do you mistake me for a heathen Chinee?...take off your hands, or I'll—I'll go for your pigtail....Hands off, you grimy thing!'"⁴⁰ The episode ends as an Indian policeman drags the Chinese man away, adding that the priest's true intentions were perhaps pick-pocketing or even murder. O'Dowd explains, "He mistook me for an idol of his," said the Doctor; "and came licking the ground at my feet. When I spurned his vile flattery, he tried to seize me in his arms."⁴¹

The 1866 report "Good News from Fuh-chau" tells a story of a convert named Lo Ling whose daughter was pledged to marry a heathen. "Her father was most anxious to have the engagement broken off, and the girl herself was equally desirous for a dissolution of the contract; but her reputed husband would not listen to it, and determined at once to marry her, and so prevent her becoming a Christian."⁴² In their version of the story, the groom's family tried to stop her religious conversion. It is possible for us to imagine the groom's family wished instead to avoid the embarrassment of a bride who refused to bow to her husband's ancestors. "During this time of his trial the Christians were in constant prayer for him, and to this I attribute his victory."⁴³ The story here was persecuted Christians waging spiritual war, not the groom's insistence on proper etiquette.

Lo Ling wanted the missionary to be present at the wedding, but he was reluctant because his presence might "excite the fury of the opposite party."⁴⁴ So several Chinese catechists attended, despite continued passive aggression. "They could do nothing. In the meantime the mob had assembled about the door, and threatened to pull down the house, which is the property of the Mission, and said something about tearing down our church."⁴⁵ Finally the bridal chair emerged, to much jeering and taunting from the locals. Someone even cried out, "'Ha! ha! come see the bride going to worship the kau tau [jiaotou],' i.e. the head of the religion, meaning the Missionary. The bridegroom and his party were infuriated."⁴⁶

Finally the wedding ceremonies took place with much abuse falling on the Christian converts. "But what of the poor girl? Why, she was dragged from her father's house amid torrents of abuse, and taken to a heathen home, where she was commanded to fall down and worship the domestic and ancestral idols. Did she at once renounce her faith in Christ? Ah! no. She at once refused to bow the knee to the idols, and said she had learned to worship the one living and true God. But this did not satisfy her cruel husband, who stood by ready to enforce his wicked commands with threats and blows. Poor girl! it was a great trial for her."[47]

The story tastefully elides the final result. Afterward, Lo Ling came to the mission to assure the missionary, "he believed his daughter would never again worship an idol."[48] This does not quite clarify if they actually succeeded in forcing her or not. She would hardly have been the first girl to have been unwillingly married into a hostile family, but in this story the idolatry and the disobeisance are the heart of the drama.

There were images in the missionary publications of children being taught to bow (Figure 5.1). But the wickedness of those who would use violence and physical strength to force converts to bow was a greater theme in missionary reportage. Wolfe reported on a widow and her twelve-year-old son, who converted. After conversion, she met with local

Figure 5.1 "Parents training their Children to worship Idols." *A Quarterly Token for Juvenile Subscribers* No. 21 (April 1861), p. 4.

opposition and persecution, and "they compelled the poor boy to bow down to the idols, and burn incense to the gods,—the poor little fellow crying, and protesting the whole time that he did not believe in them;—that he only believed in Jesus."[49] The episode warranted an illustration in *A Quarterly Token for Juvenile Subscribers*, a Church Missionary Society publication for young fundraisers. The story approved of the child's pious tantrum (Figure 5.2).

Compare Figures 5.1 and 5.2. In one, the child refuses to perform the quintessential act of filial piety, and the stern father responds with violence. This may seem harsh to our sensibilities but hardly unusual in Qing China, or Victorian England for that matter. And then we see the yielding child and the gentle guidance of a proud father. In the context of missionary publications, we are meant to respond with pity for the poor idolater-child, but the context and indeed the very production of the image cannot hide the rosy image of family harmony. What a good boy!

Figure 5.2 "Persecution in China." *A Quarterly Token for Juvenile Subscribers* No. 49 (April 1868), p. 8.

Though we usually think of conversion as an acceptance of a truth, or as a joining of a group, there is also a negative work of conversion—for example, the complex series of repudiations, abstentions, and destructions by Chinese in the process of conversion to Christianity. It was not enough for them to say yes; they also had to say no, and defining what must be rejected was a major task for missionaries in China, because the boundaries of "religion" and "culture" were not clear.

Refusing to kowtow

Any look at Western discourses against Chinese obeisance inevitably brings us to the diplomatic missions from the king of England to the emperor of China, such as the Macartney embassy of 1793 and the Amherst mission of 1816, in which the performance of the kowtow became a matter of significant contention in China and in Europe. Even Napoleon Bonaparte had an opinion.[50] The arguments about the kowtow, as well as the placement of chairs and sites of audience, seem strange, even comical. (Indeed, I have a small collection of cartoons about kowtowing.) With so much at stake, why would great nations bicker about knees? Yet the Boxer Protocol of 1901 removed the kowtow from Imperial audiences, replacing it with European protocol.

Subjects of the British throne had kowtowed to the emperor before, but those Westerners did not formally represent their monarch. The most strictly ritualized English and Chinese obeisance practices met, face to face, for the first time in 1793. King George III of England sent a high-ranking ambassador, George Macartney, to present a letter and gifts to the Emperor of China, Qianlong. The Chinese worked hard to make this visit fit the category of paying tribute from a vassal state, and the mission was not particularly successful for the British. In its later representations, the episode came to be known primarily as a conflict over obeisance: the Chinese insisting on a full prostration of "striking the head" (*ketou* or *koutou*) nine times on the ground before Qianlong and Macartney refusing to bend down any lower than he would to King George (one knee to the ground, head bowed). In the process of negotiation of an exception to the normative mode of encounter with the Son of Heaven, Macartney's knees and hands assumed political and historical significance, because the course of diplomatic relations between England and China depended on his posture at that critical moment.

In the end, Macartney gave the emperor a genuflection, kneeling on one knee, though he probably repeated the gesture three times.[51] According to later Chinese sources, Macartney "was so overcome with awe and nervousness, that his legs gave way under him, so that he groveled abjectly on the ground, thus to all intents and purposes performing an involuntary kowtow."[52]

No one claimed this was a matter of idolatry. So why were the English so stubborn about the kowtow? And why did that moment of refusal become such a topic of conversation in England? James Hevia writes that such an act would have violated the "dignity" of the English monarch and of an English gentleman. But why was it considered undignified in the first place? Hevia provides a few suggestions. For Macartney and his peers, it "seems to have conjured up all sorts of distasteful images in the imagination of the bourgeois gentlemen, not the least being the conflation of ground/low with dirt and the 'vulgar' orders."[53] Hevia described the kowtow in English imaginations as "the sign par excellence of Asia's slavish and feminized masses."[54] Near the end of his book, Hevia takes the discussion of these "conjured up" associations further:

> Kneeling had long been associated in Great Britain with subjugation, but such associations took on added urgency in the nineteenth century as a result of the transformations of physical space in the emerging bourgeois world. The opposition between kneeling and standing upright resonates with others such as high/clean and low/dirty, distinctions which figured not only social class and the geography of the nineteenth-century city, but ... the feminization of servitude in the figure of the kneeling chambermaid. The Victorian gentleman and maker of empire was just the opposite—stalwartly upright, only touching the ground with more than one knee when wounded or dead at the hands of savage barbarians.[55]

In these remarks, we see the meaning of obeisance as determined in part by a gendered "order of difference," which conflates bent posture with domestic servitude and the feminine. Macartney did not want to *put himself in the position of* a chambermaid. But feminization was mingled with religious sentiments as well. We can juxtapose the "feminization" of China with, for example, the iconoclast Andreas Karlstadt's view of "the worshippers of images as whores and adulterous women" and of idolatrous churches "as whorehouses."[56] The Fanatick Chaplain and the Protestant Divine agree that Rome is idolatrous, but the Fanatick Chaplain calls the Church of England "the younger sister to the Whore of Babylon."[57] Idolatry has been consistently gendered female.

Bourdieu has suggested that the ritual opposition between straight and bent is, at its most fundamental level, sexually determined.[58] Hevia sees the kowtow debates in terms of a fear of cultural "feminization."[59] The ideal model of middle-class womanhood was not supposed to be physically demonstrative, but women were nonetheless regarded as more emotional than rational, more tied to the body, more bent, closer to the earth, more prone to faint, and more inclined to bending down.

Was there anything like this in 662? The Five Relationships (*wulun*) included male/female, in the form of husband/wife, analogous to ruler/ruled and father/son. Certainly there was subjugation of women. Yet I have found very little explicit concern about symbolic feminization in the medieval debates. The monks might have said, being lower would be like being a woman, but I don't see how that would have strengthened their argument. And the pro-bow side apparently saw no great benefit in saying that monks should be like women. Still, the image of the chambermaid was not only about gender. It was also about class.

The general idea of "subjugation" was in fact multivalent: it was sexual, class-based, occupational, diplomatic, and political. And for Protestants, prostration was also "Catholic." As Macartney wrote:

> The paraphernalia of religion displayed here—the altars, images, tabernacles, censors, lamps, candles, and candlesticks—with the sanctimonious deportment of the priests and the solemnity used in the celebration of their mysteries, have no small resemblance to the holy mummeries of the Romish Church as practiced in those countries where it is rich and powerful.[60]

The "Romish" appearance of Chinese religious practices was noted with regularity, even predictability, throughout Protestant accounts of China. The American missionary S. Wells Williams emphasized the religious nature of the kowtow even when done before the emperor.

> What, then, becomes of the quibble of the Jesuits, who declared that it was merely a form…? There is, really, not the least difference between the

reverence paid by their subjects to the Pope and the Emperor; both demand it, on the ground that they are the viceregents of heaven, and sitting in the seat of God, and claim the honor due to gods. Knowing what these Chinese functionaries said to-day, no Christian man should ever again discuss the question of performing the *kotow*. It would be an idolatrous act.[61]

It is thus wrong to make "even a curtsey," because the meaning of it is that the Emperor is the Son of Heaven, and: "This assumption is like that of the Pope to be the Vicar of Christ."[62]

In rejecting any bow whatsoever to the emperor, I suspect Williams was not in the majority. Right or wrong, the kowtow to the emperor was nonetheless usually seen as civil ritual. But the act was performed also toward other objects. Precisely because the physical action of obeisance was the same (or similar) in approaching the Imperial throne and in prostrating to the Buddha or ancestors, some missionaries viewed the kowtow problem as fundamentally a religious issue, which is why it became so important. We have seen how the missionary W. A. P. Martin, for example, argued that obeisance to ancestral plaques was not idolatry, because it looked just like bowing to the Emperor; but more commonly, missionaries concluded that the kowtow to the Emperor was idolatrous because it looked like obeisance to idols.

The trope of heroic disobeisance

The real or imagined demand for prostration before the Chinese ruler has appeared repeatedly in the Western imagination. There grew a lore about noble disobeisance, focusing on the idealized erect body of the British Protestant, the stoical Briton with his "stiff upper lip." Take, for example, Sir Francis Hastings Doyle's "The Private of the Buffs" (1866). The poet was inspired by an incident which took place during the approach of Elgin's army to Beijing in 1860. According to the China correspondent of the London *Times*, "Some Seiks, and a private of the Buffs ... fell into the hands of the Chinese. On the next morning, they were brought before the authorities, and commanded to perform the *kotou*. The Seiks obeyed; but Moyse, the English soldier, declared that he would not prostrate himself before any Chinaman alive, was immediately knocked upon the head, and his body thrown on a dunghill."[63]

Doyle took this story (which, however, I have been unable to locate in the *Times*) and imagined an archetypal moment when ritual difference could not be ignored: an ordinary English soldier face to face with Chinese "authorities" (if not the Emperor himself):

...
To-day, beneath the foeman's frown,
He stands in Elgin's place,
Ambassador from Britain's crown,
And type of all her race.

Poor, reckless, rude, low-born, untaught,
bewildered, and alone,
A heart, with English instinct fraught,
He yet can call his own.
Ay, tear his body limb from limb,
Bring cord, or axe, or flame:
He only knows, that not through *him*
Shall England come to shame.

...
Let dusky Indians whine and kneel;
An English lad must die.
And thus, with eyes that would not shrink,
With knee to man unbent,
Unfaltering on its dreadful brink,
To his red grave he went.

Representing Queen Victoria and the English "race," a simple commoner with free "English instinct" in his heart stood unafraid of pain or death and concerned only with personal dignity and national honor. A proud white lad martyred for keeping eye contact and an erect posture. Such images confirmed national and racial identity in postural terms for colonizing Victorians and became a staple of jingoistic drama.

The novelist George MacDonald Fraser took this story and turned it around for satirical effect. In his retelling, Flashman (the notorious bully from *Tom Brown's Schooldays*) is an honored paragon of Victorian manly virtue while also a liar, coward, libertine and self-serving schemer. *Flashman and the Dragon* (1985) depicts the scene in a different light.[64] Flashman, an

Irish soldier, and Moyse (now named Moyes, and a Scot) are captured by and brought before the evil Manchu Prince Sang. A Chinese official screams at them to kowtow or be beheaded. Flashman contemplates: "There was no doubt what was demanded—and the alternative. It was enough for me: I was down and butting my way to the Antipodes before the little bastard had done speaking. I still thought we were doomed, but if a timely grovel would help, he could have it from me and welcome; you don't catch Flashy standing proud and unflinching at the gates of doom."[65] The Irish soldier also drops to the ground, but not the Scot.

> "Ye *what?*" says he, in that rasping gutter voice, and as the Prince glared and the little official jabbered, I heard the Irishman, hoarse and urgent: "Fer God's sake, Moyes, get down! Ye bloody idiot, he'll kill ye, else! Get down, man!"
> Moyes turned his head, and his eyes were wide in disbelief. By God, so were my ears. For clear as a bell, says he:
> "Tae a—in" Chink? Away, you!"
> And he stood straight as he could, stared at Prince Sang, and stuck out his dirty, unshaven chin.[66]

The executioner comes forward and holds the axe over Moyes' head. The official repeats the instructions. Despite the pleading of the Irish soldier, Moyes refuses to bow. Finally the executioner hacks off his head.

> That was how it happened—the stories that he laughed in defiance, or made a speech about not bowing his head to any heathen, or recited a prayer, or even the tale that he died drunk—they're false. I'd say he was taken flat aback at the mere notion of kow-towing, and when it sank in, he wasn't having it, not if it cost him his life. You may ask, was he a hero or just a fool, and I'll not answer—for I know this much, that each man has his price, and his was higher than yours or mine. That's all. I know one other thing—whenever I hear someone say "Proud as Lucifer", I think, no, proud as Private Moyes.[67]

Casual racism is fully within Flashman's character, so Flashman shares Moyes' contempt of the Chinese. But what is more unusual here is the respect Flashman gives to Moyes, given that Flashman had no qualms whatsoever about (as he put it) groveling. Even the cynical Flashman is impressed by the other man's foolish heroism in refusing to bow. Fraser created one of the great

Victorian anti-heroes, happy to grovel to save his life while also presenting himself as a champion of patriotic manhood. And Moyes is shown as foolish but brave and proud.

But there is no ironic inversion for the Chinese in this retelling. Fraser might have subverted the jingoism of *Tom Brown's Schooldays*, but his depiction of the Chinese is squarely in the tradition of the tyrannical Chinese, best represented by the dreadful Fu Manchu novels of Sax Rohmer (Arthur Henry Sarsfield Ward, 1883–1959). He wrote thirteen Fu Manchu novels between 1913 and 1959. In these, we find not quite the full kowtow problem but at least a consistent postural logic of forced idolatry. The manly Britons are constantly being pressed down by force. "Together, chained to the wall, two medieval captives, living mockeries of our boasted modern security, we crouched before Dr. Fu-Manchu."[68] Crouched—it's always crouched, or lay down, or looking up from the bottom of stairs: "he looked down upon us."[69] Or "the Satanic Chinaman towering over us where we lay."[70] Yet these debasements are ultimately a tease, for our heroes inevitably break free.

The 1932 film *The Mask of Fu Manchu*, based in Rohmer's 1929 story of the same name, features our stalwart hero Nayland Smith and a group of boffinish professors. The professors look forward to an expedition into China to dig up the tomb of Genghis Kahn and bring the loot back to England. But Fu Manchu's agents kidnap one of the professors and bring him to China. The throne is at one end of a room filled with Buddha images and scientific equipment; the lighting is gloomy. He encounters Fu on a throne at the top of a set of broad stairs. Fu sits formally, facing the camera. In a remarkable echo of the Macartney-Qianlong meeting, the two engage in a brief ritual struggle: the Briton walks right up to Fu. "I want to know the meaning of this!" Fu only tells him to sit down by his side on a modest stool. The Briton steps forward again, aggressively, saying, "You'll answer my question!" Fu claps his hands, the partition behind him parts to reveal two muscular guards with swords and a Buddha image directly behind the throne. Fu insists: "Sit there." As the British professor does so, the camera angle changes, so that we view them in profile, and now we clearly see Fu's higher position over the Briton. After some scheming and bluster, Fu's daughter enters the scene, performing not a kowtow nor even a *changgui* but a peculiar and fictional gesture, placing her forehead on the back of Fu's outstretched hand. Finally the professor has had enough and stands up again, saying "Fu Manchu, I'm not for sale!" At this, Fu calls in two Chinese lackeys who grip the professor. Worldlessly, Fu stands and leads them to where the professor is to be tortured.

For an effect similar to forced obeisance, Rohmer (and missionary publications) depicted Britons laid flat by the "Chinese" menace of opium. One particularly suggestive intersection of China, opium, and idolatry was the depiction of opium as a goddess in Rohmer's stories. There are many references to opium as a deity: as "Our Lady of the Poppies" as "the goddess"; taking opium is "worship" "at her shrine" or "temple." Those who work there are "priests" and the presiding evil genius of the den "might be the Spirit of Opium." And "true communicants must retreat to the temple of the goddess if they would partake of Paradise with her."[71] In *Yellow Claw*, the evil Chinese mastermind has even built a shine to opium:

> In niches of the wall were a number of grotesque Chinese idols. The floor was jet black and polished like ebony. Several tiger-skin rugs were strewn about it. But dominating the strange place, in the center of the floor stood an ivory pedestal, supporting a golden dragon of exquisite workmanship; and before it, as before a shrine, an enormous Chinese vase was placed, ... It contained a mass of exotic poppies of every shade conceivable.[72]

Fu Manchu becomes not only the most titanic genius ever known, he is also a demigod, or a god, or a demon. As they travel over England's green and pleasant lands, Petrie wonders "how an evil demigod had his sacrificial altars amid our sweetest groves."[73] Fu Manchu cackles: "I am the god of destruction!"[74]

There is a Western tradition that runs from the Rites Controversy, through the Macartney mission, through the many accusations of idolatry, that depicts the Chinese as especially fixated on obeisance. This book of mine may indeed only reinforce that view, though I believe histories of disobeisance could be written of many other, perhaps all other, cultures. Certainly it was not only China that made Victorians feel suddenly stiff. The early pages of *Dracula* (1897), which emphasize Jonathan Harker's transition from West to East, feature an episode in which a Romanian woman implores Harker not to continue on to Castle Dracula. "Finally she went down on her knees and implored me not to go .... It was all very ridiculous ... I therefore tried to raise her up."[75] Or in *She* (1886) by H. Rider Haggard, the Cambridge professor Horace Holly journeys into the African interior and eventually moves into the presence of She-who-must-be-obeyed.

> I halted, and felt scared. Indeed, my knees began to give way of their own mere motion; but reflection came to my aid. I was an Englishman, and why, I asked myself, should I creep into the presence of some savage woman...? If once I began to creep upon my knees I should always have to do so, and it would be a patent acknowledgement of inferiority. So, fortified by an insular prejudice against "koo-tooing,"... I marched in boldly.[76]

In the end, however, he brings the virile heroes to their knees.[77] This imposing woman is not, however, African but Arabian, a racial ploy by Haggard which allowed his erotic fantasy (or nightmare) woman to be other than the white Victorians but also light-skinned in comparison with the "savage" Africans whom she rules with contempt.

The civil rituals adopted by modern Chinese states have been international and modern. The Republic of China never insisted on kowtows to the President, partly because Sun Yat-sen (and later, Chiang Kai-shek) were Protestants and because the kowtow was part of an imperial past repudiated or re-negotiated in Chinese modernity. And yet, one cannot regard Chiang Kai-shek's memorial in Taipei or Mao Zedong's tomb in Beijing, as anything but religious sites, temples to great powers. Gestures of respect and offerings are made to Chiang Kai-shek but naturally such cannot be viewed as idolatry for the familiar reasons: it is no more than remembrance of the dead, and no favor is asked (explicitly). The crowds that make the pilgrimage to see Chairman Mao shuffle past, with sporadic nods of the head but (as far as I know) no kowtow.

Finally we reach a case of reverse Orientalism performed: a Chinese actor and film-maker performing the stages of a rejection of Imperial obeisance. In *Shanghai Noon* (2000), Jackie Chan plays Jiang Wen (comically mis-heard as "John Wayne"), an agent of the Qing government sent to America in 1881 to rescue abducted Manchu princess Pei Pei. He searches for the princess who is being held captive in a mining camp along with many Chinese laborers. When he has found her, in a tent, he bows his head to the ground. She says: "Please, don't draw attention! Please, stand up!" As she advances, he backs up out of the tent still on his knees, and other Chinese standing around start to bow as well. "Please, stand up! Don't bow! Get up!" So here is (if not the emperor then at least) a princess insisting on disobeisance.

Later, three Imperial guards find the princess in an empty church and kneel with one hand to the ground, as does Jackie (disguised now as a Catholic monk). But when an Imperial decree is unfurled, the guards and Jackie again bow their heads to the ground during the reading of the decree. All this takes place with the bad guys present and armed, and their face-to-ground posture provokes the blond cowboy Roy to say, "John, get up! I thought we were past this, come on!" Finally, with music surging and in defiance of Imperial etiquette, Jackie looks up and then stands up to respond to the danger—an act of disobeisance accompanied by the solemn words: "This is the West, not the East, and the sun may rise where we come from, but here is where it sets." Whatever that means. To break the deadlocked situation, princess Pei Pei grabs and burns the Imperial decree on a rack of votary candles. They then proceed to trash the church, in a six-shooter/kung-fu fight.

Shanghai Noon draws from such imagery as "The Private of the Buffs," even though in this case "China" repudiates its own ritual in favor of Western modernity—if only the bewildered Noyes had had Jackie Chan's kung fu abilities.

Conclusion

A "counter-religion" is a discourse against a particular religion that comes to take on attributes of a religious tradition itself. There is a kind of unexplored shadow-religion in Chinese history: anti-Buddhism. And anti-Taoism. At times, Confucians and Taoists sided against Buddhists; at times, Taoists and Buddhists sided against Confucians. The polemical debates and persecutions helped to determine the development of these traditions. In the Chinese anti-Christian discourse, as with the earlier anti-Buddhist discourse, one finds a complex intertextuality, with elliptical references to earlier sources and debates, as well as distinct modes of argumentation, scriptural references, epistemological assumptions, hero-figures, and practices. Clearly there were Chinese polemicists (Confucians and Buddhists) who strongly identified themselves as anti-Christian, just as anti-Buddhism came to form an important part of the identity of some Neo-Confucians. So too the Protestant missionaries in China made use of a long Western tradition of polemical literature against "the Romish Church" dating from the Reformation and an even longer oppositional literature traced back to the Ten Commandments. Arguments against Buddhism "laid much of the groundwork for future anti-heterodox thought in general and anti-Christian thought in particular."[78] One might take disobeisance as an empirical measure of the interaction of the traditions and counter-traditions of foreign and native religions in China.

When we compare Buddhist and Christian arguments, of course we find some points of similarity, but for the larger part the rhetorics are quite distinct. Some Buddhist monks' reasons for not bowing to the emperor do resemble Macartney's justifications for his disobeisance—primarily by merit of the appeals to foreign origin and allegiance to a distant ruler, in other words what I have described as diplomatic immunity and extraterritoriality. Although separated by centuries, we find continuity in the Chinese arguments why monks and Britons should bow. But when we come to the specifically Christian arguments for disobeisance, there is little by way of analogy in Medieval China. Idolatry seems wholly new to China. The rhetorical contexts are so different, one might ask if they are even talking about the same thing. At least, we always have the physical action as an empirical referent. Or do we? What is a bow?

6

Theories of Obeisance

By now it should be clear that any attempt to define obeisance with reference to any single version of what the bow *means* is in the end futile. Is it an expression of respect, or worship, or idolatry, or reverence, or gratitude, or devotion, or subjugation, or humility, or humiliation, or enlightenment? But these are all beside the point. The only common ground in all the examples are the fundamental, inherent facts: first, when you bow, you *lower* yourself. Second, you always bow *to* something. Third, when you bow, you *raise up the object* of obeisance by contrast. It takes two things and makes a difference in height. A bow is a performance of a vertical distinction. This is a minimalist, almost tautological, definition, because you still have to go on to explain what the act means in any given context. But such explanations belong to their contexts, and we still have to account for the bow's apparent universality.

It is instructive to see what explanations have been given, what theories have been proposed to account not only for the act itself but for the fact that some people bow more than others. Bowing may or may not be universal, but it is certainly widespread, either the actual performance of it, or its appearance in discourse. Why?

The vanquished bows to the conqueror

One effort to identify the "origin" of this act conceived the bow as a ritualization of a fundamental and quite specific tableaux vivant. One of the founding figures of Sociology, Herbert Spencer, in *The Principles of Sociology* (1879), wrote:

> From the beaten dog which, crawling on its belly licks its master's hand, we trace up the general truth that ceremonial forms are naturally initiated by

the relation of conqueror and conquered, and the consequent truth that they develop along with the militant type of society.¹

As a Social Darwinist, Spencer considered the behavior of social animals and humans parallel or on a continuum. So his chapter on obeisance begins with the example of a small dog cringing and offering its belly to a large dog. The primal origin of obeisance is the contrast, after physical combat, of the victor standing over the fallen and disordered body of the defeated. Here the meaning of the bow is rooted in violence of the most blatant and physical kind—actual combat.

Spencer drew a clear line from the most extreme enactments (prostration, self-mortification, removal of clothing) to faint "remnants"² of these gestures, as in the nod of the head or the touch of the cap. Conceptually, he saw all these gestures as belonging to the same logic, yet he knew a nod was not a kowtow. But what difference did it make?

He wanted to account for why some cultures bow more deeply than others. He saw an "abridgement"³ from more-lowering to less-lowering forms of the gesture, and this difference corresponded precisely to the evolution from the past to the present, from primitive to modern, from Catholic to Protestant, and from the "other" to "us" (us Britons, in this case). In Spencer's terms, the gradation of obeisance corresponded to the difference between "militant" societies based on physical coercion, fear, deception, and distrust; and "industrial" societies based on cooperation, honesty, and trust.⁴ Prostration onto the face, for example, occurred only in the most militaristic, despotic, and slavish societies.⁵ Careful attention to obeisance survived in modern Europe where "militancy" survived: among the upper classes, the army and navy, and in general, on the Continent rather than in England.⁶

> Neither the prostrations and repeated knockings of the head upon the ground by the Chinese worshipper, nor the kindred attitude of the Mahommedan at prayers, occurs where freer forms of social institutions, proper to the industrial type, have much qualified the militant type. Even going on the knees as a form of religious homage, has, among ourselves, fallen greatly into disuse; and the most unmilitant of our sects, the Quakers, make no religious obeisances whatever.⁷

So for Spencer, the precise degree at which the body bends before a ruler is an empirical barometer of the inherently non-coercive and honest nature of "industrial" social structures. The lesser angle of the torso is an geometric index of the dignity and integrity of Britain. As one reads his chapter, the associations pile up. On one end (the bottom end) of the yardstick of obeisance was full prostration, self-mortification, ritual nudity, despotism, militarism, deception, slavishness, China, Siam, Japan, primitives, Catholics, idolaters, and dogs. On the upper end was Herbert Spencer's own world: faint echoes of obeisance (growing fainter every day), freedom, industry, honesty, dignity, Britain, Protestantism (and perhaps even God). Spencer uses obeisance as a tangible index of polarities of nations, religions, sects, histories, races, and species.

When Spencer wrote all this, British colonialism was at its peak, yet his archetypal scenario, the winner of a fight towering above the beaten victim, was projected in its purer forms on the very cultures Britain was dominating or threatening. These associations justified British imperialism.

Spencer's explanation for the whole range of obeisance phenomena is almost comically reductionistic, and yet if we're honest, we can all understand it. In *Vertical Classification*, Barry Schwartz allows a measure of credence to Spencer's explanation but points out a problem. Only rarely are "symbolic categories" (such as ruler/ruled) and "physical characteristics" (such as the victor standing over the vanquished) associated directly, and the "routinization" or cultural reproduction of this association is unexplained.[8] Spencer "posits the existence of a primal social reality,"[9] which is indeed a mythic notion. In other words, our daily experience of society in general and our understanding of bowing in particular do not seem to depend on physical combat. We should certainly contest the notion that there was actually more fighting in China than in Britain or in villages than in factories.

Spencer said that obeisance is most evident in the ritual regimes of highly authoritarian societies and less evident in "modern" (industrial) societies, because the institutional basis of the reproduction of obeisance also fades. This is a little circular, though: when people never see anyone bowing to a king, naturally the act means less to them. Furthermore, Schwartz says that Spencer's explanation does not account very well for the fact of armed warriors bowing to feeble or infant emperors. Obeisance follows rather abstract distinctions of authority more than physical might or "rude power."[10] Hence, "vertical dominance denotes authority as well as power.

Spencer's origins theory, with its image of a prefigurative "primal horde," fails to appreciate this critical distinction."[11]

How might Spencer have dealt with the complicated series of symbolic moves involved with "the armored man does not bow"? Chinese soldiers bow to the emperor, except during a military campaign—if bowing is based on a scenario of combat, this soldier's disobeisance might suggest the soldier threatening to knock the emperor to the ground. But if monks do not have to kowtow to the emperor because they are like these soldiers—this might suggest that the ritual "dishevelment" (cut hair, simple robes) of the monk's body is a standing "remnant" of obeisance, as if the emperor's violence has been pre-empted by the self-mortification done by the monks to themselves—as if the asceticism was an admission of inferiority? That hardly sounds like 662. Or for that matter, how would Spencer's theory account for the eagerness of the anti-bow faction to compare monks to prisoners in chains? The beaten dog licking his master's hand is still capable of biting that hand.

Perhaps, to put Spencer in Chinese terms, victor/vanquished was his rather too literalistic way of saying ruler/ruled. Certainly, Chinese thinkers could justify any obeisance by appeal to an analogy of ruler/ruled: the father is like the ruler of the household, the wife is the husband's subject, and so on. But on the other hand, just as often they said the ruler was the father of the nation. There was no obvious priority of ruler/ruled in the Five Relationships, indeed as I have noted that Confucian traditions allowed father/son to edge out ruler/ruled in their moral calculus.

Problems arise in any attempt to posit a single archetype or scenario as the origin of obeisance. Spencer's pugilistic metaphor seems theoretically flimsy today, and very dated, but many decades later, in his influential *Oriental Despotism* (1957), Karl Wittfogel had scarcely any more nuance in his depiction of prostration as the crude display of abject weakness under a ruler's threat of violence: "The inferior man, aware that his master's wrath may destroy him, seeks to secure his good will by humbling himself; and the holder of power is more than ready to enforce and standardize the symbols of humiliation."[12] All such gestures are enactments of physical powerlessness. The open palm is only to show the lack of a weapon. "Or going to extremes, he may fall forward on all fours like an animal, strike his head on the ground, and kiss the dust."[13] Like

Spencer, he sees the geographical spread of prostration as a marker of inferior and superior societies. According to Wittfogel, the gesture tried and failed to take root in European court ritual.

Perhaps Spencer simply chose the wrong primal scenario. Having criticized Spencer, Schwartz goes on to posit a basic archetype of his own: the adult towering over the infant. Of course he does not phrase it as father/son as does the Chinese tradition.

The child bows to the adult

Although Schwartz says "we must think less of elaborating a bio-historical model and more about abandoning it altogether,"[14] he proceeds toward another essentially bio-social account of the origin of verticality as a principle of classification: in the experiences of the infant and the interactions of child and adult.[15] His goal is broader than Spencer's: to account not just for obeisance but for the prevalence of vertical classification.

> I want to argue that the physical difference between parent and child represents a code for social inequality.... Not only may we say that statural inequality in the parent-child complex is analogous to the symbolic polarity of high and low; we may also say that this analogy is introduced not by the observer but created by conditioning mechanisms in the interaction process itself.[16]

So Schwartz is not starting from the primordial division of reality into yin and yang, or the cosmological basis of natural hierarchy, or the practices of ancestral cults. In the parent–child complex, *up* (in the mother's arms) means attention and gratification; the child is put down and ignored (or punished) according to the adult's criteria of good and bad. "Social and spatial contrasts are integrated by an affective contrast. Libidinized by gratification, spatial perception is socialized by its connection to power."[17]

Verticality stands out in many media, but obeisance is the most explicit enactment. Schwartz makes the connection:

> The extreme forms of self-abasement, which involve prostration, resemble most clearly the situation of the infant laying face-down and helpless.

A variation of the same childlike tendency is to be found in the act of pleadingly groveling before another.[18]

How do you account for variations in the continuum from prostration to the nod of the head? Schwartz refers to subjective assessments of "social rank": "The precise correspondence between the social and the gestural is reaffirmed by variation in the depth of the inclination, which is very often made directly proportional to the social rank of the person to whom it is addressed."[19] In other words, we bow deeper to "higher" people. Part of what makes them "higher" is our willingness to lower ourselves, but social rank can also refer to much more abstract differences. Someone "higher" than me, for example, might cut my salary, whether I go down on my knees or not. And how exactly can we say that a tilt of the torso to a ruler in one culture is less an acknowledgment of power difference than a prostration is in another? It might be a far greater gesture depending on the norms of that culture.

In many ways, compared to Spencer's "alpha wolf" scenario, Schwartz provides a more plausible "origin" of obeisance. His aim is to account for the origin of verticality (rather than only obeisance), and so he is better able to integrate obeisance practice with a wide variety of social phenomena which reinforce the habitus of the bowing body. Verticality is evident, he notes, in "linguistic, gestural, anatomical, perceptual, statural, architectural, cosmological," and other types of representations and phenomena.[20] The basic logic of verticality is open-ended and versatile: "any object having properties isomorphic with the spatial medium of up-down can itself become a medium for the transmission of messages about social distinction."[21]

If we say the ceiling is "high above us," we take this as a simple statement about physical position. But if we are speaking of a great spiritual monk, or a ruler, words like "high" and "above us" take on social, moral, or spiritual connotations. One could easily multiply such examples, because, as Schwartz writes, "vertical classification is a semiotic code. The message it encodes concerns society's interest in affirming its own political and moral order. Given the importance of the message, it is essential that it be broadcast along different channels. This redundancy ensures reception."[22] Vertical distinction provides an easily understood way of seeing (and *thinking*) who is high and who is low.

Schwartz replaces Spencer's pugilistic "primal moment" with a much more plausible interaction. The infant-adult scenario at least has the benefit of constituting a true human universal. We have all had the basic experience of power imbalance, wherein we are smaller, lower, and vulnerable. The deep, ingrained, pre-discursive knowledge of our formative experience persists, and never entirely disappears, even when we grow up.

The bodies of children begin to receive knowledge of social categories as soon as they are born, and as we progress into adulthood, these structures become invisible, natural, and internal. The simplest and therefore most useful social categories are binary, and many such binary categories are overlaid on child/adult. We adapt our strategies of dealing with authority figures, such as bosses, priests, police officers, and heads of departments. In adulthood, it is largely a matter of improvisations on existing patterns. But earlier, in childhood, an adult stood over us and said "no, put your hand *there*." "Stand up straight." "Pull your socks up." "Let me show you." "Don't do that when we have company over." And also: "Kneel here." And earlier still, before words, the instruction began, as for example in modern Japan: "The training in this ability to communicate politely with other people does not wait until a child can speak, for it includes the commonly described pushing-down of the head of the baby on its mother's back into a bow of greeting."[23]

In some ways, the scenario of infant-adult interaction might inherit the same problems as Spencer's pugilistic theory. Though the infant-adult contrast is universal, fortunately Schwartz does not quite raise that interaction to the status of a "primal moment." He does *not* argue that

> every modality of vertical classification is uniquely derivable from early object relations but that the physical polarity which frames these relations serves as a prototype for the vertical mapping of social inequalities prior to and independently of our appreciation of nature.... Although vertical categories cannot be reduced to the ecology of the parent-child relationship, that relationship generates the formal (vertical) contrast which directs the "search" for all manner of vertical symbolism.[24]

The physical polarity of infant and adult operates throughout our lives as a "prototype," generating a contrast which is the "map" in our "search" for appropriate strategies of thought and action. This approach brings us very close to Pierre Bourdieu's notion of habitus, about which there is more below.

How historical is all this? Given the relative slightness of obeisance in modern Protestant Europe, are we to take it that these Protestants are more "adult" in some way? Or were they less conscious of their relative lack of power as children? Surely not. How can one explain Catholic-Protestant obeisance distinctions or the near-disappearance of the traditional Chinese practice of full prostration? The prototype of infant-adult interaction makes sense in the psychoanalytic field, but it functions poorly in historical, political, and institutional analysis. It seems to account for so much but cannot account for any historical details. Perhaps, in the context of in-depth psychoanalytic case-studies, one might be able to associate degrees of individual self-empowerment as a child with various attitudes toward obeisance but not at the level of a religion, a culture, a legal domain, or a time period. We should not expect too much of any theory.

In the Chinese Five Relationships (*wulun*), even more fundamental than ruler/ruled is father/son. I have remarked on the priority of this relation, so that filial piety (*xiao*) became not only about your treatment of your parents but a template for all relationships. As Kangxi remarked, even animal children mourn their parents. According to the *Xiaojing* (Classic of Filial Piety), *xiao* is the "pattern of Heaven."[25] Schwartz is not concerned with the filial nature of reality nor for that matter with its piety. The experience of helplessness as infants certainly forms one reason for a child's gratitude, though the father's donation of his "essence" and the mother's womb are even more important. In case of an orphan, the obligation of filial piety to biological parents remains even if the mother dies in childbirth and some other person raises the child. This notion of giving children their very bodies has nothing to do with Schwartz's approach. In some sense, orphans and adopted children are as powerless as first-born heirs, though perhaps they are not always as frequently picked up and cuddled.

A woman bows to a man

Pierre Bourdieu remarks of the Kabyle: "the opposition between the straight and the bent...is central to most of the marks of respect or contempt that politeness uses in many societies to symbolize relations of domination."[26] This opposition naturalizes gender distinctions:

> All the symbolic manipulations of body experience, starting with displacements within a symbolically structured space, tend to impose the integration of body space with cosmic space and social space, by applying the same categories (naturally at the price of great laxity in logic) both to the relationship between man and the natural world and to the complementary and opposed states and actions of the two sexes.[27]

So Bourdieu links the bent-unbent opposition to gender (male straight, female bent) and suggests further that "the fundamental oppositions of the social order... are always sexually overdetermined, as if the body language of sexual domination and submission had provided the fundamental principles of both the body language and the verbal language of social domination and submission."[28]

Certainly obeisance frequently follows gender distinctions, just as it follows distinctions in seniority, institutional title, and many other classifications. Since female bows to male and junior bows to senior, one might say that obeisance practice "feminizes" the junior or one might say that it "infantalizes" the female. It is not clear how one might assign priority to one opposing pair over another. We cannot take sexual difference as the necessary "origin" of the meaning of the bent-unbent or high-low distinctions. Still, the pairing of female-male and bent-unbent is empirically evident in Kabyle society, and China, and elsewhere, as is the pairing of ruler-ruled or father-son in other contexts. The question is not whether the association of men with height (or the unbent) can be demonstrated as active in a culture. The question is whether or not gender can be posited as the generating principle of obeisance per se. Is gender any better an explanatory principle than victor/vanquished or child/adult interaction?

Bourdieu however broadens his explanation beyond gender, and, like Schwartz, considers vertical distinction as a semiotic code which draws strongly from gender as well as other sources of difference. Patriarchy operates sometimes in inefficient, direct ways such as physical abuse but more pervasively by gendering the less powerful of any pair as female. The vocabulary of vertical distinctions is full of terms which are both physical and cultural (and spiritual, social, political, and gendered). Postural patterns are charged with social meanings through the association of bodily posture and social position—physically lower with "socially lower," and so on. Hence, when the patterns of straightening, bending, and flattening are commonly associated with certain social meanings, the body acts out the social order.

While there is no Spencerian "primal moment" or fundamental image here, Bourdieu assigns priority to the male-as-sexually dominant/female-as-sexually submissive. Put in this way, it would seem that the Kabyle male's physical strength, and especially the male's sexual conduct, lead to the meaning of the bent/unbent distinction, which then transfers into other specific contexts (such as obeisance). Because verticality is a semiotic code, it leads to the possibility of metaphoric enactment from obeisance to gender or sexual position as well as to and from distinctions of age, rank, ordination, and so on. Indeed, Bourdieu cites age as a natural or "given" distinction: "The act of institution is an act of social magic that can create difference *ex nihilo*, or else (as is more often the case) by exploiting as it were pre-existing differences, like the biological differences between the sexes or ... the difference in age."[29] In other words, "The distinctions that are the most efficacious socially are those which give the appearance of being based on objective differences."[30] Bourdieu's language is cautious and obscure here—"magic"—"as it were"—"give the appearance"—because, as much recent work on the body has shown, it is difficult to say that anything about the body is innate, natural, or "given."[31] The body now seems so profoundly constructed and produced. It is always easy to point to cases where "gender," for example, is manipulated and manufactured, from Barbie/G. I. Joe and blue/pink to debates over marriage equality or rules about wives bowing to husbands.

Spencer sees bowing as colonized culture; Schwartz is more of a psychoanalyst of childhood experience; Bourdieu posits gender as the most important of the "given" differences which make obeisance "natural" but, like Schwartz, backs away from assigning a fixed "origin" of obeisance. In other words, obeisance makes sense not because of any specific analogy to fighting or being a baby or experiencing sexual difference but rather by analogy to vertical distinction. High/low functions much like yin/yang as an intermediary currency between otherwise distinct relations. It is because of the abstraction of a distinction like high/low that we can move easily from one kind of relationship to another. Naturally, sometimes people speak of bowing as a kind of defeated submission to brute force, and as a kind of feminine position, and as like being a baby. With recourse to images of obeisance, Victorian Protestants could speak of Catholics being like the Chinese. And we find these analogies mixed together, reinforcing each other. Authority is so essential to social order that it is always over-determined.

We are never just dealing with two pairs of distinctions but with multitudes. So far, we have looked at Spencer's ruler/ruled, Schwartz's father/son, and Bourdieu's husband/wife. If we add older-younger, plus the category friends, we have the traditional Confucian list of five fundamental human relations (*wulun*).[32] At first sight, the category "friend" appears as something of an exception, but friendship was often modeled on brotherhood, with the two terms *xiong* (older brother) and *di* (younger brother) functioning to indicate an older friend and a younger friend.[33] In other words, "friends" and the kinship structure would seem to follow the same logic, although undoubtedly "friends" is much looser and less codified.

Theorizing obeisance

According to the context, the body is a display of membership in certain group categories in seemingly natural, native or biological ways: pigmentation, hair, physical features, the size and appearance of the body. These features are of course ambiguous, having in themselves no absolute meaning. It is not only that we can manipulate our bodies to change a physical feature but also (and more importantly) that we can change the meaning of a bodily datum. In the previous chapters I have mentioned ordination and capping as examples of rituals (deployments of bodies following scripts) which transform the person, marking a clear line between before and after. And in some cases, the body is marked by this border-crossing, such as by a shaven head or by clothes. Bourdieu said that rituals which consecrate a body (as thereby belonging to a distinct new category) draw lines which can seem arbitrary, yet become real in the performance and in the changed social meanings.[34] As Foucault remarked, "the body is also directly involved in a political field; power relations have an immediate hold upon it; they invest it, mark it, train it, torture it, force it to carry out tasks, to perform ceremonies, to emit signs."[35] To make these movements habitual and thus "natural," we drill them into our bodies: in that sense, Foucault described the modern soldier as a *product*.[36]

What is the relationship between bodies and boundaries (such as the boundaries between bodies)? If we say that acts *represent* social distinctions, it would seem that such boundaries already exist "elsewhere," at a more natural, real or significant level, which ritual acts then "reflect." This other "level" might be conceived of as, for example, imbalances in economic capital, genetic superiority, seniority, real or perceived strength in combat, or presence of the divine—in other words, insert your reality here. In this representational view, the bow has meaning only as a reflecting enactment of authority, or as an expression of an inner feeling of respect or awe, or as a representation of a power imbalance. This is the basis of those arguments in 662 which sought to portray disobeisance as unnatural. Chinese ritual theory included the idea that ritual reflected reality but also that ritual participated in reality, in a cosmic sense. For most Confucians, the correct performance of ritual was a moral act, and furthermore Heaven could sense and respond to morality.

Bourdieu certainly saw ritual action as representation.[37] But he tended to privilege economic capital as the grounds and measure of accumulation of other capitals. In his treatments of intellectual and educational fields, for example, he described how the structure of these fields is determined by imbalances of wealth. Ritual action, in those fields and in general, was a representation of economic difference. However, he stressed the ability of representations and rituals to have real effects.[38] Rituals are not *mere* rituals. To ordain is to make a claim of transition from one category to another, of crossing a boundary created in part by such acts of occasionally crossing it, as in an ordination ritual or by monastic disrobing. The dimensions of that "other" that one has now become are displayed in the details of one's body. The discipline of ritual creates both a body and a representation of a body—inseparably. And not only a body but a self: in Foucault's terms, the individual is "fabricated" by discipline.[39]

Catherine Bell wrote about the function of the bow, not only to signify or refer elsewhere but to embody hierarchy by the very act itself: "required kneeling does not merely *communicate* subordination to the kneeler. For all intents and purposes, kneeling produces a subordinated kneeler in and through the act itself."⁴⁰ Within a given context, obeisance practice creates at least two subject positions: the one bowing and the one bowed to. (There are also observers, and though I have said little of them, it must surely be that the pro-bow officials wanted very much to *see* monks bow to the emperor because they felt the monks' disobeisance challenged their own position in the social order and the moral welfare of the state.)

Foucault wanted to account for historical changes in the "self" through investigation of changes in the treatment of the body and in the material and classificatory structures which give the body some context and mediate the body to others. He wrote: "The individual is not a pre-given entity which is seized on by the exercise of power. The individual, with his identity and characteristics, is the product of a relation of power exercised over bodies, multiplicities, movements, desires, forces."⁴¹ As *Discipline and Punish* demonstrates, this exercise of power may be analyzed in its specific mechanisms, its strategies rather than as an abstract force acting on an individual conceived of apart from the exercise of power. The mechanisms matter. And here, we look at the negotiation over what specific bows were allowed (the monk's *changyi* to the emperor but not his *ketou*; the knee bending but not the torso). Foucault said, "Discipline is a political anatomy of detail."⁴²

One of the interesting features of obeisance as an object of analysis is that is gives us a vivid picture and quantifiable measure of social differences. In Thailand, for example, you could almost literally use a yardstick. You can watch people greet each other and quantify the vertical difference. The standard gesture of greeting is called a *wai*. This consists of putting the palms together and bending forward. But there are many kinds of *wai*, and they are ordered in three ways: first, the vertical distinction: the *wai* can be as high as your forehead—to the King or a senior monk. To parents and elders, the hands come together directly in front of your face. To those who are comparable in seniority or slightly higher, the ends of your fingers are at the chin. And to children or obvious inferiors, the *wai* was is in the center of your chest. Second, the tilt forward. In many social interactions only the head bows, but when greeting monks or superiors, the torso tilts as well. Third, sequence: the junior initiates the *wai*, and the senior returns it at the same or lower level. So you never return a *wai* any higher than the *wai* offered to you. Of course, there are many ways to fudge it, if seniority is unclear or if you don't want to come off all haughty. But here is a vertical distinction built into a gesture that has become so iconic of Siamese culture they use it in their airline advertisements.

Combining the representational and embodied approaches to ritual treats bowing as a strategy which both creates and reflects distinctions: you bow to the senior monk because he is senior, but the meaning of seniority is constituted by such acts as the obeisance of juniors—especially when we are dealing with, say, a fifty-year-old monk who ordained last year bowing to a thirty-year-old monk who ordained ten summers ago. For a new monk, a new kind of seniority became applicable at his ordination, and it was visible in the world as a bow.

The relationship of embodiment and representation brings us to the homology, in which two pairs of qualitatively different distinctions, such as up-down and future-past, are paired, so that (in a certain context) it makes sense to say that up is future, down is past. Or, as evident in the Chinese terms, that up is past and down is future: *shang* is up and the past, *xia* is down and the future.[43] In the Chinese language, one's ancestors are high up in front of you, and descendants lower and behind you. You would not turn your back on, or look down on, your ancestors. We can homologize up/down to all sorts of other distinctions, moral, social, or spiritual. The correlation of sets of oppositions is a particular forté of traditional Chinese thought: *yin* and *yang* are above all floating signifiers, always able to be applied to any given distinction.

Up/down can be widely applied to many different pairs of contrasts (male/female, monk/laity, etc.) but also to other schemata, such as inner/outer, front/back, and before/after. Generally speaking, in China, to be higher was also to be inner, because of the strong assertion of centrality in Chinese culture. The outer was generally the lesser, so that for example Buddhists called non-Buddhist teachings *waidao*, outer paths. In chapter one, I noted the injunction to step into a temple as far from the center as possible, as a manifestation of humility. Left and right were also asymmetrical, as for example in the term *pangmen zuodao*, "side doors and left-hand paths," meaning heresy, sorcery, or deviance—although the emperor's left was the more honored side in court. Up/down is always a more obvious schema than left/right. Although a left/right distinction can signal hierarchical status, so can any distinction. Differences in color, use of ritual or valuable objects, titles, access to specific locations, who has a corner office, who the waiter presents the bill to, anything can signal status difference. But "only vertical opposition will do for the representation of equality itself."[44]

The Sangha's internal organization consisted of correlated sets of distinctions (high/low, male/female, etc.) which functioned as criteria for determining who bows to whom. Monastic training thereby emplaced "the most fundamental structures of the group in the primary experiences of the body"[45] —first, by mapping reverence onto the body in the form of head-foot distinctions, and second, by making distinctions (of age, gender) the monk's guide to bodily action and orientation.

Just as, in conventional use, topography is the representation of differences of land elevation, ritual topography is the charting of systems of ordering bodies according to distinctions of height. In obeisance, vertical distinction is the primary metaphoric principle of the homology, which, crucially, can be embodied (because it is spatial) and can be spoken of and associated with other pairs of distinctions, such as:

| up | old | male | monk |
| down | young | female | laity |

The matching of these pairs occurs in a diffuse manner wherever anyone bows. This matching is performed as a focus of attention (or at least, of perception), even if only of one's own attention. The bow points upward to an object, and in so doing, participates in the creation of that object, and in the creation of the relationship between self and object. The subject of a bow and its object are not absolute entities but are made by their physical mediation. The bowing debates thus concerned the subjective and objective constitution of both sovereign and monk. The "lofty" really *were* higher—measurably, in feet and inches, on a throne, or by sitting when another person lies flat on the floor.

Labor was required to make sure the physical reality matched the homology. Bowing requires some stage management. The "playing field" of social interactions is indeed not level anywhere, but the flat balance of the floor serves as a starting point for a demonstration of imbalance. During a full prostration, even the floor rises and falls, closer or farther away from one's forehead.

So far, I have posited obeisance as constituting a subject and an object and the relation between them and that refusing to bow (in a situation where obeisance is expected) is simply the non-participation in that relationship. But disobeisance creates another kind of body, neither the subject nor object of obeisance. Perhaps *dis-* is the wrong prefix—if it were not such an ugly coinage, I might suggest ab-obeisance.[46] After all, a monk not bowing to the emperor was only a problem when they actually faced each other. Outside of that situation, not bowing to the emperor was a non-event. The monks did not merely not-bow but positioned themselves pointedly "outside" the bowing relationship, in the game but not playing it. Viewed this way, we can see the logic of non-dualism in their rhetoric of being "guests." Neither master nor servant but in the house nonetheless.

7

Disobeisance Today

An analogous case

Meeting a king is not like meeting a president. Sometimes it seems the modern West has somehow dispensed with bowing altogether, but we still see it: people in church, actors at the end of a play, and at the martial arts dojo, and in period dramas and fantasy films, and when CNN runs a story about Islam or Japanese businessmen or samurai or royalty, and when Fox runs a story about Obama in Saudi Arabia or Japan. But if we use my more conceptual definition, if bowing is the performance of a vertical distinction, we see it whenever someone lowers their gaze out of deference or fear. Or when people speak of God, and look up. Daoxuan told his novices to look down, and the lowered gaze has not become a sign of superiority.

And after all, first on Daoxuan's list of "expressions of respect" was a *word*. (*Namu*.) If we also allow for discursive obeisance, rhetorical one-downmanship, we hear it whenever anyone speaks of hierarchy. It is ingrained in our languages, in the ways we think. Vertical distinction certainly has not gone away.

Bowing, and a discomfort with bowing, permeate modern Western culture. Even though one doesn't do it, the semiotic system survives. If the debate of 662 was happening now, I wonder how Fox News would report it. It might depend on who was president at the time. It could be presented as a weird non-Christian group's scandalous failure to respect the dignity of the office of the President; or it might be an example of the President's overweening pride and ambition in contrast to those patriotic Americans who regard the Federal government with suspicion. Even on Fox, there would be outrage if any American president actually *demanded* obeisance by an

American citizen, beyond a general "respect for the office" which would not involve actual kneeling. Respect for the office is usually invoked in a partisan way to rebuke criticism of a particular president, and it is hard to imagine a President actually demanding a kowtow. We have found other ways to signal our supplication.

In America, much of the sacrality of the king has been transferred to the flag. We have something in recent history quite analogous to the 662 debate, in the cultural politics of the American flag. Many writers on this topic have noted how the flag is a sacred object, if only in the context of what Robert Bellah and others have called civil religion. When we look, for example, at a text like *Manual on Flag Etiquette* issued by the Georgia State Department of Education (Atlanta, 1938), we find a straightforward proposition, "the flag of the United States is a thing that men die for, and it is a sacred thing. Disrespect for the flag symbolizes disrespect of law and indifference and ill will toward our great national establishment of government and country."[1]

The *Manual* gives rules about where the US flag should be displayed, relative to other flags, in general "at the center or at the highest point"[2] No others should be above it on a pole. When displayed with a flag of another nation in a time of peace, the two should be precisely equal in height, according to "international usage."[3] So the logic is explicitly vertical—this flag above others—and then an exception is made due to something like diplomatic immunity, or more specifically to the sovereign equality of states, as enshrined for example in Article two of the United Nations charter. The theory of the equality of nations (and the placement of flags) is horizontal, even as the practice of international relations is endlessly vertical. Yet the American flag does not "dip" in the Olympic opening ceremonies, as other flags do in recognition of the host country. The American skier Bill Koch declared his intention to dip the American flag at the 1992 Winter Olympics in France but changed his mind under media and peer pressure.[4]

In rules for the flag's orientation, and in other directions, we find a kind of body or subject position attributed to the flag. The flag is given a subjective position of it's own, as when the manual refers to the placement of objects relative "to the flag's own right—i.e., to the observer's left."[5] The top of the flag is correlated with the head of a person, or more precisely a corpse: "When used to cover a casket, the flag should be placed so that the union is at the head and over the left shoulder. The flag should not be lowered into the grave or allowed to touch the ground."[6] Graves are for dead things, the ground is for the fallen.

With the prohibition on putting a flag in a grave, we come close to acknowledging the consciousness and agency of an insentient object. In his book on the anthropology of objects, Alfred Gell describes how consciousness follows the path of our gaze upon inanimate things:

> Animacy takes its origin from this ocular exchange, because, even if one does not take a mystical attitude towards images, one is none the less entitled to apply action verbs like "look" (or "smile," "gesticulate," etc.) to them. A perfect sceptic can say, in fact is obliged to say, that an idol "looks" in a particular direction; the remark would pass unnoticed because everybody accepts that the criterion for idols "looking" is that their eyes should be open and pointed in a particular direction.[7]

The flag has no eyes but certainly a "face." If the flag has a face and a head, has purity which should not be violated, might die if it touched the ground, is looked upon and in turn looks upon us, the civil animism of flag-saluting takes us to the edge of the purported separation of church and state. The *Manual on Flag Etiquette* says, "A flag is more than a piece of cloth with something printed on it."[8] There have been attempts to make the flag mystical and holy, linking it to Masonic symbols, or to the Bible.[9] This effort may be comparable to the notion of the cosmic status of the Chinese emperor, though the analogy is not at all precise. It is an assertion of a kind of non-duality of flag and nation, like icon and Buddha. In either case, to refuse to kowtow or salute is regarded as refusing the dignity of the very cosmos, like shunning God. Pat Buchanan linked flag with "mother," so that refusing to salute became a kind of filial impiety.[10] He might have had more to say on the topic if he had read the Medieval Chinese bowing debates, with their easy correlation of rulers and parents.

It is hardly surprising that in America the primary language of disobeisance is that of idolatry. During the debates about flag desecration in the 1980s, Congressman George Brown stated, "No flag that symbolizes a ruler or state is sacred. To even speak in such terms denies the primacy of God in the world, demeans the spiritual basis of freedom and democracy and smacks of idolatry."[11] Congressman Ron Paul had similar objections, based more on a hostility to the deification of government than to worries about God's primacy.

I don't have a lot of interest in talking to the missionaries who knock on my door on Sundays, but if I find they're Jehovah's Witnesses, at least I have one thing to talk about. They don't salute the flag. When I ask them about it, they're always well prepared, so this is clearly something they're known for, and part of their identity. On one occasion the missionary had a ring-binder with well-designed pages printed on card stock, indexed by topic, and one of the tabs was for the page about not saluting the flag. Watchtower Online Library also has a section on this problematic abstention. "Jehovah's Witnesses believe that bowing down to a flag or saluting it, often in conjunction with an anthem, is a religious act that ascribes salvation, not to God, but to the State or to its leaders."[12]

In the late 1930s and 1940s, many American states requires all students to recite the pledge of allegiance and salute the American flag. Many Jehovah's Witness children would not, and around two thousand children were expelled from schools by 1940. A Supreme Court ruling in 1943 struck down the compulsory flag salute, arguing from the principle of individual liberty. The irony was often noted, of being forced to salute a flag which stands for freedom, including the freedom from being forced to salute it.[13]

On the one hand, I can't help thinking the idea is absurd, that they can somehow suspend their participation in political idolatry simply by sitting down when everyone else stands up. On the other hand, I'm not much of a nationalist myself, and I like that there's this group of people who don't treat the icons of nation-states as holy objects. Like the Jehovah's Witnesses, I certainly consider saluting the flag as a form of bowing. True, we don't lower ourselves, but we spend a stiff, solemn moment looking up, to the top of a pole (a device whose sole purpose is to raise a flag). Saluting the flag is a formal occasion on which we pointedly focus on an object deliberately raised up higher than ourselves. And the gesture is sometimes accompanied by a spoken formula, pledging "allegiance" to it, "and to the Republic for which it stands." The notion that one might *have* allegiance to what it stands for but not *show* allegiance to the object itself is precisely the gist of the Supreme Court decision of 1943, and also the gist of the monks' argument that respect unperformed is not respect unfelt, and also the gist of the moderate Reformers' argument that a bow of the body is not necessarily a bow of the heart.

This "idolatry" is also periodically contested in public performances such as placing the flag underfoot. There was a moral panic over the flag in art, during the 1980s. Protesters chanted: "One, two, three, four, get the flag up off the floor."[14] The horror at the flag on the floor and the likelihood of someone stepping on it was countered with the rhetorics of both artistic freedom, and idolatry. Much of modern art has been about provocative dethronement. Obviously, the art motive has nothing in common with 662. The monks expressed no concept of individual freedom of expression. They did not refuse to kowtow to the emperor in order to demonstrate that the emperor should not be kowtowed to.

I have a basic personal sympathy for those who object to the idolatry of the flag. On the other hand, sometimes I think, what's your problem? Get over it. Once I went to a ball game with a cousin of mine, and his girlfriend. We were running a few minutes late, so we were not quite in the stadium when the national anthem started. Over the fence, we could see the flag. My cousin was fresh out of the Marines, and he stopped right there. He said, "Excuse me, I gotta do this." He saluted and stood tall, there in the parking lot. I stood around a little baffled—I'd never saluted the Union Jack. A bunch of boys went past, snickering, and without changing his saluting posture my cousin said "fuck you" to them, out of the side of his mouth. The anthem ended, and the rest of the afternoon has vanished from my memory. In a small way, it took principle and a kind of moral courage to salute the flag.

Bowing and me

Sometimes I conjure up a very appealing tableau vivant: the most powerful man in the world on his throne, and everyone is on the floor bowing to him except this one monk, who merely puts his hands together and smiles. The image includes a few frowns on the faces of the stuffed shirts and professional ass-kissers. It appeals to a certain "tribal" affiliation I feel toward the Buddhist monks in this particular case.

I began to contemplate Buddhist bowing when I started visiting temples in Thailand, in 1980. Like many Westerners, for me, Buddhism was at first a kind of psychological philosophy, or philosophical psychology, associated with meditation but also with haiku, motorcycle maintenance, Thoreau, and Yoda. Alan Watts, Aldous Huxley, and Thomas Merton may have been wise men, but they weren't anthropologists. Perennial Philosophers never gave much attention to what the millions of Buddhists in Asia actually did. So naturally I had a bit of a culture shock when I arrived in Thailand, a "Buddhist country," filled with Buddhists who as far as I could tell knew almost nothing of the Dharma. I never saw anyone meditate. The only thing they ever did that was at all Buddhist was going to the temples and bowing. Sometimes they even *asked for stuff*. For the briefest moment I contemplated the possibility that I (and the Western men I'd been reading) were right, and all these millions were wrong. But instead I adjusted, and enlarged my concept of what "Buddhism" is. I have never been able to believe that there's anything "actually there" in the Buddha image, but at least I got over myself and joined in when my Thai friends bowed. To say that I was a Buddhist and yet not bow in a temple would have struck them as bizarre.

On occasion I had my doubts about "being a Buddhist." Was the "tribal" affiliation contrary to my own practice? I never thought I was violating some innate human dignity by bowing. I was never concerned about idolatry. In my most religious moments of bowing, I just took it as an occasion for a little bit of humble introspection, but at the same time I always felt like a "participant observer," because of my fundamental lack of belief. In later years I have thought that maybe belief is not that important.

It used to be a reasonable generalization that in the West, Buddhism was treated as mediation only, or philosophy, or psychology. In the early history of the spread of Buddhism in America, for example, outside of "ethnic communities," few were interested in bowing—it was too devotional. Many of the early converts or enthusiasts were interested in Buddhism not only in itself but as a way to think their way out of Christianity, and in that counter-religious mode there was little patience for all that groveling. The more explicitly devotional forms of Buddhism have taken longer to spread, such as Jodo Shinshu, and Tibetan Buddhism. Still today there is very limited interest in Chinese Pure Land outside of China. Zen, the supposedly most "iconoclastic" form of Buddhism, has in practice embraced the bow, as a visit to almost any zendo in America will show. A student of Zen, Andi Young, wrote *The Sacred Art of Bowing: Preparing to Practice*. Her path was not that different from my own: She discovered meditation as a teenager; "I thought that Buddhism was *only* meditation."[15] Then during a four-month stay in Nepal, face to face with actual practice, she started to take bowing more seriously.

And yet, listen to this explanation. At her Korean Zen center, "We also bow to the Buddha on the altar, not because he is superior to us, but because we, like the Buddha, have Buddha-nature, or the potential to "wake up" and attain enlightenment."[16] The idea of bowing without thought of superiority seems paradoxical, and yet such a non-dual understanding was the very pinnacle of bowing according to Daoxuan. Here the bow is an assertion of equality, at least in potential. "But we shouldn't think too much about bowing. All the symbolism and meaning involved in bowing is just explanation; bowing, really, is *just bowing*, putting our hands together and bending our knees."[17] She treats bowing the same way she treats zazen. You should *just bow* the way you should *just sit*. And yet, having worked through Daoxuan, surely there is a long-standing basis of this meditation-oriented view.

And Young is a more dedicated practitioner than me. In the end, I suspect the best I have ever managed was *changheli*, "the bow of chanting together," or social bowing. According to Daoxuan, I should not expect too much of it. "The demeanor is roughly correct, the body and mind are reverent, and rising and falling are co-ordinated, [but still,] ... the blessing is thin and meager. It is not a true offering."[18]

I'll do it anyway.

Appendix: Further Information on the Debate Participants

Each debate participant is listed with his institution and rank. The speeches are listed according to the hierarchical sequence: ministries (*bu*), courts (*si*), directories (*jian*), military units, and provincial administrative units (prefecture [*fu*], county [*xian*]).

Speakers from the six Ministries (*bu*) are listed: Rites, Revenue, War and Justice (anti-bow), and Personnel and Works (pro-bow). The ranks of these speaker vary, with a somewhat higher show for the anti-bow side: speakers included a vice-minister and a "Dynasty-founding Marquis."

Grand Executive Attendant (i.e. Minister) Wang Peicha and Grand Master (Bureau Director) Kong Zhiyue are listed under the Ministry of Rites but are also from the highest ranking unit, *Zhongtai* (variant name for Department of State Affairs, higher in rank than the Six Ministries). These two seem to have spoken for other units as well: following their listing on the "contents page" at the beginning of fascicle three of the *Collection*, is the note. "The Courageous Guard of the Right, the Gate Guard of the Right, the Personal Guard of the Right and the Guanfusi[1]; these four offices ask to agree with the argument of the Ministry of Rites" (i.e. Wang Peicha and Kong Zhiyue). This note supports the idea that each speaker spoke for his administrative unit, although representatives of the Personal Guard of the Right (anti-bow) and the Gate Guard of the Right (pro-bow) also give presentations later.[2]

Courts. Anti-bow: Imperial Sacrifices, Judicial Review, Imperial Granaries, Imperial Treasury. Pro-bow: Imperial Sacrifices, Imperial Entertainments, Imperial Regalia, Imperial Stud, Judicial Review, and Diplomatic Relations. (Missing: Court of the Imperial Clan, Court of State Ceremonials.) Pro- and anti- overlap here in two cases: Imperial Sacrifices and Judicial Review. Setting those aside, we see Granaries and Treasury supporting the monks, opposed to a series of Courts very directly associated with the emperor's ritual body: Entertainments, Regalia, Stud,[3] and Diplomatic Relations.

Appendix: Further Information on the Debate Participants 147

It is interesting that no one from the Courts of the Imperial Clan (*Zongzhengsi*) and of State Ceremonials (*Honglusi*) spoke in the debate. The *Zongzhengsi* maintained the imperial genealogy and dealt with imperial relatives, who also formed most of the staff. Supervised by the Ministry of Rites, the *Honglusi* dealt with audiences with foreign dignitaries, state funerals, and other state rituals. One would expect these two Courts to be represented in the debate, and one can only speculate on why they were not.

Directorates. Anti-bow: Palace Buildings, Education. Pro-bow: Imperial Manufactures, Waterways. (Missing: Armaments.) It seems peculiar that the Chancellor (Linghu Defen) and a "probationary erudite" of the Directorate of Education (two speeches) should argue against forcing monks to bow. We would expect the influence of rationalized, ideological Confucianism to be strong in imperially sponsored scholarly circles.

Military units. The most striking difference between the pro- and anti-bow representatives of military units is the predominance on the pro-bow side of representatives from military units associated with the Heir Apparent Li Hong (Prince Pei, eldest son of Wu Zetian). These are: Left and Right Military Guard, Left and Right Office of Protectorate Guard, Left Police Patrol Guard Command,[4] Left and Right Guard Honoring the Inner Apartments, and the Left and Right Good Fortune Guard. Also there are four non-military units associated with the Heir Apparent on the pro-bow side: Household Administration of the Heir Apparent, Left and Right Secretariat of the Heir Apparent, and the Court of the Watches. The anti-bow side has the Right Secretariat of the Heir Apparent, and the Livery Service of the Heir Apparent, and eight military units but no military units explicitly identifiable as assigned to the Heir Apparent. In other words, there seems to have been a strong pro-bow lobby coming from the Heir Apparent or from his assigned bureaucratic and guard units.[5] Since at this time, Li Hong was only nine years old, this strong lobby certainly indicates Wu Zhao "active behind the scenes."[6]

Regional officials. Seven officials from four regional offices spoke as anti-bow; one official spoke as pro-bow.

148 Appendix: Further Information on the Debate Participants

i. Institutional affiliations and ranks of debate participants

(a) List of lay officials arguing for not-bowing. *Jishamen buyingbaisu dengshi*, fascicle 3, 454c. and 459c.

1. Wang Peicha — Dept. of State Affairs, Min. of Rites, Grand Executive Attendant (= Minister), of Longxi
2. Kong Zhiyue — Dept. of State Affairs, Min. of Rites, Grand Master (= Bureau Director)
3. Dou Dexuan — Min. of Revenue, Grand Executive Attendant
4. Zhang Shanshou — Min. of Revenue, Junior Executive Attendant
5. Zheng Qintai — Min. of War, Bureau of Military Appointments, Junior Executive Attendant
6. Qin Huaike — Min. of War, Vice-Minister
7. Liu Xiangdao — Min. of Justice, Bureau of Judicial Administration, Grand Executive Attendant; Dynasty-founding Marquis of Chengyang xian
8. Gao Yaoshang — Palace Administration, Vice-Director, Military Protector
9. Hu Xuanliang — Palace Domestic Service, Executive Attendant, Erudite
10. Liu Qingdao — Court of Imperial Sacrifices, Aide
11. Hao Chujie — Court of Imperial Sacrifices, Recorder
12. Wang Qianshi — Court of Judicial Review, Aide
13. Zhang Daosun — Court of Judicial Review, Aide
14. Liang Xiaoren — Court of the Imperial Granaries, Chief Minister
15. Zhao Xingben — Imperial Graneries Office, Director
16. Wei Siqi — Court of Imperial Treasury, Chief Minister
17. Jia Ju — Court of Imperial Treasury, Recorder.
18. Liu Shen — Directorate for the Palace Buildings, Director; Acting as high official to the Tujue
19. Linghu Defen — Directorate of Education, Chancellor
20. Fan Yijun — Directorate of Education, probationary erudite.
21. Zhang Yenshi — Guard of the Left, General-in-chief
22. Cui Xiuye — Guard of the Right, Administrator
23. Wang Xuan — Courageous Guard of the Left, Administrator
24. Cao Xiaoguan — Courageous Guard of the Left, Horseman [*ceqi*]

Appendix: Further Information on the Debate Participants 149

25.	Xu Qing	Militant Guard of the Right, Administrator
26.	Li Hui	Militant and Awesome Guard of the Right, General.
27.	Du Junchuo	Martial Guard of the Left, General-in-chief
28.	Chuan Shancai	Imperial Insignia Guard of the Left, General; Supreme Pillar of State, Dynasty-founding Marquis
29.	Xin Hongliang	Personal Guard of the Right, General
30.	Xie Shou	Secretariat of the Heir Apparent of the Right, Secretary
31.	Wang Sitai	Livery Service of the Heir Apparent, Grand Master
32.	Niu Xuanzhang	Livery Service of the Heir Apparent, Aide
33.	Yuan Chengxin	Wannian (xian) District Magistrate
34.	Wang Fangze	Chang-an xian, Aide
35.	Cui Daomei	Chang-an xian, Aide
36.	Huang Fu	Peiwang fu, Administrator
37.	Chen Zhide	Peiwang fu, Instructor
38.	Yuan Zhenxin	Zhouwang fu, Administrator
39.	Yuan Sijing	Zhouwang fu, adjunct

(b) List of lay officials arguing for compromise positions. juan 5. 464c-465a.

1.	Cui Andu	Awesome Guard of the Left, Administrator
2.	Chen Xuanming	Awesome Guard of the Left, Office Manager
3.	Li Xia Police	Patrol Guard Command of the Right [of the Heir Apparent], Administrator
4.	Zhang Songshou	Chang-an District Magistrate

(c) List of lay officials arguing for bowing. juan 5. 465a.

1.	Yang Sixuan	Dept. of State Affairs, Min. of Personnel, Junior Executive Attendant
2.	Yang Shouzhuo	Dept. of State Affairs, Min. of Personnel, Bureau of Evaluations, Grand Master
3.	Yan Liben	Ministry of Works, Grand Executive Attendant
4.	Li Chunfeng	Orchid Pavilion (Palace Library), Director of the Astrological Service
5.	Lü Cai	Court of Imperial Sacrifices, erudite

6.	Dou Lujian	Court of Imperial Entertainments, Aide.
7.	Yang Sijian	Court of Imperial Regalia, Chief Minister
8.	Han Chuxuan	Court of the Imperial Stud, Aide
9.	Yuan *dashi*	Court of Judicial Review, Vice-Minister
10.	Xie You	Court of Diplomatic Relations, Aide
11.	Liu Yuanzhen	Directorate for Imperial Manufactures, Aide
12.	Li Renfang	Directorate of Waterways, [no rank listed]
13.	Zhao Chongsu	Militant Guard of the Right, Military Service Section, adjunct.
14.	Li Yifan	Martial Guard of the Right, Administrator
15.	Xuegu Wuren	Imperial Insignia Guard of the Right, General
16.	Liu Wenzong	Imperial Insignia Guard of the Right, Administrator
17.	Neng Xuanyi	Palace Gate Guard of the Right, Commandant
18.	Li Kuan	Household Administration of the Heir Apparent, Supervisor of the Household
19.	He Lanmin	Secretariat of the Heir Apparent of the Left, Mentor (=Head of the Secretariat)
20.	Yang Lingjie	Secretariat of the Heir Apparent of the Left, Admonisher
21.	Hao Chujun	Secretariat of the Heir Apparent of the Right, Mentor
22.	Yang Sizheng	Secretariat of the Heir Apparent of the Right, Admonisher
23.	Zhang Yue	Court of the Watches [headed by Director/*ling* of Household Administration of the Heir Apparent], Aide
24.	Wang Jiusi	Militant Guard of the Left [in establishment of the Heir Apparent], Granaries Section, [no rank given]
25.	Husi Jingze	Militant Guard of the Right, General
26.	Ma *dashi*	Office of the Protectorate Guard of the Left [of the Heir Apparent], Administrator
27.	Cui Chongye	Office of the Protectorate Guard of the Right, Administrator
28.	Jiang Zhenzhou	Police Patrol Guard Command of the Left [of Heir Apparent], Administrator

Appendix: Further Information on the Debate Participants   151

29. Dou Shangyi   Guard Honoring the Inner Apartments of the Left [of Heir Apparent], Administrator
30. Li Xingmin   Guard Honoring the Inner Apartments of the Right, Administrator
31. Qiu Shenjing   Good Fortune Guard of the Left [of Heir Apparent], Administrator
32. Wei Huaijing   Good Fortune Guard of the Right, Commandant
33. Liu Renrui   Yongzhou, Personnel Manager

Notes

Chapter 1

1 Zhu Hong, *Shami lüyi yaolue* (Essential Summary of Sramanera discipline). Cited in *Deren Foxue Xingzhuyishi*, p. 108.
2 T. vol. 45, no. 1897.
3 Ibid., section 4, no. 30, p. 870b.
4 Ibid., section 5, no. 51, p. 870c.
5 Ibid., section 5, no. 55, p. 871a.
6 Ibid., section 3, no. 32, p. 869c.
7 Ibid., section 1, no. 1, p. 869b.
8 Ibid., section 14, no. 3, p. 872c.
9 Ibid., section 14, no. 4, pp. 872c–873a.
10 Ibid., section 14, no. 11, p. 873a.
11 Daoxuan, *Xingshichao*, T. vol. 40, no. 1806, pp. 140c–141a. The full title is: *Sifenlü shanfan buque xingshichao* ("Guide to Practice of the Four-part Vinaya, with Troublesome Points Removed and Deficiencies Rectified"). See also Shi Zhiyu, *Nanshan lüxue cidian*, (Dictionary of the Nanshan school of Vinaya) (Taipei: Xilian jinglan chubanshe, 1996), pp. 870–871.
12 Daoxuan, *Xingshichao*, p. 141b; *Nanshan lüxue cidian*, p. 873.
13 *Xingshichao*, p. 141b. *Nanshan lüxue cidian*, pp. 872–873.
14 Daoxuan, *Jiaojie lüyi* ("Admonitions for the New Student-Monks to Maintain Discipline"), section 1, no. 8, p. 869b.
15 Ibid., section 4, no. 17, p. 870a.
16 Ibid., section 4, no. 18, p. 870a. The difference between these two terms, *menkun* and *menxian*, is still unclear. There are also other terms for door-sill: *menkan* (two variants).
17 Lu Xun, "The New-Year Sacrifice," in *Selected Works*, vol. 1, trans. Yang Xianyi and Gladys Yang (Beijing: Foreign Languages Press, 1956), p. 185.
18 Daoxuan, *Jiaojie lüyi*, section 5, no. 39, p. 870c.
19 Ibid., section 5, no. 41, p. 870c.
20 Ibid., section 5, no. 42, p. 870c.

21 Ibid., section 1, no. 5, p. 869b.
22 Ibid., section 3, no. 24, p. 869c.
23 Ibid., section 3, no. 31, p. 869c.
24 Ronald G. Knapp, *China's Living Houses: Folk Beliefs, Symbols, and Household Ornamentation* (Honolulu: University of Hawaii Press, 1999), p. 36.
25 Michel Foucault, *Discipline and Punish: The Birth of the Prison*, trans. Alan Sheridan (New York: Vintage Books, 1979), p. 152. Or: the "instrumental coding of the body. It consists of a breakdown of the total gesture into two parallel series: that of the parts of the body to be used [or conspicuously not used, e.g. one's foot] … and that of the parts of the object manipulated." Ibid., p. 153.
26 Ibid., p. 153.
27 Ibid., p. 172.
28 Knapp, *China's Living Houses*, p. 7.
29 Daoxuan, *Shimen guijingyi* ("Buddhist Rites of Obeisance"), T. 45, no. 1896, pp. 854–868.
30 Daoxuan, *Jiaojie lüyi*, section 1, no. 6, p. 869b.
31 Ibid., section 18, p. 873b. A similar list appears in *Lijing Fota*, (Putian: Guanghua Temple, n.d.), p. 1.
32 Daoxuan, *Jiaojie lüyi*, section 3, no. 3–4, p. 869c.
33 Barry Schwartz, Abraham Tesser and Evan Powell, "Dominance Cues in Nonverbal Behavior," *Social Psychology Quarterly*, vol. 45, no. 2 (1982), p. 115.
34 Daoxuan, *Jiaojie lüyi*, section 4, no. 9, p. 870a.
35 Zanning, *Song gaosengzhuan* (Biographies of eminent monks compiled in the Song), T. 50, no. 2061, p. 790c, 791b.
36 Daoxuan, *Jiaojie lüyi*, section 7, no. 18, p. 871b.
37 Ibid., section 6, no. 29, p. 871a.
38 Ibid., section 8, no. 11, p. 871c.
39 This image was famously depicted by Thomas Kubota, in *Chinese and Indian Architecture* by Nelson Wu (1963).
40 Yifa, *The Origins of the Buddhist Monastic Codes in China: A Annotated Translation and Study of the Chanyuan Qinggui*. A Kuroda Institute Book (Honolulu: University of Hawaii, 2002), pp. 87–90.
41 See Ronald G. Knapp, *Chinese Houses: The Architectural Heritage of a Nation* (North Clarendon: Tuttle, 2005), pp. 20–31.
42 Pierre Bourdieu, *The Logic of Practice*. trans. Richard Nice (Stanford: Stanford University, 1990), pp. 30–33; Pierre Bourdieu, *Language and Symbolic Power*, edited by John B. Thompson, trans. Gino Raymond and Matthew Adamson (Cambridge: Harvard University, 1991), pp. 43–46.

Chapter 2

1 Howard J. Wechsler, *Offerings of Jade and Silk: Ritual and Symbol in the Legitimation of the T'ang Dynasty* (New Haven: Yale University Press, 1985), p. 232.

2 Robert M. Somers, "Time, Space and Structure in the Consolidation of the T'ang Dynasty (A.D. 617–700)" in *State and Society in Early Medieval China*, Albert E. Dien ed. (Stanford: Stanford University Press, 1990), p. 372.

3 Preface to *Guizhengpian* (article on reverting to the correct path), in *Guanghongmingji*, T. vol. 52, no. 2103, p. 98a.

4 Howard J. Wechsler, "T'ai-tsung (Reign 626–649) the Consolidator" in *The Cambridge History of China* Vol. 3: Sui and T'ang China, 589–906, Part 1, Denis Twitchett eds (Cambridge: Cambridge University Press, 1979), p. 218.

5 T. vol. 45, no. 1896, pp. 854–869. There are two commentaries. (a) Yanqi (Song), *Shimen guijingyi hufaji*, ("A record of the protection of the Dharma in 'Buddhist Rites of Obeisance' "), first fascicle, *Xuzangjing* [Supplement to the Canon] (Taipei: Xinwenfeng chuban gongsi, 1983) vol. 105, no. 1079, pp. 142–176. (b) Liaoran (Song), *Shimen guijingyi tongzhenji*, compiled by Huiguang (Japan), 3 fascicles, *Xuzangjing*, vol. 105, no. 1080, pp. 177–311.

6 Daoxuan, *Guijingyi*, p. 862a.

7 Third of four fruitions or rewards, ranks of Hinayana attainment.

8 Ibid., p. 855b. From the *Dazhidulun*, T. vol. 25, no. 1509, p. 131a.

9 Daoxuan, *Guijingyi*, p. 855c. Actually, the *Dabeijing* does not have this passage exactly. Daoxuan was paraphrasing from the text, circa p. 959 of T. vol. 12, no. 380.

10 The autobiography of the modern monk Xu Yun features several cases of animals reverently bowing when Xu Yun administers the precepts to them. Xu Yun *Empty Cloud: The Autobiography of the Chinese Zen Master*, trans. Charles Luk (Longmead: Element Books, 1988), pp. 53–54 (cock), p. 75 (cow), p. 91 (raven), pp. 101–102 (geese).

11 Daoxuan, *Guijingyi*, p. 855b. Daoxuan says this story is from the *Fojian pingshawang jing* (The Sutra of the Buddha Meeting King Bimbisara), but I have found no such text. Perhaps Daoxuan is paraphrasing, very loosely, from a passage in *Foshuo pinpoluowang jing* (Sutra spoken by Buddha to King Bimbisara), T. vol 1, no. 41, p. 825c.

12 Daoxuan, *Guijingyi*, p. 855c.

13 Ibid., 855c. See also *Vinaya Texts*, trans. T. W. Rhys Davids and Hermann Oldenberg, Sacred Books of the East, part III (Oxford: Clarendon Press,

1881–1885), pp. 193–194. Some details of the story differ; I have followed the Chinese version. Notably, the Pali version omits the visual image of the bird on the head of the monkey, on the back of the elephant.

14 Daoxuan, *Guijingyi*, p. 464b.
15 There is a similar line in *Yujia shidilun* 瑜伽師地論, T. vol. 30, no. 1579, p. 499b.
16 Daoxuan, *Guijingyi*, p. 861b.
17 Ibid.
18 *Foshuo guanpuxian pusa xingfajing*, (Sutra spoken by Buddha on the method of the practice of contemplating Samantabhadra bodhisattva), T. vol. 9, no. 277, p. 392c.
19 *Shizhu piposha lun*, T. vol. 26. no. 1521.
20 Daoxuan, *Guijingyi*, p. 859c.
21 T. vol. 24, no. 1495, translated by the Sui monk Dunajueduo (Jnanagupta, 523–600), p. 1101b. See also the very similar *Foshuo zhenggongjing jing* (Sutra Spoken by Buddha on the Correct Offering of Respect), T. vol. 24, no. 1496, pp. 1102–1104, translated in the early sixth century by Fotashanduo (Buddhasanta).
22 See Yifa, *The Origins of Buddhist Monastic Codes in China*, pp. 23–24.
23 Daoxuan, *Guijingyi*, pp. 862c–864c. Daoxuan lists twelve forms at ibid., p. 862c, and follows that sequence but loses track of his numbering, so that the explanations which follow blend together 3 and 4, 11 and 12; and though discussing 8 (*hugui*), he skips it in the numbering sequence. I have used the list of twelve at Ibid., p. 862c.
24 Heng Sure, "Sacred Literature into Liturgy: Jingyuan (1011–1088) and the Development of the Avatamsaka Liturgy in Song China," (Ph.D. dissertation. Graduate Theological Union, 2003), pp. 360–362.
25 Daoxuan, *Guijingyi*, p. 862c.
26 Daoxuan notes the meaning of *ji* as "reach," so that in this bow, the head touches the ground. ibid., p. 863a. He gives as a synonym *dunshou*, but notes a change in usage: the "present day practice of *dunshou* is light, it just refers to standing up and bowing the head to empty air." This (strictly speaking) misnamed erect obeisance is also called *changyi* "long salute."
27 Ibid.
28 Ibid., pp. 863a–b.
29 Ibid., p. 863b.
30 Ibid. See also Sure, "Sacred Literature," pp. 155–162.
31 Daoxuan, *Guijingyi*, p. 863c.

32 Ibid., pp. 863c–864a.
33 Ibid., p. 864a.
34 Ibid., pp. 864a–b.
35 Ibid., p., 864b.
36 Ibid., pp. 863b–c.
37 Daoxuan, *Xingshichao* pp. 429–463.
38 Daoxuan, *Guijingyi*, pp. 858c–859a.
39 Ibid., p. 859a.
40 Ibid., p. 856a.
41 Ibid., p. 859a.
42 Ibid., p. 859b.
43 i.e. the lower three of the six paths. Ibid., pp. 858c–859a.
44 Ibid., p. 859a.
45 Ibid., p. 862a. Again, "when roots are blunt and the times are degenerate, firmness in trust is hard to actualize. When practice is shallow and virtue is inferior, it is easy to be deluded about correctness in wisdom." Ibid., p. 860b.
46 Ibid., p. 856a. The overturned vessel is a metaphor for someone who is not receptive to the Dharma, just as water poured on an overturned vessel will not collect in the vessel.
47 Ibid. A reference to the proud arhats in Chapter 2 of the *Lotus Sutra*. 5,000 clerics and laity did obeisance and withdrew, with "deep and grave roots of sin and overweaning pride." Buddha remains silent and does not restrain them. They are the "branches and leaves," so only the "firm fruit" remain. Buddha remarks "it is just as well" they left. *Scripture of the Lotus Blossom of the Fine Dharma*, trans. Leon Hurvitz (New York: Columbia University Press, 1976), p. 29.
48 Daoxuan, *Guijingyi*, p. 860c. And: "seeing defilement-boundaries, know they are not from the outside. Boundaries are not from outside the mind, they are from the forms of the mind (*xinxiang*)." Ibid., p. 860c.
49 Ibid. The *Taisho* does not contain this exact quote, though the sentiment is pervasive.
50 His encounter with Falin: *Gujin tushu jicheng*, section on Zhongnanshan. On his encounter with Shanwuwei, see Chou I-liang, "Tantra in China," *Harvard Journal of Asiatic Studies*, vol. 8 (1945), pp. 241–332. His encounter on Wutaishan: Yinguang, *Sidamingshanzhi*, vol. 4. (Taipei: Fojiao chubanshe, 1978), pp. 96–97.
51 Daoxuan, *Jiaojielüyi*, p. 869b.
52 Daoxuan, *Guijingyi*, pp. 865a–865c. See Sure, "Sacred Literature," pp. 367–376.
53 As noted above, the five wheels are: both feet, both hands, forehead.

54 Daoxuan, *Guijingyi*, p. 865a.
55 Sure, "Sacred Literature," p. 371.
56 Daoxuan, *Guijingyi*, p. 865a.
57 *Entry into the Realm of Reality*, trans. Thomas Cleary (Boston: Shambhala, 1989), pp. 365–374.
58 Daoxuan, *Guijingyi*, p. 865a.
59 Ibid., pp. 865a–b.
60 Ibid., p. 865b.
61 This saying appears in many Mahayana sutras, for example the *Renwang huguo banruoboluomiduo jing*, trans Kumarajiva, T. vol. 8, no. 245, p. 652b.
62 This reference would seem to indicate *Wenshushili pusa wuxiang shili* (The Ten Formless Bows of the Bodhisattva Manjusri), T. vol. 85, no. 2844 文殊師利菩薩無相十禮。However, this quotation does not appear in that text but in, for example, Dharmaruci's *Rulai zhuangyan zhihui guangming ruyiqie Fojingjie jing* (The Sutra of the Tathagata's Imposing Wisdom Illuminating All Buddha-worlds, 如來莊嚴智慧光明入一切佛境界經, T. vol. 12, no. 357, p. 247c.
63 Daoxuan, *Guijingyi*, pp. 865b–c.
64 Ibid., pp. 856b–858a.
65 Ibid., p. 857a.
66 Ibid., p. 857c.
67 Ibid., p. 857c.
68 This section is particularly interesting because anti-Buddhists of the period emphasized the materiality of the monks' objects of obeisance. For example, Fu Yi "did not by nature believe in Buddhism, invariably treating monks and nuns with disrespect, and even going so far as to treat stone images of the Buddha as if they were bricks or tiles." The materiality of objects of obeisance made them vulnerable to both rhetorical and physical attack. Tang Lin, *Miraculous Retribution: A Study and Translation of T'ang Lin's Ming-pao chi*, trans. Donald E. Gjertson. Berkeley Buddhist Studies Series (Berkeley: University of California Press, 1989), p. 264.
69 Daoxuan, *Guijingyi*, p. 857c.
70 Ibid.
71 *Sidamingshanzhi*, vol. 4, pp. 96–97.
72 *Foshuo wushangyi jing*, T. vol. 16, no. 669, p. 468b. trans. by Paramartha.
73 Daoxuan, *Guijingyi*, p. 858a. I have not found any source for this precise quote; it could be that Daoxuan is once more paraphrasing.
74 The *Zuofo xingxiang jing* is extant only in Chinese. The earliest translation dates from the early third-century CE: T. vol. 16, no. 692, pp. 788a–c. See Robert H.

Sharf, trans. & intro., "The Scripture on the production of Buddha Images" in *Religions of China in Practice* Donald S. Lopez, Jr., ed. (Princeton: Princeton University Press, 1996), pp. 261–267. Among the benefits are: "clear eyes and a handsome appearance," a pure body without defilements, rebirth in the seventh Brahma Heaven, birth into a rich noble family, and one will "always be the color of reddish gold, handsome without peer." (Ibid., p. 265). One will be well-loved, born in India, into royal or aristocratic family, will become a respected emperor, a cakravartin; "He will always guard his chastity, and his thoughts will always be on his desire to follow the Buddhist path," he will "always honor the Buddha and revere the scriptures. He will continually make offerings to the relics of the Buddha of variegated silk, fine flowers, exquisite incense, lamps, and all the precious jewels and rare objects of the world." (Ibid., p. 266).

75 Daoxuan, *Guijingyi*, p. 855b. The reference here to "lords and fathers" reminds us of the contemporary political situation.

76 Ibid., p. 855c. Daoxuan is paraphrasing, but the *Zengyi ahanjing* says something to this effect, T. vol. 2, no. 125, p. 673a.

77 Daoxuan, Guijingyi, p. 855a.

78 Ibid., p. 862b.

79 Ibid., p. 860b.

80 Ibid., p. 855a.

81 The *qingmiao* refers to the Imperial ancestral temple, as described in Ode 266 of the *Shijing*.

82 Compare to *Lunyu* 3:12: "'Sacrifice as if present' is taken to mean 'sacrifice to the gods as if the gods were present.'" *The Analects*, trans. D.C. Lau, p. 69. Or, in Wing-tsit Chan's translation: "When Confucius offered sacrifice to his ancestors, he felt as if his ancestral spirits were actually present." *A Source Book in Chinese Philosophy*, trans. & ed. Wing-tsit Chan (Princeton: Princeton University Press, 1963), p. 25.

83 Daoxuan, *Guijingyi*, p. 858a.

84 Sharf, introduction to "Scripture on the Production of Buddha Images," p. 261.

85 See Fabio Rambelli and Eric Reinders, *Buddhism and Iconoclasm in East Asia: A History* (London: Bloomsbury, 2012), pp. 16–22.

86 *Guijingyi*, 858a.

87 There is no exact match for this quote in the Taisho, but a close match in the *Dapan niepan jing jijie* 大般涅槃經集解, T. vol. 37, no. 1763, p. 457c.

88 Daoxuan, *Guijingyi*, p. 857a.

89 Faure phrases this tension more aggressively: "Chan monks have always had the secret desire to convert local deities, to wipe out the memory of places, to

deconsecrate or reconvert spaces, to decode and reencode legends. We have here a confrontation between two incompatible worldviews (even though the coexist in practice): the utopian, unlocalized, and universalist conception derived from Buddhism, and the 'locative' and localized conception of local religion–two visions of space, two different anthropologies." Bernard Faure, *Visions of Power: Imagining Medieval Japanese Buddhism*, trans. by Phyllis Brooks (Princeton: Princeton University Press, 1996), p. 179.

90 修行本起經 Xiuxing benqijing, T. vol. 3, no. 184, p. 463c. Daoxuan is paraphrasing.

91 Daoxuan, *Guijingyi*, p. 855a.

92 Ibid. Yenqi says: "'body-form and bones break apart' is the thought of not having the feeling of caring with respect to your body. It can be called returning your fate to Buddha." *Hufaji*, p. 146b.

93 Literally, a salutation in which the host proposes a toast to the guest; to pledge with wine; a salutation.

94 Daoxuan, *Guijingyi*, p. 855a.

95 Liaoran says this is a quote from the *Xiaojing*, Chapter 12: "propriety (*li*) is respect (*jing*) and that is all. Thus in respecting the father, the son is happy; in respecting the older brother, the younger brother is happy; in respecting the lord, the minister is happy; in respecting the one man then the myriad people are happy. Those that are respected are few, and those that are happy are a multitude. This is called the essential way (*yaodao*)." *Tongzhenji*, p. 217b. While the citation may be basically correct, Daoxuan does not quote exactly the *Xiaojing*. Liaoran sees this quote followed by one from the *Miaofa lianhua jing* as a contrast: "although Ru and Shi have distinct (forms of) respect, the meaning is not different." Ibid.

96 Daoxuan, *Guijingyi*, p. 858a. Quoted from chapter 17 of *Miaofa lianhua jing*, T. vol. 9, no. 261, p. 46a. (One who) "humbly reveres the stupa-shrines,/defers to the bhiksus" (shall have great merit). *Scripture of the Lotus Blossom of the Fine Dharma*, trans. Hurvitz, p. 256.

97 Yenqi glosses *shengchang* as the same as above, *suxi* ("common custom"), hence the norms (*chang*) of beings (*sheng*). *Hufaji*, p. 147b.

98 Daoxuan, *Guijingyi*, p. 855a.

99 "The *determination of the ethical substance*; that is, the way in which the individual has to constitute this or that part of himself as the prime material of his moral conduct." Michel Foucault, *The History of Sexuality*, vol. 2, *The Use of Pleasure*, trans. Robert Hurley (New York: Vintage Books, 1985), p. 26.

100 Daoxuan, *Guijingyi*, p. 862b.
101 Ibid., p. 855b, small print.
102 Ibid., p. 856a.
103 Geoffrey Galt Harpham, *The Ascetic Imperative in Culture and Criticism* (Chicago: University of Chicago Press, 1987), p. xv.
104 Zenryu Tsukamoto, *A History of Early Chinese Buddhism: From Its Introduction to the Death of Hui-yuan* (Tokyo: Kodansha International, 1985), p. 837.

Chapter 3

1 The documents are preserved in *Hongmingji*, T. vol. 52, no. 2102, pp. 79b–80b; and *Jishamen buyingbaisudengshi*, T. vol. 52, no. 2108, pp. 443c–444c. Much of the correspondence has been translated by Erik Zürcher, *The Buddhist Conquest of China: The Spread and Adaptation of Buddhism in Early Medieval China* (Leiden: E. J. Brill, 1959), pp. 160–163.
2 The Wang clan, headed by Wang Dao and Wang Dun, had lost power to the Yu in ca. 325; the Wang and their allies the He seem to have been committed to support for Buddhist institutions. Although some members of the Yu were well-disposed toward Buddhist monks, during their brief period of ascendance (ca. 325–345) they turned on the religious ideology of their rivals. In 344, He Chong installed two-year-old emperor Mu. Through the child emperor, He Chong used the last two years of his life promoting not only his own clan but also Buddhism.
3 Cai Mu biography is in *Guanghongmingji*, p. 126c. See Zürcher, *Buddhist Conquest*, p. 107; Tsukamoto, *History*, p. 343.
4 Ibid., p. 341.
5 The Chinese text does not actually specify "principle of government," which is Zürcher's interpolation.
6 Zürcher, *Buddhist Conquest*, p. 162. Bracketed remarks added.
7 The Huan Xuan - Huiyuan correspondence is treated in Tsukamoto, *History*, pp. 828–844, and in Zürcher, *Buddhist Conquest*, pp. 231–239.
8 *Hongmingji*, T. vol. 52, no. 2102, pp. 29–32. See: Leon Hurvitz, " 'Render unto Caesar' in early Chinese Buddhism. Hui-Yuan's treatise on the exemption of the Buddhist clergy from the requirements of civil etiquette." *Sino-Indian Studies* V, no. 3–4 (1957), pp. 80–114.
9 R. W. L. Guisso, *Wu Tse-t'ien and the Politics of Legitimation in T'ang China* (Bellingham: Western Washington University, 1978), p. 32.

10 Zanning, *Song Gaosengzhuan*, p. 812b.
11 Stanley Weinstein, *Buddhism Under the T'ang* (Cambridge: Cambridge University Press, 1987), p. 32.
12 Wang Yarong, *Lüzong Nanshanzong chuzu: Daoxuan dashizhuan* (The founder of the Nanshan lineage of the Vinaya lineage: the biography of great master Daoxuan) (Taipei: Foguang, 1998), pp. 196–198.
13 Dou Lujian, *Jishamen*, 455b.
14 Ibid., p. 455c.
15 Ibid., p. 455b.
16 Ibid., p. 454c.
17 Ibid., p. 455b.
18 Ibid., p. 456a.
19 Ibid.
20 Ibid.
21 Guisso, *Wu Tse-t'ien*, p. 32. She caused the dethronement and death of Gaozong's original empress in 656, demoted and exiled the Heir Apparent Li Zhong, and installed her own three-year-old son Li Hong as Heir Apparent. Although in some respects Wu Zhao could be considered a supporter of Buddhism, most of her active support was during her own dynasty, the Zhou (690–705), and was entirely subordinate to her quest for political legitimacy.
22 Dou Lujian, *Jishamen*, pp. 456a–b.
23 Ibid., p. 472a. See also Weinstein, *Buddhism Under the T'ang*, p. 33.
24 In Dou Lujian, *Jishamen*, pp. 472b–c, and *Guanghongmingji*, pp. 289c–290a, called "His Majesty's order to Buddhist monks to cease doing obeisance before the ruler" but in *Chuan Tangwen* 12, pp. 7b–8a, "An Imperial order to members of the Buddhist and Taoist clergies to reverence their parents." Weinstein, *Buddhism Under the T'ang*, p. 161.
25 Ibid., p. 34.
26 Dou Lujian, *Jishamen*, pp. 473a–b.
27 Weinstein, *Buddhism Under the T'ang*, p. 34.
28 Ibid.
29 Erik Zürcher, "Buddhism in China," in *Encyclopedia of Religion*, vol. 2, Mircea Eliade, ed. (Chicago: University of Chicago, 1987), p. 416.
30 Similar overlap is evident in the Court of Judicial Review (Xiangxingsi), with an anti-bow Aide and pro-bow Vice-Minister; and in the Militant Guard of the Right, with an anti-bow administrator (*changshi*) and a pro-bow general (*jiangjun*); and in the Secretariat of the Heir Apparent of the Right, with an anti-bow secretary (*zhushi*) and a pro-bow Mentor (*zhonghu*) and Admonisher (*zanshan*).

31 The Right Police Patrol Guard Command appears among the so-called "compromise" positions, which was basically pro-bow.
32 There is one case of direct overlap: the Secretariat of the Heir Apparent of the Right, with an anti-bow secretary (*zhushi*) and a pro-bow Mentor (*zhonghu*) and Admonisher (*zanshan*).
33 T. vol. 52, no. 2108, pp. 443–474. Also in *Xuzangjing* 28/1.
34 Zanning, *Song Gaosengzhuan*, T. vol. 50, no. 2061, p. 728.
35 *Daciensi sanzang fashi zhuan* ("Biography of the Tripitaka Dharma Master of Daci-en Monastery") in ten fascicles. T. vol. 50, no. 2053, pp. 220–280. The Daci-en si was dedicated in 648. At one point, Huili was *weina* of Ximingsi, the abbot of which was Daoxuan. See Huili biography in Zanning, *Song Gaosengzhuan*, p. 813a.
36 *Hufa shamen Falin biezhuan* ("An Alternative Biography of Falin, the Sramana who Protected the Dharma") in three fascicles. T. vol. 50, no. 2051, pp. 198–213. The fiery Daoist-turned-Buddhist Falin (572–640) was the primary contemporary opponent of Fu Yi. Falin was the author of *Poxielun* ("Treatise on Breaking Falsity," circa 626; T. vol. 52, no. 2109, pp. 474–489) and *Bianzhenglun* ("Treatise on Establishing the Correct," T. vol. 52, no. 2110, pp. 489–550). In 639 he was exiled, ostensibly for lese majeste.
37 See *Xiaojing*, ch. 11: "There are three thousand offenses subject to the five punishments, but of these none is greater than lack of filial piety." "The Classic of Filial Piety," trans. Patricia Buckley Ebrey, in *Chinese Civilization: A Sourcebook*, second editions, ed. Patricia Buckley Ebrey (New York: The Free Press, 1993), p. 67.
38 First of the "compromise" position speeches, Dou Lujian, *Jishamen*, pp. 464c–465a.
39 Ibid., p. 466b.
40 Ibid., p. 455a.
41 Ibid., p. 468a. By assigning father/son to Heaven and ruler/ruled to Earth, Li Yifan places the father-son relationship higher than that of the ruler-ruled. Perhaps this is because for Li Yifan, Heaven was more like a father than a ruler.
42 Roger T. Ames, "The Meaning of Body in Classical Chinese Philosophy" in *Self as Body in Asian Theory and Practice*, Thomas Kasulis et al., eds (Albany: State University of New York, 1993), p. 164. Ames elaborates on *li* as "formal behaviors which define interpersonal relationships in community" (Ibid., p. 169); "a *li* action is an em*bodi*ment or *form*alization of meaning and value." (Ibid., p. 169)
43 Dou Lujian, *Jishamen*, p. 467a.

44 Ibid., p. 468b. It is interesting to note that Daoxuan also wrote *Shimen zhangfuyi* ("Buddhist Rites of Clothing," T. vol. 45, no. 1894, pp. 834–839) in 656. Also, Huiyuan wrote *Shamen danfu lun*, ("Treatise on the Sramanas' removal of clothing"), *Hongmingji*, pp. 32–33.
45 Dou Lujian, *Jishamen*, p. 467a.
46 An alternate version of the text has *wugeng* (five classes of experienced men) instead of *wujing* (five classics).
47 Zheng Qintai & Qin Huaike, Ibid., p. 458c.
48 For example in the Yueji chapter: *Li Chi: Book of Rites*, trans. James Legge (New Hyde Park: University Books, 1967), vol. 2, pp. 124–125.
49 Dou Lujian, *Jishamen*, p. 459a.
50 Dou Lujian, Ibid., p. 467a.
51 Dou Lujian, *Jishamen*, Ibid., p. 466a.
52 Dou Lujian, Ibid., 467a.
53 Ibid., p. 455a.
54 Ibid., p. 466a.
55 Ibid., p. 469b.
56 Ibid., pp. 460a–b.
57 Ibid., p. 460a.
58 Ibid., p. 468a.
59 Ibid., p. 455a.
60 Ibid., p. 466b.
61 Ibid., p. 468a.
62 Ibid., p. 469a.
63 Ibid.
64 Ibid., p. 456a. Or possibly, "a protective umbrella."
65 Ibid., p. 455c.
66 Ibid., p. 466a.
67 Ibid., p. 466b.
68 Ibid.
69 Dou Lujian, Ibid., p. 467a.
70 Sun and Moon; and from this image, yang and yin. Yin-yang motifs pervade this quotation.
71 Ibid., p. 469a.
72 The Buddha's teaching, the practice of it, and the realization of it.
73 Ibid., p. 455c.
74 Ibid., p. 455b.

75 Ibid., p. 456a.
76 Ibid., p. 466b.
77 Ibid., pp. 461c–462a.
78 Ibid., p. 460b.
79 Ibid., p. 469a.
80 Here "jade pass" refers to those who are "within the pass" (*guannei*), i.e. "China proper."
81 Ibid., p. 455c.
82 Ibid., p. 456a.
83 Ibid., p. 460b.
84 Ibid., p. 456a.
85 Ibid., p. 455c.
86 Ibid., p. 455b. The 657 order also briefly mentions historical precedent: "The Song court for a time changed this custom (*feng*, lit. wind), but after a little while, they returned to honoring the old custom (*guan*, lit. threaded string)." Ibid., p. 455a.
87 Ibid., p. 466b.
88 *Tao Te Ching*, ch. XXV. trans. D.C. Lau (London: Penguin, 1963), p. 82.
89 Ibid., p. 466c.
90 Ibid., p. 455b.
91 Ibid., p. 456a.
92 Ibid., p. 469a.
93 Ibid., pp. 466b-c. There is no precise match for the quote from the Renwangjing.
94 Ibid., p. 466c.
95 A close match for this quote is vol. 12, no. 365, p. 341c.
96 Dou Lujian, *Jishamen*, 466c.
97 Ibid., p. 462a. The reference to drumming pots is from Zhuangzi, who behaved abnormally after his wife died. *Wandering on the Way*, trans. Victor H. Mair (New York: Bantam, 1994), pp. 168–169.

Chapter 4

1 Dou Lujian, *Jishamen*, p. 474a.
2 A set expression comes down to us: "Sengzhao, approaching punishment, recites a *gatha*" (religious verse). The *gatha* which Sengzhao recited is as follows: The Four Elements originally have no master; The Five Skandhas are basically empty.

When my head meets the white blade, It will merely be like beheading the spring wind. Daoxuan wrote a poem praising Sengzhao for this self-possession in the face of worldly power. *Guanghongmingji*, T. vol. 52, no. 2103, p. 360c.

3 Dou Lujian, *Jishamen*, p. 474b.
4 Ibid., p. 474c. The *Liji* quote is the very first line of the Classic: *Li Chi*, vol. 1, p. 61.
5 Ibid., p. 461b.
6 Ibid., p. 474b.
7 For example, the Jitong chapter: *Li Chi: Book of Rites*, vol. 2, p. 246–247.
8 It was generally preferable that the impersonator of the dead father should be the eldest son, so that obeisance to the "father" was simultaneously obeisance to the father's successor as living patriarch. But there were ritual provisions for others to play the role, and it is these exceptions that are referred to here. As Fan Lijun remarked, it might be a grandson.
9 Dou Lujian, *Jishamen*, p. 466a.
10 Ibid., p. 474b.
11 Ibid.
12 *The Analects* (Lunyü), XIII:18, trans. D. C. Lau, p. 121.
13 Dou Lujian, *Jishamen*, p. 474b. On capping, see for example *Liji*, Guanyi chapter: *Li Chi*, vol. 2, p. 426.
14 *The Analects* 7.1.
15 Xueji chapter. Based on the Legge translation, modified by the author. *Li Chi*, vol. 2, p. 88.
16 Zürcher, *Buddhist Conquest*, 258.
17 Ibid., p. 258.
18 Ibid., p. 259.
19 *Sibu* here refers to the four stages of enlightenment, from stream-winner to arhat. More commonly the term refers to the four classes of Confucian literature.
20 Dou Lujian, *Jishamen*, p. 474b. The special treatment of the lords of Qi and Song are mentioned in *Kongzi jiayu* (Confucian School Sayings), section 1. Compiled by Wang Su (195–256).
21 Legge's translation of *guobin* is inconsistent. The Ming commentator Wang Fuzhi glosses *guobin* as lords and great officers who have come for imperial audiences and for ambassadorial purposes. *Liji zhangju*, (Changsha: Xinhua shudian, 1991), p. 1050
22 *Liji* 22:9. *Li Chi: Book of Rites*, vol. 2, p. 176–177.
23 Dou Lujian, *Jishamen*, p. 470c.

24 Ibid., p. 474b. Xu You is mentioned in *Zhuangzi*, turning down Yao. *Wandering on the* Way, p. 6. Quote from Houhanshu, 逸民列傳 Biographies of hermits, vol. 83, section 1.
25 *Scripture of the Lotus Blossom of the Fine Dharma*, p. 206.
26 Dou Lujian, *Jishamen*, p. 474b; the monk Xuan Fan uses the same allusion and analogy, ibid., p. 471b.
27 Ibid., pp. 461.b–c.
28 Ibid., p. 458b.
29 Sima Qian, *The Record of the Grand Historian*, trans. Burton Watson (New York: Columbia University Press, 1961), p. 432.
30 Ibid., p. 434.
31 Ibid., p. 435.
32 David McMullen, "The Cult of Ch'i T'ai-kung and T'ang Attitudes to the Military." *T'ang Studies*, vol. 7 (1989), p. 63. See also Howard Wechsler, "The Confucian Impact on Early T'ang Decision-making," *T'oung Pao*, vol. 66, no. 1–3 (1980), pp. 26–29.
33 *Tao Te Ching*, chapter XXXI, p. 89. Vilma Fritsch discusses this particular left-right distinction in *Left and Right in Science and Life* (London: Barrie & Rockliff, 1968), pp. 42–46.
34 Dou Lujian, *Jishamen*, p. 474b.
35 For a discussion of the political ambiguities of the "spectacle of the scaffold" in France, see Foucault, *Discipline and Punish*, pp. 32–69.
36 Dou Lujian, *Jishamen*, p. 469a.
37 Ibid., p. 458c.
38 Erving Goffman, "The Nature of Deference and Demeanor" in *Interactional Ritual: Essays on Face-to-face Behavior* (Garden City, New York: Anchor, 1967), p. 93.
39 Michel Foucault, "Political Technology of Individuals" in *Technologies of the Self: A Seminar with Michel Foucault*, Luther H. Martin, Huck Gutman and Patrick H. Hutton, eds (Amherst: University of Massachusetts Press, 1988), p. 153.
40 Michel Foucault, "Technologies of the Self" in *Technologies of the Self: A Seminar with Michel Foucault*, Luther H. Martin, Huck Gutman and Patrick H. Hutton, eds (Amherst: University of Massachusetts Press, 1988), p. 17.

Chapter 5

1 Matteo Ricci, S. J., *The True Meaning of the Lord of Heaven (T'ien-chu Shih-i)* trans. & intro by Douglas Lancashire & Peter Hu Kuo-chen, S. J.; Chinese-English

edition ed. by Edward J.Malatesta, S. J. Variétés Sinologiques New Series 72. (Taipei: Ricci Institute, 1985), p. 241.

2   Yang Guangxian, quoted in Paul A. Cohen, *China and Christianity: The Missionary Movement and the Growth of Chinese Antiforeignism, 1860–1870* (Cambridge: Harvard University Press, 1963), p. 26.

3   Eric Reinders, *Borrowed Gods and Foreign Bodies: Christian Missionaries Imagine Chinese Religion* (Berkeley: University of California Press 2004), pp. 146–169; and Eric Reinders, "Blessed Are the Meat-Eaters: Christian Anti-Vegetarianism and the Missionary Encounter with Chinese Buddhism," *Positions: East Asia Cultures Critique*, vol. 12, no. 2 (Fall 2004), pp. 509–537.

4   Exodus 20:4, and Deuteronomy 5:8–9. See also, for example, Leviticus 19:4, 26:1.

5   Reinders, *Borrowed Gods and Foreign Bodies*, pp. 8–11.

6   Ibid., pp. 101–112.

7   Lee Palmer Wandel, *Voracious Idols and Violent Hands: Iconoclasm in Reformation Zurich, Strasbourg, and Basel* (Cambridge: Cambridge University Press, 1995), pp. 146–147, 195.

8   Henry Burton, *Jesu-Worship Confuted, or, Certain Arguments Against Bowing at the Name Jesus, Proving It to Be Idolatrous and Superstitious, and So Utterly Unlawfull, with Objections to the Contrary fully Answered* (London: H.C., 1660), p. 1. Answered by: For example, John Evans, *The Case of Kneeling at the Holy Sacrament, Stated and Resolved* (London, 1683).

9   Edward Stillingfleet, *Several Conferences Between a Romish Priest, A Fanatick Chaplain, and a Divine of the Church of England, Concerning the Idolatry of the Church of Rome: Being a Full Answer to the Late Dialogues of T. G[odwin]* (London: 1679), p. 38. For a rich treatment of the ritual and politics of the host in the late Medieval period, see Charles Zika, "Hosts, Processions and Pilgrimages: Controlling the Sacred in Fifteenth-Century Germany," *Past & Present*, vol. 118 (February 1988), pp. 25–64. In particular, Zika treats the host as a clerical instrument of control: "It served as a demonstration of priestly power" (ibid., p. 60) See also Ann Kibbey, *The Interpretation of Material Shapes in Puritanism: A Study of Rhetoric, Prejudice, and Violence* (Cambidge: Cambridge University Press, 1986), pp. 44–59.

10 This Revised Standard Version translation of the Greek is peculiar, because the word *kampsei* only means bend, not bow. And it is strange to say that the knee bows. You bow, by bending the knee; the knee itself does not bow any more than your hands pray.

11 *Several Conferences*, p. 44.

12 ibid., p. 37.
13 ibid., p. 224.
14 Alain Peyrefitte, *The Collision of Two Civilizations: The British Expedition to China in 1792–4*, trans. Jon Rothschild (London: Harvill, 1993), p. 251.
15 John Francis Davis, *The Chinese: A General Description of the Empire of China and Its Inhabitants*, vol. II (London: Charles Knight, 1836–1840), p. 83.
16 William Burder, *The History of All Religions of the World: With Accounts of the Ceremonies and Customs, or the Forms of Worship, Practiced by the Several Nations of the Known World, from the Earliest Records to the Present Time* (New York: Gay Brothers1870), p. 679. W. Gilbert Walshe's article "China" in *Encyclopædia of Religion and Ethics*, James Hastings, ed. (Edinburgh: T & T Clark, 1913–22) upholds this view: the later developments of Buddhism and Daoism "served to degrade the primitive simplicity and purity" of an original monotheism. ibid., vol. 3, p. 550. Among the "new inventions" was, for example, the ledger of merit, prompting Davis to remark: "This method of keeping a score with heaven is as foolish and dangerous a system of morality as that of penances and indulgences in the Roman church." Davis, *The Chinese*, vol. 2, p. 171.
17 Karl Gützlaff, *Journal of Three Voyages along the Coast of China, in 1831, 1832, & 1833, with Notices of Siam, Corea, and the Loo-Choo Islands* (London: Frederick Westley and A. H. Davis, 1832; Reprint Taipei: Ch'eng-Wen, 1968), pp. 371–372. John MacGowan had a similar view: "The best days for China were in the ancient past, according to the sacred books of the nation, when God and heaven were the predominant words in the religious life of the people, and when the idols had not yet come from India to lower the conceptions of the Divine." John MacGowan, *Sidelights on Chinese Culture* (London: Kegan Paul, Trench, Trübner & Co., 1907), p. 338.
18 Antonio Sisto Rosso, O.F.M. *Apostolic Legations to China of the Eighteenth Century* (South Pasadena: P. D. and Ione Perkins, 1948), pp. 71–72.
19 Ibid., p. 73.
20 Ibid., 340. Also Jonathan D. Spence, *Emperor of China: Self-Portrait of K'ang-hsi* (New York: Vintage Books, 1975), p. 79.
21 Rosso, *Apostolic Legations*, p. 111.
22 Ibid., 340.
23 Dou Lujian, *Jishamen*, p. 468b.
24 Rosso, *Apostolic Legations*, pp. 339–340. Also Spence, *Emperor of China*, p. 79.
25 W. A. P. Martin, "The Worship of Ancestors—A Plea for Toleration" in *Records of the General Conference of the Protestant Missionaries of China, Held at Shanghai, May 7–20, 1890* (Shanghai: American Presbyterian Mission Press, 1890), p. 628.

26 Martin, ibid., p. 626.
27 Martin, ibid. p. 626.
28 Henry Blodget, "The Attitude of Christianity toward Ancestral Worship," *Records of the General Conference of the Protestant Missionaries of China, Held at Shanghai, May 7–20, 1890*, pp. 649–654.
29 *Records of the General Conference of the Protestant Missionaries of China, Held at Shanghai, May 7–20, 1890*, pp. 690–692.
30 H. V. Noyes, "How Far Should Christians Be Required to Abandon Native Customs?" *Records of the General Conference of the Protestant Missionaries of China, Held at Shanghai, May 7–20, 1890*, p. 612. The "V." in her name here is typographic error for her actual middle initial, N.
31 Noyes, "How Far … ", p. 614.
32 *Records of the General Conference of the Protestant Missionaries of China, Held at Shanghai, May 7–20, 1890*, p. 659.
33 "Praying for Rain in China," *Church Missionary Gleaner*, April 1874, p. 40.
34 "The Story of the Fuh-Chow Mission: II.—Sowing the Seed," *Church Missionary Gleaner*, April 1876, p. 44.
35 W. Ellis, in Gützlaff, *Journal of Three Voyages*, p. xxvi.
36 Thomas W. Blakiston, *Five Months on the Yang-tsze; with a Narrative of the Exploration of Its Upper waters, and Notices of the Present Rebellions in China* (London: John Murray, 1862), p. 179, see also p. 183.
37 "Chinese Missionary Work," *Church Missionary Gleaner*, January 1851, p. 113.
38 "Cyril" [Henry E. Dennehy], *A Flower of Asia: An Indian Story* (London: Burns & Oates, 1901), p. 267.
39 ibid.
40 ibid., p. 268.
41 ibid.
42 "Good News from Fuh-chau," *Church Missionary Gleaner*, February 1866, p. 16.
43 Ibid., p. 17.
44 Ibid., p. 17.
45 Ibid., p. 17.
46 Ibid., p. 17.
47 Ibid., pp. 17–18.
48 Ibid., p. 18.
49 "Persecution in China." *A Quarterly Token for Juvenile Subscribers*, April 1868. p. 7.
50 Immanuel C. Y. Hsü, *The Rise of Modern China* (New York: Oxford University Press, 1970), p. 211. Also Peyrefitte, *The Collision of Two Civilizations*, pp. 513–516.

51. Ibid., pp. 223–231; James L. Hevia, *Cherishing Men From Afar: Qing Guest Ritual and the Macartney Embassy of 1793* (Durham: Duke University Press, 1995), pp. 105–108.
52. Quoted in Peyrefitte, *The Collision of Two Civilizations*, p. 206.
53. Hevia, *Cherishing Men from Afar*, p. 79.
54. ibid.
55. ibid., p. 234.
56. Bryan D. Mangrum and Giuseppe Scavizzi, intro & trans., *A Reformation Debate: Karlstadt, Emser, and Eck on Sacred Images: Three Treatises in Translation* (Toronto: Victoria University, 1991), p. 35.
57. Stillingfleet, *Several Conferences*, p. 37. The same Fanatick voice says: "What the cup of fornication means, that is Idolatry, and to bow at the name of Jesus, and to bow to the Altar, that is Idolatry." ibid., p. 35.
58. Bourdieu, *The Logic of Practice*, p. 72.
59. Hevia, *Cherishing Men from Afar*, pp. 73–74.
60. Peyrefitte, *Collision of Two Civilizations*, p. 251. Peyrefitte then comments: "Macartney's frequent antipapist flourishes were typical of the time. It was the age of Voltaire." (ibid).
61. S. Wells Williams, in Williams, Frederick Wells, *The Life and Letters of Samuel Wells Williams, LL.D.: Missionary, Diplomatist, Sinologue* (New York: G. P. Putnam's Sons, 1889), p. 319. 'it has never been easy to impress upon Western minds the genuine apprehensions which agitated the imperial counsellors [sic] as to the disturbing effect which a concession of audience without prostration would produce upon a people educated to regard its ruler as a divinity. It is hardly too much, indeed, to say that a slight to a Roman Augustus, or to a Pope in the middle ages, might have been allowed with less danger to the dignity of the potentate than this act of approach without low obeisance to the "Dragon Throne."' Frederick Wells Williams, in ibid., p. 318.
62. S. Wells Williams, in ibid., p. 405.
63. Sir Francis Hastings Doyle, *The Return of the Guards and Other Poems* (London: Macmillam, 1866), p. 105.
64. George MacDonald Fraser, *Flashman and the Dragon* (London: Collins Harvill, 1985)
65. Ibid., p. 154.
66. Ibid.
67. Ibid., p. 155.
68. Sax Rohmer, *The Insidious Dr. Fu-Manchu*, (Mineola: Dover Mystery Classics, 1997), p. 84.

69 Ibid., p. 85.
70 Ibid., p. 131. See Eric Reinders, "The Chinese Macabre in Missionary Publications and Horror Fiction" in *Beating Devils and Burning Their Books*, Anthony Clark eds (Ann Arbor: Association for Asian Studies/University of Michigan, 2010), pp. 15–41.
71 There are references to a cult of "Our Lady of the Poppies." (*Yellow Claw*, p. 174, 175, 251). Ho-Pin calls opium "the goddess." (Ibid., p. 175). "In common with the lesser deities," he continued, "our Lady of the Poppies is exacting. After a protracted sojourn at her shrine, so keen are the delights which she opens up to her worshipers, that a period of lassitude, of exhaustion, inevitably ensues. This precludes the proper worship of the goddess in the home, and necessitates—I say *necessitates*—the presence, in such a capital as London, of a suitable temple. You have the honor, Soames, to be a minor priest of that Temple!" (Ibid., pp. 175–176). And so, "as the worshipers of old came by the gate of Fear into the invisible presence of Moloch, so he—of equally untutored mind—had entered the presence of Mr. King!" (Ibid., p. 184). Moloch (which means "king") was a pagan god in the Old Testament. (2 Chron. 28:3, 33:6.) Mr. Gianapolis, an unpleasant Greek character, calls Mr. King "a high priest of the cult." (Ibid., p. 278). "Mr. King might be the Spirit of Opium." (Ibid., p. 312). Gianapolis: "true communicants must retreat to the temple of the goddess if they would partake of Paradise with her." (Ibid., p. 276).
72 "It was a cavern!—but a cavern the like of which he had never seen, never imagined. The walls had the appearance of being rough-hewn from virgin rock—from black rock—from rock black as the rocks of Shellal—black as the gates of Erebus." (Ibid., p. 145). Erebus = Hades. There are pillars and arched latticework above. "In niches of the wall were a number of grotesque Chinese idols. The floor was jet black and polished like ebony. Several tiger-skin rugs were strewn about it. But dominating the strange place, in the center of the floor stood an ivory pedestal, supporting a golden dragon of exquisite workmanship; and before it, as before a shrine, an enormous Chinese vase was placed, of the hue, at the base, of deepest violet, fading, upward, through all the shades of rose pink seen in an Egyptian sunset, to a tint more elusive than a maiden's blush. It contained a mass of exotic poppies of every shade conceivable, from purple so dark as to seem black, to poppies of the whiteness of show." Ibid., p. 145.
73 Rohmer, *Mystery*, p. 161. Blood sacrifice tainting England; "that enemy of the white race who was writing his name over England in characters of blood." Rohmer, *Mystery*, p. 161.

74 Sax Rohmer, *The Mystery of Dr Fu-Manchu* (London: Methuen, 1913), p. 265.
75 Bram Stoker, *Dracula* (New York: Bantam, 1981), p. 5.
76 H. Rider Haggard, *She: A History of Adventure* (New York: Penguin Books, 2007. First published, 1886), p. 168.
77 Ibid., pp. 230–231, 278–279, 291.
78 Paul A. Cohen, *China and Christianity*, p. 6.

Chapter 6

1   Herbert Spencer, *The Principles of Sociology*, vol. 2 (New York: D. Appleton, 1900. Reprint from 1879), p. 220.
2   Ibid., p. 131.
3   Ibid., p. 122.
4   Ibid., p. 143, pp. 223–224.
5   Ibid., p. 118; also pp. 140–141, associating an emphasis on prostration with militarism.
6   Ibid., pp. 141–142.
7   Ibid., p. 143.
8   Barry Schwartz, *Vertical Classification: A Study in Structuralism and the Sociology of Knowledge* (Chicago: University of Chicago, 1981), p. 85.
9   Ibid.
10 Ibid., 86.
11 Ibid.
12 Karl Wittfogel, *Oriental Despotism: A Comparative Study of Total Power* (New Haven: Yale University Press, 1957), p. 152.
13 Ibid.
14 Schwartz, *Vertical Classification*, p. 86.
15 Ibid., pp. 100–106.
16 Ibid., p. 100.
17 Ibid., p. 104.
18 Ibid., p. 115.
19 Ibid., p. 116.
20 Ibid., p. 45.
21 Ibid., p. 62.
22 Ibid., p. 74.
23 Joy Hendry, *Becoming Japanese: The World of the Pre-school Child* (Honolulu: University of Hawaii Press, 1986), p. 73.

24 Schwartz, *Vertical Classification*, p. 118.
25 "The Classic of Filial Piety," trans. Patrica Ebrey, p. 65.
26 Bourdieu, *The Logic of Practice*, p. 72.
27 Ibid., p. 77.
28 Ibid., p. 72.
29 Ibid., pp. 119–120.
30 Ibid., p. 120.
31 These phrases of caution—"as it were" and "give the appearance"—signal Bourdieu's reluctance to definitively posit *a priori* social categories, even if in his works he takes many differences as empirically given.
32 Hsü Dau-lin has persuasively argued that the now-standard set of five *lun* (*wulun*) was not established until as late as the Song. Prior to that, the various lists of *lun* were somewhat flexible in number, content, and order, although showing a basic continuity. See Hsü Dau-lin, "The Myth of the Five Human Relationships of Confucianism" *Monumenta Serica*, vol. 29 (1970–1971), pp. 27–37.
33 Also, in modern Chinese, *xiongdi jiemei*, "older-and-younger-brothers and older-and-younger-sisters" used to address a crowd of friends or an audience, etc., of roughly comparable age, e.g. game show hosts to an expected audience of college students. The same applies to the whole vocabulary of kinship: "aunt," "uncle," "grandma," etc. (Usually the kinship terms used to denote non-kin are derived from the mother's side of the family, so that "a-yi" means both "auntie" in the broadest metaphorical sense and (younger?) sister of one's mother (or a wife's sister). The vocabulary of the male side of the family generally is not used in metaphorical senses to denote non-kin. Certainly in late Imperial fiction, the discourse of friendship was explicitly fraternal: *The Carnal Prayer Mat* describes a pact of friendship: "Since the Knave [the thief] was older than Vesperus [the student], they addressed each other as younger brother and elder brother respectively." Li Yu, *The Carnal Prayer Mat*, trans. Patrick Hanan (New York: Ballantine Books, 1990), p. 66. Friendship is a major theme in many stories from the late imperial period. See "The story of Wu Pao-an" and "The Journey of the Corpse" in *Stories from a Ming Collection: The Art of the Chinese Story-Teller*, trans. Cyril Birch (Grove Press, 1958), pp. 117–150; "Yang Jiao Throws Away His Life in Fulfillment of a Friendship" in *Perfect Lady by Mistake and Other Stories*, trans. W. Dolby (London: Elek Book, 1976), pp. 144–158. For a treatment of such rituals, see David Jordon "Sworn brothers: A study in Chinese ritual kinship," in *The Chinese Family and Its Ritual Behavior*, Hsieh Jih-chang and Chuang

Ying-chang, eds (Taibei: Academia Sinica, 1985), pp. 232–262. In many groups of sworn brothers, each individual is numbered (First Brother, Second Brother, etc.). Jordon comments: "Among sworn siblings, as among natural siblings, this hierarchical ordering is self-conscious but weak." (Ibid., p. 240). See also Joseph P. McDermott, "Friendship and Its Friends in the Late Ming," in *Family Process and Political Process in Modern Chinese History*, part 1 (Taipei: Academia Sinica, 1992), pp. 67–96.

34 Such as "between the last person to pass and the first person to fail" an exam. Bourdieu, *Language and Symbolic Power*, p. 120.
35 Foucault, *Discipline and Punish*. p. 25.
36 Ibid., p. 135.
37 Bourdieu, *Language and Symbolic Power*, p. 170.
38 Even our scholarly "social science must take account of the symbolic efficacy of rites of institution, that is, the power they possess to act on reality by acting on its representation." Bourdieu, *Language and Symbolic Power*, p. 119. Here Bourdieu draws upon the work of Austin on the performative aspects of language.
39 Foucault, *Discipline and Punish*, p. 194, 217.
40 Catherine Bell, *Ritual Theory, Ritual Practice* (Oxford: Oxford University, 1992), p. 100.
41 Michel Foucault, *Power/Knowledge: Selected Interviews and Other Writings 1972–1977*, Colin Gordon, ed. (New York: Pantheon Books, 1980), p. 74.
42 Ibid., p. 139.
43 There is a similar difference between Chinese and English in the pairing of past/future with front/back. In conventional English usage, the future is "in front of" you; but the Chinese term for front (*qian*), refers to the past, as in *yiqian*, "in the past."
44 Barry Schwartz et al., "Dominance Cues in Nonverbal Behavior," *Social Psychology Quarterly*, vol. 45, no. 2 (1982), p. 115.
45 Bourdieu, *The Logic of Practice*, p. 71.
46 China Mieville, "On Monsters: Or, Nine or More (Monstrous) Not Cannies." *Journal of the Fantastic in the Arts*, vol. 23, no. 3 (2012), pp. 377–393.

Chapter 7

1 *Manual on Flag Etiquette* (Atlanta, Georgia State Department of Education Division of Information and Publications, 1938), p. 12.
2 Ibid., p. 13.
3 Ibid., p. 13.

4   Carolyn Marvin and David W. Ingle, *Blood Sacrifice and the Nation: Myth, Ritual, and the American Flag* (Cambridge: Cambridge University Press, 1998), pp. 147–148.
5   *Manual on Flag Etiquette*, p. 13.
6   *Manual on Flag Etiquette*, p. 14.
7   Alfred Gell, *Art and Agency: An Anthropological Theory* (Oxford: Clarendon Press, 1998), p. 118.
8   *Manual on Flag Etiquette*, p. 8.
9   Michael Welch, *Flag Burning: Moral Panic and the Criminalization of Protest* (New York: Aldine de Gruyter, 2000), p. 37.
10 Ibid., pp. 104–105.
11 Ibid., p. 143.
12 http://wol.jw.org/en/wol/d/r1/lp-e/1102008085, accessed August 30, 2013.
13 Welch, *Flag Burning*, p. 39.
14 Ibid., p. 76.
15 Young Andi, *The Sacred Art of Bowing: Preparing to Practice* (Woodstock: Skylight Paths, 2003), p. 10.
16 Ibid., p. 22.
17 Ibid., p. 24.
18 Ibid.

Appendix

1   Charles O. Hucker's *A Dictionary of Official Titles in Imperial China* (Stanford: Stanford University Press, 1985) does not identify Guanfusi. He gives Guanfu as a general term for government or the "responsible authorities," but here Guanfusi clearly refers to a particular office.
2   An administrator of the Courageous Guard of the *Left* gives an anti-bow speech later.
3   Part of the work of the Court of the Imperial Stud was maintenance of the emperor's chariots.
4   The Right Police Patrol Guard Command appears among the so-called "compromise" positions, which was basically pro-bow.
5   There is one case of direct overlap: the Secretariat of the Heir Apparent of the Right, with an anti-bow secretary (*zhushi*) and a pro-bow Mentor (*zhonghu*) and Admonisher (*zanshan*).
6   Guisso, *Wu Tse-t'ien*, p. 32.

Bibliography

Abbreviation

T. *Taisho shinshu daizokyo* [Buddhist Canon of the Taisho Era], edited under the direction of Takakusu Junjiro, Watanabe Kaigyoku, & Ono Gemyo in 100 vols. (Tokyo: Taisho issaikyo kankokai, 1924–1935)

Primary sources

Anonymous (1866), "Good News from Fuh-chau," *Church Missionary Gleaner*, pp. 17–18.

Daoxuan, Shi, compiler. *Guanghongmingji* ("The Larger Record of Spreading Illumination"), T. 52, no. 2103, pp. 97–363.

———. *Jiaojie xinxue biqiu xinghu lüyi* ("Admonitions for the New Student-Monks to Maintain Discipline"), T. 45, no. 1897, pp. 869–874.

———. *Shimen guijingyi* ("Buddhist Rites of Obeisance"), T. 45, no. 1896, pp. 854–868.

———. *Sifenlü shanfan buque xingshichao* ("Guide to Practice of the Four-part Vinaya, with Troublesome Points Removed and Deficiencies Rectified"), T. 40, no. 1806, pp. 429–463.

Foshuo zhenggongjing jing ("Sutra Spoken by Buddha on the Correct Offering of Respect"), translated by Fotashanduo (Buddhasanta), T. 24, no. 1496, pp. 1102–1104.

Fuzhi Wang. (1991), *Liji zhangju*. Changsha: Xinhua shudian.

Liaoran (Song). (1983), *Shimen guijingyi tongzhenji* ("A Record of the Transmission of the Truth of 'Buddhist Rites of Obeisance'"), edited by Huiguang (Japan), *Xuzangjing* [Supplement to the Canon] (Taipei: Xinwenfeng chuban gongsi), T. 105, no. 1080, pp. 177–311.

Sengyou, ed. *Hongmingji*, T. 52, no. 2102, pp. 1–96.

Shangongjing jing ("Sutra on Properly Offering Respect"), trans. Dunajueduo (Jnanagupta), T. 24, no. 1495, pp. 1100–1102.

Shigao An, *Da biqiu sanqian weiyi* ("Three Thousand Rules of Dignified Conduct for the Great Monk"), T. 24, no. 1470, pp. 912–926.

Yanzong, Shi, *Jishamen buying baisu dengshi*, ("A Collection on the Matter of Why Monks Should Not Bow to Laity"), T. 52, no. 2108, pp. 443–474. Also in *Xuzangjing* [Supplement to the Canon] (Taipei: Xinwenfeng chuban gongsi, 1983) 28/1.

———. *Tang hufa shamen Falin biezhuan* ("Alternate biography of Falin, the Tang monk who protected the Dharma"), T. 50, no. 2051, pp. 198–214.

Yenqi (Song). (1983), *Shimen guijingyi hufaji* ("A Record of the Protection of the Dharma in 'Buddhist Rites of Obeisance'") first fascicle, Xuzangjing [Supplement to the Canon] (Taipei: Xinwenfeng chuban gongsi) T. 105, no. 1079, pp. 142–176. Abbreviated as *Hufaji*.

Zanning, *Song gaosengzhuan* ("Biographies of Eminent Monks Compiled in the Song"), T. 50, no. 2061, pp. 709–900.

Primary sources in translation

Confucius. (1979), *The Analects (Lun yü)*. Translated by D. C. Lau. London: Penguin.

Huiyuan. (1957), "'Render unto Caesar' in Early Chinese Buddhism. Hui-Yuan's Treatise on the Exemption of the Buddhist Clergy from the Requirements of Civil Etiquette." Translated by Leon Hurvitz. *Leibenthal Festschrift: Sino-Indian Studies* V/3–4, pp. 80–114.

Li Chi: Book of Rites. (1967). Translated by James Legge. New Hyde Park: University Books.

Qian, Sima. (1961), *Records of the Grand Historian* [*Shiji*]. Translated by Burton Watson. New York: Columbia University Press.

Scripture of the Lotus Blossom of the Fine Dharma. (1976). Translated by Leon Hurvitz. New York: Columbia University Press.

"The Scripture on the Production of Buddha Images," (1996). Translated by Robert H. Sharf in Lopez, Donald S., Jr. (ed.), *Religions of China in Practice*, Princeton: Princeton University Press, pp. 261–267.

T'ang, Lin. (1989), *Miraculous Retribution: A Study and Translation of T'ang Lin's Ming-pao chi*. Translated by Donald E. Gjertson. Berkeley Buddhist Studies Series. Berkeley: University of California.

Tzu, Chuang. (1994), *Wandering on the Way*. Translated by Victor H. Mair. New York: Bantam.

Tzu, Lao. (1963), *Tao Te Ching*. Translated by D. C. Lau. London: Penguin.

Secondary sources

Ames, Roger T. (1993), "The Meaning of Body in Classical Chinese Philosophy," in Thomas, Kasulis et al., (eds), *Self as Body in Asian Theory and Practice*. Albany: State University of New York, pp. 157–177.

Bell, Catherine. (1992), *Ritual Theory, Ritual Practice*. Oxford: Oxford University Press.

Blakiston, Thomas W. (1862), *Five Months on the Yang-tsze; with a Narrative of the Exploration of Its Upper waters, and Notices of the Present Rebellions in China*. London: John Murray.

Bourdieu, Pierre. (1990), *The Logic of Practice*. Translated by Richard Nice. Stanford: Stanford University Press.

——. (1991), *Language and Symbolic Power*. Edited by John B. Thompson, translated by Gino Raymond and Matthew Adamson. Cambridge: Harvard University.

Burder, William. (1870), *The History of All Religions of the World: With Accounts of the Ceremonies and Customs, or the Forms of Worship, Practiced by the Several Nations of the Known World, from the Earliest Records to the Present Time*. New York: Gay Brothers.

Burton, Henry. (1660), *Jesu-Worship Confuted, or, Certain Arguments Against Bowing at the Name Jesus, Proving It to Be Idolatrous and Superstitious, and so Utterly Unlawfull, with Objections to the Contrary fully Answered*. London: H.C.

Ch'en, Kenneth. (1964), *Buddhism in China: A Historical Survey*. Princeton: Princeton University Press.

"Chinese Missionary Work." (1851), *Church Missionary Gleaner*, Jan: 111–113.

Cohen, Paul A. (1963), *China and Christianity: The Missionary Movement and the Growth of Chinese Antiforeignism, 1860–1870*. Cambridge: Harvard University Press.

"Cyril" [Henry E. Dennehy]. (1901), *A Flower of Asia: An Indian Story*. London: Burns & Oates.

Doyle, Sir Francis Hastings. (1866), *The Return of the Guards and Other Poems*. London: Macmillan.

Ebrey, Patricia Buckley. (ed.). (1993), *Chinese Civilization: A Sourcebook*, second edition. New York: The Free Press.

Evans, John. (1683), *The Case of Kneeling at the Holy Sacrament, Stated and Resolved*. London: Fincham Gardiner.

Faure, Bernard. (1996), *Visions of Power: Imagining Medieval Japanese Buddhism*. Translated by Phyllis Brooks. Princeton: Princeton University.

Foucault, Michel. (1979), *Discipline and Punish: The Birth of the Prison*. Translated by Alan Sheridan. New York: Vintage Books.

———. (1985), *The History of Sexuality*, vol. 2, *The Use of Pleasure*. Translated by Robert Hurley. New York: Vintage Books.

———. (1988), "Political Technology of Individuals," in Martin, Luther H., Gutman, Huck and Hutton, Patrick H. (eds), *Technologies of the Self: A Seminar with Michel Foucault*. Amherst: University of Massachusetts Press, pp. 145–162.

———. (1980), *Power/Knowledge: Selected Interviews and Other Writings 1972-1977*. Edited by Colin Gordon. New York: Pantheon Books.

———. (1988), "Technologies of the Self," in Martin, Luther H., Gutman, Huck, and Hutton, Patrick H. (eds), *Technologies of the Self: A Seminar with Michel Foucault*. Amherst: University of Massachusetts Press, pp. 16–49.

Francis, Davis John. (1836–1840), *The Chinese: A General Description of the Empire of China and Its Inhabitants*. Two volumes. London: Charles Knight.

Fraser, George MacDonald. (1985), *Flashman and the Dragon*. London: Collins Harvill.

Fritsch, Vilma. (1968), *Left and Right in Science and Life*. London: Barrie & Rockliff.

Gell, Alfred. (1998), *Art and Agency: An Anthropological Theory*. Oxford: Clarendon Press.

Georgia State Department of Education (1938), *Manual on Flag Etiquette*. Atlanta: Georgia State Department of Education Division of Information and Publications.

Gilbert, Walshe W. (1913–1922), "China," in Hastings, James (ed.), *Encyclopædia of Religion and Ethics*, vol. 3. Edinburgh: T & T Clark, pp. 549–552.

Goffman, Erving. (1967), "The Nature of Deference and Demeanor," in *Interactional Ritual: Essays on Face-to-face Behavior*. Garden City: Anchor, pp. 47–96.

Guisso, R. W. L. (1978), *Wu Tse-t'ien and the Politics of Legitimation in T'ang China*. Bellingham: Western Washington University.

Gützlaff, Karl. (1834), *Journal of Three Voyages along the Coast of China, in 1831, 1832, & 1833, with Notices of Siam, Corea, and the Loo-Choo Islands*. London: Frederick Westley and A. H. Davis.

Harpham, Geoffrey Galt. (1987), *The Ascetic Imperative in Culture and Criticism*. Chicago: University of Chicago Press.

Hendry, Joy. (1986), *Becoming Japanese: The World of the Pre-school Child*. Honolulu: University of Hawaii Press.

Hevia, James L. (1995), *Cherishing Men From Afar: Qing Guest Ritual and the Macartney Embassy of 1793*. Durham: Duke University Press.

Hsü, Dau-lin. (1970–1971), "The Myth of the 'Five Human Relations' of Confucius." *Monumenta Serica* 29, pp. 27–37.

Hsü, Immanuel C. Y. (1970), *The Rise of Modern China*. New York: Oxford University Press.

Huidan, Shi. (n.d.), *Fojiao Yishi xuzhi* (What you should know about Buddhist rituals). Taipei: Fojiao chubanshe.

Jordon, David. (1985), "Sworn Brothers: A Study in Chinese Ritual Kinship," in Hsieh, Jih-chang and Ying-chang, Chuang (eds), *The Chinese Family and Its Ritual Behavior*. Taipei: Academia Sinica, pp. 232–262.

Kibbey, Ann. (1986), *The Interpretation of Material Shapes in Puritanism: A Study of Rhetoric, Prejudice, and Violence*. Cambridge: Cambridge University Press.

Kipnis, Andrew. (1994), "(Re)inventing *Li: Koutou* and Subjectification in Rural Shandong," in Zito, Angela and Barlow, Tani E. (eds), *Body, Subject and Power in China*. Chicago: University of Chicago Press, pp. 201–223.

Knapp, Ronald G. (1999), *China's Living Houses: Folk Beliefs, Symbols, and Household Ornamentation*. Honolulu: University of Hawaii Press.

———. (2005), *Chinese Houses: The Architectural Heritage of a Nation*. North Clarendon: Tuttle.

(n.d.), *Lijing Fota* (Bowing to Buddha). Putian: Guanghua Temple.

MacGowan, John. (1907), *Sidelights on Chinese Culture*. London: Kegan Paul, Trench, Trübner & Co.

Mangrum, Bryan D. and Scavizzi Giuseppe. (1991), *A Reformation Debate: Karlstadt, Emser, and Eck on Sacred Images: Three Treatises in Translation*. Toronto: Victoria University.

Marvin, Carolyn and David W. Ingle. (1998), *Blood Sacrifice and the Nation: Myth, Ritual, and the American Flag*. Cambridge: Cambridge University Press.

McDermott, Joseph P. (1992), "Friendship and Its Friends in the Late Ming," in Institute of Modern History, Academia Sinica *Family Process and Political Process in Modern Chinese History*, part 1. Taipei: Academia Sinica, pp. 67–96.

McMullen, David. (1989), "The Cult of Ch'i T'ai-kung and T'ang Attitudes to the Military." *T'ang Studies* 7, pp. 59–103.

Moule, Arthur Evans. (1874), "Praying for Rain in China," *Church Missionary Gleaner* 1, April, p. 40.

(1996), *Nanshan Lüxue Cidian* (Dictionary of the Nanshan School of Vinaya). Edited by Shi Zhiyu. Taipei: Xilian jinglan chubanshe.

Peyrefitte, Alain. (1993), *The Collision of Two Civilizations: The British Expedition to China in 1792–4*. Translated by Jon Rothschild. London: Harvill.

(1978), *Qingliangshanzhi* (Gazetteer of Clear and Cool Mountain) (*Sidamingshanzhi* vol. 4) Revised by Yinguang. Taipei: Fojiao chubanshe.

Lewis, W. J., Barber, W. T. A. and Hykes, J. R. (ed.). (1890), *Records of the General Conference of the Protestant Missionaries of China, Held at Shanghai, May 7–20, 1890*. Shanghai: American Presbyterian Mission Press.

Reinders, Eric. (2004), *Borrowed Gods and Foreign Bodies: Christian Missionaries Imagine Chinese Religion*. Berkeley: University of California Press.

———. (2010), "The Chinese Macabre in Missionary Publications and Horror Fiction," In Clark, Anthony (ed.), *Beating Devils and Burning Their Books: Views of China, Japan, and the West*. Ann Arbor: Association for Asian Studies/University of Michigan, pp. 15–41.

Ricci Matteo, S. J. (1985), *The True Meaning of the Lord of Heaven (T'ien-chu Shih-i)*. Translated by Douglas Lancashire and Peter Hu Kuo-chen, S. J.; Chinese-English edition by Edward J. Malatesta, S. J. Variétés Sinologiques New Series 72. Taipei: Ricci Institute.

Haggard, H. Rider. (2007), *She: A History of Adventure*. New York: Penguin Books. First published 1886.

Rohmer, Sax. (1915), *The Yellow Claw*. New York: McKinlay, Stone & Mackenzie.

Rohmer, Sax. (1916), *The Return of Dr. Fu-Manchu*. New York: Robert M. McBride.

———. (1997), *The Insidious Dr. Fu Manchu*. Mineola: Dover. (Originally published 1913, *The Mystery of Dr Fu-Manchu*. London: Methuen).

Rosso, Antonio Sisto. (1948), *O.F.M., Apostolic Legations to China of the Eighteenth Century*. South Pasadena: P. D. and Ione Perkins.

Schwartz, Barry. (1981), *Vertical Classification: A Study in Structuralism and the Sociology of Knowledge*. Chicago: University of Chicago.

Schwartz, Barry, Tesser, Abraham and Powell, Evan. (1982), "Dominance Cues in Nonverbal Behavior," *Social Psychology Quarterly*, 45/2, pp. 114–120.

Somers, Robert M. (1990), "Time, Space and Structure in the Consolidation of the T'ang Dynasty (A.D. 617–700)," in Dien, Albert E. (ed.), *State and Society in Early Medieval China*. Stanford: Stanford University Press, pp. 369–399.

Spence, Jonathan D. (1975), *Emperor of China: Self-Portrait of K'ang-hsi*. New York: Vintage Books.

Spencer, Herbert. (1900), *The Principles of Sociology*. New York: D. Appleton. (Reprint from 1879 original).

Stillingfleet, Edward. (1679), *Several Conferences Between a Romish Priest, A Fanatick Chaplain, and a Divine of the Church of England, Concerning the Idolatry of the Church of Rome: Being a Full Answer to the Late Dialogues of T. G[odwin]*. London.

(1876), "The Story of the Fuh-Chow Mission: II.—Sowing the Seed," *Church Missionary Gleaner*, 3, p. 44.

Sure, Heng. (2003), "Sacred Literature into Liturgy: Jingyuan (1011–1088) and the Development of the Avatamsaka Liturgy in Song China." Ph.D. dissertation. Graduate Theological Union.

Tsukamoto, Zenryu. (1985), *A History of Early Chinese Buddhism: From Its Introduction to the Death of Hui-yuan*. Tokyo: Kodansha International.

Wandel, Lee Palmer. (1995), *Voracious Idols and Violent Hands: Iconoclasm in Reformation Zurich, Strasbourg, and Basel*. Cambridge: Cambridge University Press.

Wechsler, Howard J. (1980), "Confucian Impact on Early T'ang Decision-making," *T'oung Pao* 66/1–3, pp. 1–40.

———. (1985), *Offerings of Jade and Silk: Ritual and Symbol in the Legitimation of the T'ang Dynasty*. New Haven: Yale University Press.

Weinstein, Stanley. (1987), *Buddhism Under the T'ang*. Cambridge: Cambridge University Press.

Welch, Michael. (2000), *Flag Burning: Moral Panic and the Criminalization of Protest*. New York: Aldine de Gruyter.

Williams, Frederick Wells. (1889), *The Life and Letters of Samuel Wells Williams, LL.D.: Missionary, Diplomatist, Sinologue*. New York: G. P. Putnam's Sons.

Wittfogel, Karl. (1957), *Oriental Despotism: A Comparative Study of Total Power*. New Haven: Yale University Press.

Wolfe, John Richard. (1868), "Persecution in China." *A Quarterly Token for Juvenile Subscribers* 13, pp. 7–8.

Yarong, Wang. (1998), *Lüzong Nanshanzong chuzu: Daoxuan dashizhuan* (The Founder of the Nanshan Lineage of the Vinaya Lineage: The Biography of Great Master Daoxuan). Taipei: Foguang.

Yifa. (2002), *The Origins of the Buddhist Monastic Codes in China: A Annotated Translation and Study of the Chanyuan Qinggui*. A Kuroda Institute Book. Honolulu: University of Hawaii.

Young, Andi. (2003), *The Sacred Art of Bowing: Preparing to Practice*. Woodstock: Skylight Paths.

Yun, Xu. (1988), *Empty Cloud: The Autobiography of the Chinese Zen Master*. Translated by Charles Luk. Longmead: Element Books.

Zika, Charles. (1988), "Hosts, Processions and Pilgrimages: Controlling the Sacred in Fifteenth-Century Germany." *Past & Present* 118, pp. 25–64.

Zürcher, Erik. (1959), *The Buddhist Conquest of China: The Spread and Adaptation of Buddhism in Early Medieval China*. Leiden: E. J. Brill.

———. (1987), "Buddhism in China," in Eliade, Mircea (ed.), *Encyclopedia of Religion*, vol. 2, Chicago: University of Chicago Press, pp. 414–421.

Index

altars 12, 23, 70, 103
alterity and foreignness 2, 11, 23, 24, 29, 34, 48, 52, 53, 79, 85–87, 92, 95, 138
Amherst mission 112
Analects 45
ancestral cult 44, 45, 61, 70, 77, 81, 83, 97, 102–107
animals 29–31, 44, 104, 105, 123, 124, 130
anti-Catholicism 98–101, 107, 108, 114
arhats 29
armor 63, 77, 88–90, 126
audiences with imperial figures 54, 55, 93

baidian 17
baring one's right side 32, 34
Bell, Catherine 134, 135
Benqijing 46
Bianru fajie lijing gongliang (the offering of obeisance for wholly entering the Dharma realm) 40
Bible 25, 95, 97, 98, 141
Bimbisara, King 29
bin (guest) 72, 77, 85, 86, 138
Blodget, Henry 107
bodhicitta 44
bodhisattva 37, 38, 56, 74
bodies and architecture 1, 6–9, 11, 23
bodies as unreal 79, 80, 83
bodies of monks 59, 60
body as constructed or performed object 48, 62, 69, 70, 93, 133–135
Bourdieu, Pierre 21, 23, 114, 130–132, 134
bowing, as subject-object relation 5, 40–43, 46, 47, 135, 138
bowing, definitions 123–138, 145
bowing, depth of 14, 25, 124, 125, 128
bowing, duration of 14, 16, 17
bowing, for laity 3, 4, 28, 66

bowing, for women 4, 30, 34, 89, 113, 114, 118, 120
bowing, frequency of 32
bowing, location of 32, 33
bowing to buddha 28, 29, 39, 46
bowing to feet 32, 34
bowing to parents 24, 29, 47, 53, 56, 59, 60, 135
bowing to senior monks 2, 4, 9, 10, 24, 29, 30, 33, 135
bowing to the emperor 24, 27, 55, 56, 97
bowing when entering 3–5, 7
bowl 2, 8, 9, 11, 63
Boxer Protocol 112
Boyi 88
Buddha as the "one man" (yiren) 27
Buddha icons 5, 7–9, 22, 24, 43–46
Buddha, three bodies 32, 39, 42, 43
Burder, William 101

Cai Mu 51
Cakravartin 66
Cao Xiaoguan 70, 74
Capping ceremony 81, 83, 133
celibacy 96
centrality 1, 12, 95, 140
Chan, Jackie 120, 121
Changheli (the bow of chanting together) 39, 145
Chao Fu 87, 88
Chiang Kai-shek 120
children 110, 111, 127, 128, 129, 135
Chongba 58
Christian refusal to bow to idols 25, 109, 110, 111
Christian refusal to bow to the emperor 25, 97
Christian ritual 21, 96
circumambulation 3, 34

Index

Confucianism 54, 64, 66–69, 78–80, 84, 93, 94, 102–104, 126, 134
Confucius 27, 45, 78, 83, 102, 103, 106
consecration rituals 45, 46, 48, 70
counter-religion 121, 122

Dabeijing 29
Daoism 14, 18, 21, 22, 24, 53, 54, 59, 60, 62, 64, 73, 74, 102
Daosengge 28
Daoxuan 1–6, 8–11, 24, 25, 28–51, 53–56, 58–59, 63, 66, 68–69, 71–73, 145
Davis, John Francis 101
Dazhidulun 28
Debate of 662 24, 25, 28, 51–94, 99, 100, 105, 114, 126, 134, 139, 141, 143
Debate participants 56–58, 146–151
Decline of the Dharma 36, 72, 88
Department of State Affairs 55
dignity (*weiyi*) 3, 46, 79, 98, 113, 116, 125, 139, 144
diplomatic immunity 78, 86
donations 36
doors, gates 1–7, 11–14, 16, 19, 23, 54, 55, 136
doorsill 5–7
Dou Lujian 61, 63
Dracula, by Bram Stoker 119, 120
dualism and non-dualism 37, 38, 40, 42, 46, 47, 67–69, 141

emperor, as "one man" (*yiren*) 27, 61, 62
ethnocentrism 95, 96, 100

facing, frontal 13, 16–18, 21, 22, 24, 41
Faith, *see* trust
Falin 37, 58
Fan Yijun 88
Fazhi qingjing jieda fojingjie lifo (the bow to Buddha which emanates wisdom and purity so that one can penetrate into the Buddha's realm) 39
feet, stepping 1, 6, 7, 31, 32, 34, 35, 45
feminization 113, 114, 131
filial piety 48, 52, 59, 61, 63, 65, 68, 73, 103, 106, 130, 141
five punishments 59, 91, 92
Five Relationships 114, 126, 130, 133

five wheels (or points) touch the ground 34
flag 25, 140–143
Flashman and the Dragon, by George MacDonald Fraser 116–118
A Flower of Asia: An Indian Story by Henry Dennehy 108, 109
Foucault, Michel 7, 32, 94, 133, 134, 135
four postures 40
funerals 67, 81, 82, 86, 89, 104, 107

Gao Yaoshang 64, 71, 72
Gaozong, emperor 24, 28, 53, 55, 56
gaze 3, 11, 23, 34, 36, 54, 139, 141
General Conference of the Protestant Missionaries of China 106
George III, King 112
Guandugong 19
Guanghongmingji 51
Guanyin 13, 16–19, 22, 23
guest, *see bin* (guest)

hands (palms) together 3, 15, 23, 30, 32, 34, 135
He Chong 51, 71
head 31, 34, 45, 62
Heaven 12, 47, 61, 65, 66, 68, 87, 105, 130
hermits 78, 87, 88
Hinayana 37, 38, 43, 56, 100
historical narratives 71–73, 95
Huan Xuan 49, 52, 71
Huatuo 18
Huayanjing 39
Huili 58
Huiyuan 52, 71, 79, 85, 90

idolatry 25, 46, 97–103, 105–108, 110, 113, 115, 141–143
imperial orders 24, 28, 53, 55, 56, 64, 65
imperial palace 7, 8, 12, 13, 20, 34, 53–55, 90, 91
impersonator of the dead 77, 81, 82, 89
incense 16, 18, 19, 21, 23, 39, 45
India 34, 35, 95, 96, 100, 108, 109, 116
insects 11
inversion of ritual 62, 81–84, 86, 88–90

Jade Emperor 18
Jehovah's Witnesses 25, 142, 143

Jiang Zhenzhou 64
Jiaojie xinxue biqiu xinghu lüyi
    (Admonitions for new student-monks to maintain discipline) 2–4, 6–11, 35
Jishamen buying baisu dengshi
    (A Collection on the Matter of Why Monks Should Not Bow to Laity) 58

Kangxi, Emperor 104, 105, 130
karma 38, 39, 44
Kasyapa 29, 30
kneeling 16, 17, 32, 55, 56, 99, 134

Laozi 27, 59, 64, 73, 90
laughter 4
left/right 1, 3, 19, 34, 90, 136, 137
Li (ritual), concepts of 61
Li Chunfeng 59–60, 70
Li Yifan 61, 65, 66
Lifo guanmen 38
Liji 62, 79, 81, 84, 86, 88, 89
Longshan Temple 13–19
Lotus sutra 48, 74, 88
Lu Cai 73, 74
Lu Xun 6

Ma Dashi 66, 68, 71, 91, 92
Macartney mission 24, 112, 113, 114, 115
Mahayana 37, 38, 45, 56, 100
Maillard de Tournon, Carlo T. 105
Maitreya 39
Manjusri Ten Bows 41
Manual on Flag Etiquette 140, 141
Mao Zedong 120
Martin, William Alexander Parsons 106, 107
Mask of Fu Manchu, the 118, 119
Mazu 19
military analogy 63, 77, 88–91, 124, 126
mind and body 36, 39, 40, 44, 48, 78, 99
Ming, Emperor 71
missionaries 25, 95
monastic space 2, 7, 8, 16, 24
monastic/lay distinction 61, 63, 66, 67, 69, 70, 77, 85, 93
monks, legal status of 2, 28, 43, 51
Moule, Arthur Evans 108
mountain 12

movement through temple space 2–4, 12–20, 105
M'Clatchie, Thomas 108

namo 33
natural sentiments or feelings 52, 60, 70, 94
Neng Xuanyi 61, 66, 105
Nine Bows 79
North-South axis 9, 12–14, 16, 18, 22, 23, 82, 84, 90
Noyes, Harriet 107
nuns 30, 34, 60, 74

one bow three steps (*yili sanbu*) 14
opium 119

Pei, Prince 54, 57, 58
photography 21, 23
physical presence of bodies 43, 51, 52, 65, 66, 79, 80, 87
pride 35, 36, 37, 38, 39, 41, 56, 63, 67, 73
principle/practice or phenomenon 44, 47, 64, 68, 69
prisoners 78, 91, 92
Private of the Buffs, the, by Francis Hastings Doyle 115, 116
Pure Land 74
purity/pollution 37, 71
pyramid 12, 13, 22, 27, 78, 92, 93

Qianlong, Emperor 112, 113
Qin Huaike 89, 92

Ratnamati 38
rebirth 36, 71, 74
Renwang banruo jing 73
respect (*jing*) 44, 66, 79
Ricci, Mateo 95, 102–104
Rites Controversy 102–104
ritual static 21
ritual topography 9–14, 25, 30, 31, 78, 136–138
robes 6, 7, 8, 61–63, 66, 69–71, 87, 91, 92, 105
Rohmer, Sax 118, 119, 120
Rongguo, Lady 54, 55, 58, 69, 72, 73

Sariputra 29
sarira 29

Schwartz, Barry 125, 127, 128
seniority 8–10, 24, 29–32, 94, 131, 134–136
seven kinds of bowing to Buddha 38–42
Shamen bujing wangzhe lun (Treatise on the fact that sramanas do not pay respect to kings) 52
Shanghai Noon 120, 121
Shangongjing jing 33
She, by H. Rider Haggard 120
Shengyen, Chan Master 48–49
Shenxin gongjingli (the bow of offering respect with body and mind) 39
Shiji 89
Shimen guijingyi (Buddhist Rites of Obeisance) 8, 28, 35, 48
Shixiang sanbao zita pingdengli (the bow of the true form of the Three Treasures, with self and other equal) 41
shoes 11, 32, 34
Shuqi 88
sincerity 23
sitting cloth 3, 33
sitting/standing 10, 11, 28, 29, 30, 107
social order 68, 91, 129, 137
Song gaoseng zhuan (Biographies of Eminent Monks Compiled in the Song Dynasty) 11
Spencer, Herbert 123–127, 132
stairs 19, 34, 54, 86, 105
straight/bent 130, 131
Subaraksimha (Shanwuwei) 37
Sun Yat-sen 120

Taizong, Emperor 28, 56
talking, prohibition of 4
Tangible Three Treasures 42–43
Taylor, Hudson 107
teacher/student relationship 8, 10, 11, 77, 84, 85
terms of address 30, 33–35, 105, 139
territory 51, 52, 65, 66, 79, 87
Thailand 11, 135, 144
Three Olds 62, 84
Three Treasures 29, 39, 42–45, 47, 48, 72, 81, 83
Three woods 91, 92
throne 12, 105

Tiangong 18, 19, 22
toilet 3, 4, 8, 9
transmission and lineage 69, 70, 77, 81–87
Treatise on Ten Stages 33
trust 44, 45
twelve expressions of respect 33–35
Two Truths 45

verticality 9, 10–13, 25, 30, 31, 63, 78, 127–129, 135–137, 139
Vimalakirti 74

walls 1, 5
Wang Mi 52, 71, 73
Wang Xuan 70, 74
washing 6, 8, 9
wedding 109, 110
Weixiu 53, 54, 59, 69, 73
Wen Chang 18
Wen/wu (civil/military) 90
When *not* to bow 8, 9, 23, 30, 33
Williams, S. Wells 114, 115
Womanli (the bow of self-pride) 38
Wu Zetian 55–58
Wu, King 88
Wuliangshou guanjing 74
Wutaishan 37, 43

Xiaojing (Classic of Filial Piety) 48, 130
Ximingsi 53
Xingshichao (Guide to practice) 3, 35
Xu You 87, 88
Xuan Fan 87
Xuanzang 58
Xuanzong, Emperor 56

Yan Liben 58, 65, 67
Yang Shouzhuo 63, 64, 83
Yang Sixuan 63, 64, 83
Yanzong 54, 57–60, 67, 70, 71, 74, 77, 79–87, 91–93
Yao 87, 88
Yen, Y. K. 107
Young, Andi 145
Yu Bing 51, 71, 73

Zengyi ahan jing 44
Zhang Songshou 67

Zheng Qintai 89, 92
Zhengguanli zishenfo (bow of correct contemplation that one's own body is Buddha) 40

Zhou Bo 89, 90
Zhou Yafu 88, 89, 90
Zong (lineage) 82, 83
Zuofo xingxiang jing 43–44